A NEW WINDOW
ON THE WORLD OF DIETING . . .

With this guide, you can compare 18 kinds of ice cream, 80 types of canned vegetables. You'll learn about margarine, soups, and cheeses. You'll find out whether *your* favorite brand counts higher or lower than rivals. You'll discover a surprising number of dishes you can safely add to your weight-loss menus—even though they aren't on most conventional diets!

Go low—in calorie and carbohydrates—and you won't go wrong!

BRAND-NAME GUIDE

to

CALORIES

and

CARBOHYDRATES

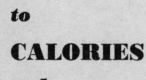

WILLIAM I. KAUFMAN

A JOVE BOOK

BRAND-NAME GUIDE TO CALORIES
AND CARBOHYDRATES

A Jove Book / published by arrangement with
the author

PRINTING HISTORY
Two previous paperback printings
Jove edition / October 1977
Fourth printing / February 1985

ISBN: 0-515-08262-7

Jove books are published by The Berkley Publishing Group,
200 Madison Avenue, New York, N.Y. 10016.
The words "A JOVE BOOK" and the "J" with sunburst
are trademarks belonging to Jove Publications, Inc.

PRINTED IN THE UNITED STATES OF AMERICA

INTRODUCTION

Have you ever asked your diet-minded self, as you shop at your supermarket: Which brand of tomatoes or meat or spaghetti should I choose? What kind of frozen dinner or juice? Should I buy chicken and noodles, or beef with peppers? Must I avoid pastries and rolls, ice cream, and cocktails? Are some cheeses and yogurts less fattening than others?

This calorie and carbohydrate-gram counter to more than 5,000 brand-name foods and beverages gives you the answers.

In order to simplify your life, I have compiled in this book the calorie and carbohydrate-gram counts of brand-name foods most frequently found in the modern grocery. For short-term weight loss, count carbohydrate grams. (You may lose as much as 10 pounds in 2 weeks, if you stick to 60 carbohydrate grams a day.) For the long pull, count calories. (The proper number to consume per day or week will depend on your height and build.) You can break away from the usual routine of dieting and plan attractive menus. Your shopping list will be full of things you love to eat even though the list has "built-in" weight-conrol factors.

But remember, there is no magic gimmick or pill for safe and constant weight loss. The *only* answer lies in portion control. And calorie and carbohydrate-gram counting is your only tool and your only ally in taking off—and keeping off—those unwanted pounds.

Your doctor will tell you that this is the only way, although well-meaning friends may offer methods that suggest easier ways to take off weight. Save yourself a great deal of time and frustration. Do it the safe, accurate, medically acceptable way. COUNT—and do it at the very beginning of your campaign. Start in your market basket.

My work as a food writer makes it almost impossible for me to lose weight when I am on a business trip or acting in my role of official food critic. This book provides you with the same information I use when I want to knock off extra weight. I place myself immediately on a 1500-calorie or 60-carbohydrate-gram-per-day diet, and I stay on it faithfully until I have lost the 10 or 15 pounds I want to lose.

WHAT'S IN A NAME?

Different brands of the "same" food *do* vary in calorie or carbohydrate count; each food processor has his own recipe or method which accounts for the difference, and gives each brand its distinctive flavor. There are differences, too, in calorie and carbohydrate count with foods such as canned or frozen fruits and vegetables. This is because manufacturers prepare foods in different sections of the country when the produce ripens. As the size of fruits and vegetables varies from region to region, so will their calorie or carbohydrate count. Switching brands may allow you to eat more and still stay within your daily quota.

Plan your meals in advance and follow through with your selections from your supermarket shelves, counting your calories and/or carbohydrate grams while you stroll along the aisles. If you are concerned about the health of a loved one, this book will make it easier for you to adhere to special diets. You will get the most for your food dollar because you will buy only those items that are necessary for the weight control of every member of the family.

You can fill your supermarket basket with a wide variety of delicious foods and still lose weight. Self discipline, wise shopping, and careful eating will bring the desired results. The world of dieting is full of all kinds of no-nos. I hope this book will surprise and please you with more than a few yes-yeses.

WILLIAM I. KAUFMAN

BRAND-NAME
CALORIE COUNTER
TABLE OF CONTENTS

HORS D'OEUVRE, DIPS, SPREADS

Anchovies, Flat (Reese), 2 oz.	100
Bacon and Smoke Dip 'n Dressing (Sealtest), 8 oz.	379
Beef, Chipped, Dip 'n Dressing (Sealtest), 8 oz.	366
Blue Cheese Dip 'n Dressing (Sealtest), 8 oz.	394
Blue Tang Dip (Dean), 2 tbsp.	60
Casino Dip 'n Dressing (Sealtest), 8 oz.	350
Caviar (Northland Queen), 1 oz.	74
Chicken Livers, Chopped (Reese), 1 oz.	47
Chicken Spread (Underwood), 1 tbsp.	31
Corned Beef Spread (Underwood), 1 tbsp.	27
Ham and Cheese Spread (Oscar Mayer), 1 oz.	73
Ham, Deviled (Underwood), 1 tbsp.	45
Ham Salad Spread (Oscar Mayer), 1 oz.	47
French Onion Dip (Dean), 2 tbsp.	55
French Onion Dip (Sealtest), 8 oz.	378
Onion and Garlic Dip 'n Dressing (Sealtest), 8 oz.	367
Jalapeño Bean Dip (El Paso), 1 oz.	35
Jalapeño Bean Dip, Fritos (Frito-Lay), 100 grams	127
Liver Pâté (Sell's), 1 tbsp.	42
Liverwurst Spread (Underwood), 1 tbsp.	42
Sandwich Spread (Oscar Mayer), 1 oz.	42
Sandwich Spread (Best Foods), 1 tbsp.	60
Sandwich Spread (Hellmann's), 1 tbsp.	60

HORS D'OEUVRE, Frozen, 1 piece

Calories

Bean and Bacon Burrito Rolls (Patio)	47
Beef Burrito Rolls (Patio)	48
Beef Puffs (Durkee)	47
Cheese Puffs (Durkee)	59
Cheese Straws (Durkee)	29
Chicken Burrito Rolls (Patio)	49

	Calories
Chicken Puffs (Durkee)	49
Chicken Liver Puffs (Durkee)	48
Cocktail Tacos (Patio)	39
Franks-N-Blankets (Durkee)	45
Shrimp Puffs (Durkee)	44

SOUPS AND CHOWDERS,
Canned

	Calories
Alphabet Vegetable (Lipton), 1 envelope	205
Asparagus, Cream of (Campbell's), 3½ oz.	70
Bean (Manischewitz), 8 oz.	112
Bean with Bacon (Campbell's), 3½ oz.	133
Bean with Smoked Ham (Great American Soups), 1 cup	201
Bean, Hot Dog (Campbell's), 3½ oz.	153
Bean with Smoked Pork (Heinz), 1 cup	165
Beef (Campbell's), 3½ oz.	87
Beef Barley (Manischewitz), 8 oz.	83
Beef Bouillon, Cubes (Korr-Swiss), 8 oz.	18
Beef Bouillon, Cubes (Maggi), 1 cube	7
Beef Bouillon, Instant (Maggi), 1 tsp.	7
Beef Broth (Campbell's), 3½ oz.	22
Beef Broth (College Inn), 1 cup	11
Beef Cabbage (Manischewitz), 8 oz.	62
Beef Noodle (Campbell's), 3½ oz.	58
Beef Noodle (Heinz), 1 cup	74
Beef Noodle (Lipton), 1 envelope	197
Beef Noodle (Manischewitz), 8 oz.	64
Beef Noodle with Dumplings (Great American Soups), 1 cup	100
Beef Vegetable (Manischewitz), 8 oz.	59
Black Bean (Campbell's), 3½ oz.	80
Black Bean (Crosse & Blackwell), 6½ oz., ½ can	96
Borscht, bottled (Manischewitz), 8 oz.	72
Celery, Cream of (Campbell's), 3½ oz.	66
Celery, Cream of (Heinz), 1 cup	101

Calories

Cheddar Cheese (Campbell's), 3½ oz.	125
Chicken Barley (Manischewitz), 8 oz.	83
Chicken Bouillon, Cubes (Knorr-Swiss), 8 oz.	18
Chicken Bouillon, Cubes (Maggi), 1 cube	8
Chicken Bouillon, Instant (Maggi), 1 tsp.	8
Chicken Broth (Campbell's) 3½ oz.	36
Chicken Broth (College Inn), 1 cup	30
Chicken Broth (Richardson & Robbins), 1 cup	17
Chicken, Cream of (Campbell's), 3½ oz.	76
Chicken, Cream of (Great American Soups), 1 cup	102
Chicken, Cream of (Heinz), 1 cup	93
Chicken Gumbo (Campbell's), 3½ oz.	49
Chicken 'n Dumplings (Campbell's), 3½ oz.	83
Chicken Kasha (Manischewitz), 8 oz.	41
Chicken Noodle (Campbell's), 3½ oz.	54
Chicken Noodle (Heinz), 1 cup	75
Chicken Noodle (Lipton), 1 envelope	217
Chicken Noodle (Manischewitz), 8 oz.	46
Chicken Noodle-O's (Campbell's), 3½ oz.	59
Chicken Noodle with Diced Chicken Meat (Lipton), 1 envelope	206
Chicken Noodle with Dumplings (Great American Soups), 1 cup	89
Chicken Rice (Lipton), 1 envelope	189
Chicken Rice (Manischewitz), 8 oz.	48
Chicken with Rice (Campbell's), 3½ oz.	43
Chicken with Rice (Heinz), 1 cup	61
Chicken with Rice (Richardson & Robbins), 1 cup	45
Chicken Rice with Mushrooms (Great American Soups), 1 cup	96
Chicken with Stars (Campbell's), 3½ oz.	50
Chicken and Star Noodle (Heinz), 1 cup	66
Chicken Vegetable (Campbell's), 3½ oz.	60
Chicken Vegetable (Heinz), 1 cup	85

Calories

Chicken Vegetable (Lipton), 1 envelope	210
Chicken Vegetable (Manischewitz), 8 oz.	55
Chili Beef (Campbell's), 3½ oz.	131
Chili Beef (Great American Soups), 1 cup	163
Chili with Beef (Heinz), 1 cup	161
Clam Chowder, Manhattan Style (Campbell's), 3½ oz.	63
Clam Chowder, Manhattan Style (Crosse & Blackwell), 6½ oz., ½ can	61
Clam Chowder, Manhattan Style, without milk (Snow), 1 lb. container	299
Clam Chowder, New England Style (Crosse & Blackwell), 6½ oz., ½ can	101
Consomme (Campbell's), 3½ oz.	28
Consomme Madrilene, Clear (Crosse & Blackwell), 6½ oz., ½ can	33
Consomme Madrilene, Red (Crosse & Blackwell), 6½ oz., ½ can	33
Consomme, Beef Flavor, Instant Soupmix (Knorr-Swiss), 6 oz.	15
Consomme Celestine, Instant Soupmix (Knorr-Swiss), 6 oz.	39
Consomme, Chicken Flavor, Instant Soupmix (Knorr-Swiss), 6 oz.	15
Consomme, Oxtail Flavor, Instant Soupmix (Knorr-Swiss), 6 oz.	15
Crab (Crosse & Blackwell), 6½ oz., ½ can	59
Gazpacho (Crosse & Blackwell), 6½ oz., ½ can	61
Green Pea (Campbell's), 3½ oz.	116
Green Pea Soupmix (Knorr-Swiss), 6 oz.	54
Green Pea (Lipton), 1 envelope	408
Leek Soupmix (Knorr-Swiss), 6 oz.	54
Lentil (Manischewitz), 8 oz.	166
Lima Bean (Manischewitz), 8 oz.	93
Lobster, Cream of (Crosse & Blackwell), 6½ oz., ½ can	92
Minestrone (Campbell's), 3½ oz.	72

Calories

Mushroom (Campbell's), 3½ oz.	70
Mushroom (Lipton), 1 envelope	124
Mushroom, Cream of (Campbell's), 3½ oz.	115
Mushroom, Cream of (Great American Soups), 1 cup	120
Mushroom, Cream of (Heinz), 1 cup	124
Mushroom Barley (Manischewitz), 8 oz.	72
Mushroom Bisque (Crosse & Blackwell), 6½ oz., ½ can	103
Noodle Soupmix (Knorr-Swiss), 6 oz.	38
Noodles & Ground Beef (Campbell's), 3½ oz.	80
Onion, (Campbell's), 3½ oz.	37
Onion, French (Crosse & Blackwell), 6½ oz., ½ can	46
Onion Soupmix and Dip Mix (Knorr-Swiss), 6 oz.	30
Onion (Lipton), 1 envelope	140
Oxtail Soupmix (Knorr-Swiss), 6 oz.	53
Oyster Stew (Campbell's), 3½ oz.	57
Pepper Pot (Campbell's), 3½ oz.	83
Petite Marmite (Crosse & Blackwell), 6½ oz., ½ can	33
Potato (Lipton), 1 envelope	300
Potato, Cream of (Campbell's), 3½ oz.	58
Schav, bottled (Manischewitz), 8 oz.	11
Scotch Broth (Campbell's), 3½ oz.	74
Senegalese (Crosse & Blackwell), 6½ oz., ½ can	61
Shrimp, Cream of (Crosse & Blackwell), 6½ oz., ½ can	92
Split Pea (Manischewitz), 8 oz.	133
Split Pea with Ham (Campbell's), 3½ oz.	141
Split Pea with Ham (Heinz), 1 cup	153
Split Pea with Smoked Ham (Great American Soups), 1 cup	186
Tomato (Campbell's), 3½ oz.	69
Tomato (Heinz), 1 cup	97
Tomato (Manischewitz), 8 oz.	61

	Calories
Tomato Beef Noodle-O's (Campbell's), 3½ oz.	96
Tomato, Bisque of Campbell's), 3½ oz.	101
Tomato Rice, Old Fashioned (Campbell's), 3½ oz.	87
Tomato Rice (Manischewitz), 8 oz.	78
Tomato with Vegetables (Great American Soups), 1 cup	126
Tomato Vegetable (Lipton), 1 envelope	276
Tuna Creole (Crosse & Blackwell), 6½ oz., ½can	57
Turkey Noodle (Campbell's), 3½ oz.	63
Turkey Noodle (Great American Soups), 1 cup	89
Turkey Noodle (Heinz), 1 cup	83
Turkey Vegetable (Campbell's), 3½ oz.	64
Vegetable (Campbell's), 3½ oz.	68
Vegetable Soupmix (Knorr-Swiss), 6 oz.	28
Vegetable, Old Fashioned (Campbell's), 3½ oz.	53
Vegetable Beef (Campbell's), 3½ oz.	66
Vegetable Beef (Great American Soups), 1 cup	126
Vegetable Beef (Campbell's), 3½ oz.	66
Vegetable Beef (Lipton), 1 envelope	159
Vegetable with Beef Broth (Great American Soups), 1 cup	132
Vegetable and Beef Stockpot (Campbell's), 3½ oz.	79
Vegetable with Beef Stock (Heinz), 1 cup	83
Vegetable, Golden, Noodle O's (Campbell's), 3½ oz.	62
Vegetable with Ground Beef (Great American Soups), 1 cup	139
Vegetarian Vegetable (Campbell's), 3½ oz.	62
Vegetarian Vegetable (Great American Soups), 1 cup	119
Vegetable Vegetarian (Heinz), 1 cup	83
Vegetable Vegetarian (Manischewitz), 8 oz.	63
Vermicelli Soupmix with Meat balls (Knorr-Swiss), 6 oz.	48

LOW-SODIUM SOUPS,
Campbell's), ready to serve, 8 oz.   *Calories*

Green Pea	152
Mushroom, Cream of	138
Tomato	99
Turkey Noodle	64
Vegetable	85
Vegetable Beef	97

SOUPS AND CHOWDERS,
Frozen (Campbell's),
1/3 can, 1 serving   *Calories*

Clam Chowder, New England Style	108
Green Pea with Ham	109
Oyster Stew	102
Potato, Cream of	90
Shrimp, Cream of	132
Vegetable with Beef, Old Fashioned	68

MEATS, Packaged and Fresh
Per slice, except as noted   *Calories*

Bacon (Oscar Mayer), cooked	53
Bacon, Canadian (Oscar Mayer, 6-oz. pkg.)	41
Bacon, Canadian (Oscar Mayer, 5-oz. pkg.)	35
Bar-B-Q Loaf (Oscar Mayer)	48
Beef Jerky (Slim Jim), 1 piece	25
Beef Loaf, Jellied (Oscar Mayer)	41
Beef, Thin-Sliced (Oscar Mayer), 1 oz.	39
Bologna, All Meat (Armour), 100 grams	349
Bologna, Bar-S (Cudahy)	94
Bologna, All Meat (Oscar Mayer)	70
Bologna, Pure Beef (Oscar Mayer)	70
Bologna, Pure Beef Lebanon (Oscar Mayer)	49
Cheese Smokies (Oscar Mayer), 1 link	138
Cocktail Loaf (Oscar Mayer)	63
Corned Beef, Jellied Loaf (Oscar Mayer)	41

Calories

Franks, All Meat (Armour Star), 100 grams	345
Franks, Pure Beef (Oscar Mayer), 1 link	146
Franks, Machiaeh Brand, Pure Beef (Oscar Mayer), 1 link	174
Ham, Boneless, Jubilee (Oscar Mayer, whole), 1 oz.	63
Ham and Cheese Loaf (Oscar Mayer)	72
Ham, Chopped (Oscar Mayer)	64
Ham, Minced (Oscar Mayer)	64
Ham, Smoked Cooked (Oscar Mayer, 6-oz. package)	30
Ham, Smoked Cooked (Oscar Mayer, 5-oz. package)	40
Ham, Thin-Sliced (Oscar Mayer)	12
Ham and Cheese Roll (Oscar Mayer, ½ lb., meat spread), 1 oz.	65
Head Cheese (Oscar Mayer)	51
Honey Loaf (Oscar Mayer)	45
Liver Cheese (Oscar Mayer)	62
Liver Loaf, Bar-S (Cudahy)	92
Luncheon Meat, All Meat (Oscar Mayer)	106
Luncheon Meat, Pure Beef (Oscar Mayer)	79
Luxury Loaf (Oscar Mayer)	40
Old Fashioned Loaf (Oscar Mayer)	55
Olive Loaf (Oscar Mayer)	51
Olive Loaf, Bar-S (Cudahy)	103
Peppered Loaf (Oscar Mayer)	46
Pickle and Pimento Loaf (Oscar Mayer)	63
Picnic Loaf (Oscar Mayer)	58
Pork Loin, Thin-Sliced (Oscar Mayer)	14
Pork, Tend'r Lean (Swift), 3½ oz. cooked	240
Pork Shoulder Butt, Sweet Morsel (Oscar Mayer, 1-3 lbs.), 1 oz.	89
Pro Ten Beef (Swift), 3½ oz., cooked	266
Salami for Beef (Oscar Mayer)	53
Salami, Cotto, Pure Beef (Oscar Mayer)	51
Salami, Cotto, Bar-S (Cudahy)	81

Calories

Salami, Cotto, All Meat (Oscar Mayer)	51
Salami, Hard, All Meat (Oscar Mayer)	38
Salami, Machiaeh Brand, Pure Beef (Oscar Mayer)	54
Sausage, Smoked Breakfast, All Meat (Oscar Mayer), 1 link	66
Sausage, Braunschweiger Liver (Oscar Mayer), 1 oz.	105
Sausage, Chubbies, All Meat (Oscar Mayer), 1 link	235
Sausage, Luncheon Roll (Oscar Mayer)	25
Sausage, Minced Roll, All Meat (Oscar Mayer)	53
Sausage, New England Brand, All Meat (Oscar Mayer)	31
Sausage, Polish, All Meat (Oscar Mayer), ¾ lb. ring	960
Sausage, Polish, All Meat (Oscar Mayer), 1 link	480
Sausage, All Beef Polish (Slim Jim), 1 piece	108
Sausage, Pork (Armour Star), 100 grams	470
Sausage, Pork, Pure (Oscar Mayer), 1 link cooked	55
Sausage, Smokie Links, All Meat (Oscar Mayer), 1 link	137
Sausage, Little Smokies, All Meat (Oscar Mayer), 1 link	29
Sausage, Thuringer Cervelat, All Meat (Oscar Mayer)	70
Sausage, Thuringer Cervelat, Pure Beef Summer (Oscar Mayer)	69
Slim Jims (Slim Jim), 1 piece	83
Turkey Breast Meat, cured-pressed-smoked-cooked (Oscar Mayer)	22
Wieners, All Meat (Oscar Mayer), 1 link	146
Wieners, All Meat, Bar-S (Cudahy), 1 link	145
Little Wieners, All Meat (Oscar Mayer), 1 link	31

Barbecue Manwich (Hunt's), 15 oz.	289
Beef, Chopped (Armour), 12 oz.	1042
Beef Goulash (Heinz), 1 can	253
Beef Stew (Armour Star), 24 oz.	623
Beef Stew (B & M), 1 cup	163
Beef Stew (Bounty), ⅓-½ cup	79
Beef Stew (Heinz), 1 can	253
Beef Stew (Libby, McNeill & Libby), 1 cup	179
Beef Stew (Morton House), 15 oz.	570
Beef Stroganoff (Lipton), 1 package	760
Chicken à la King (College Inn), 1 cup	266
Chicken à la King (Richardson & Robbins), 1 cup	332
Chicken Baronet (Lipton), 1 package	641
Chicken, Boned (Richardson & Robbins), 3 oz.	179
Chicken, Boned (College Inn), 1 oz.	75
Chicken and Dumpling Dinner (Morton House), 12¾ oz.	545
Chicken Fricassee (Richardson & Robbins), 1 cup	229
Chicken Fricassee (College Inn), 1 cup	234
Chicken Noodle Dinner (Heinz), 1 can	186
Chicken & Egg Noodles (College Inn), 1 cup	301
Chicken & Rice with Vegetables (Morton House), 12¾ oz.	690
Chicken Stew (B & M), 1 cup	168
Chicken Stew (Bounty), ⅓-½ cup	82
Chicken Stew with Dumplings (Heinz), 1 can	202
Chicken Stroganoff (Lipton), 1 package	775
Chicken Supreme (Lipton), 1 package	678
Corned Beef (Armour), 12 oz.	967
Corned Beef Hash (Armour), 15½ oz.	872
Corned Beef Hash (Bounty), ⅓-½ can	180
Corned Beef Hash (Morton House), 15 oz.	890
Corned Beef Hash (Van Camp), ½ cup	80

Calories

Ham (Armour Star), 100 grams	188
Ham (Armour Golden Star), 100 grams	126
Ham, Jubilee (Oscar Mayer, all sizes), 1 oz.	42
Ham, Boneless Jubilee Ham Slice (Oscar Mayer), 1 oz.	43
Ham Chedderton (Lipton), 1 package	660
Ham, Chopped (Armour), 12 oz.	922
Deviled Ham (Armour), 3 oz.	278
Ham, Parti-Style (Armour), 100 grams	147
Lamb Stew (B & M), 1 cup	247
Macaroni with Beef (Morton House), 12¾ oz.	745
Manwich (Hunt's), 15 oz.	243
Potted Meat (Armour), 3¼ oz.	198
Potatoes and Ham (Morton House), 12¾ oz.	660
Salisbury Steak and Mushroom Gravy (Morton House), 12¾ oz.	835
Sausage, Vienna (Armour), 4 oz.	244
Sausage, Vienna (Libby, Mc Neill & Libby), 1 sausage	39
Scrapple (Oscar Mayer, 1 lb.), 1 oz.	44
Treet (Armour), 12 oz.	1001
Turkey Primavera (Lipton), 1 package	786

MEATS AND POULTRY, Frozen

Calories

Beans with Franks Dinner (Morton), 11 oz.	428
Beans and Franks, TV Brand (Swanson), 1 complete dinner	610
Beans and Franks (Banquet), 10.75 oz.	687
Beef in Red Wine Sauce (Seabrook Farms), ½ cup	176
Beef Dinner, TV Brand (Swanson), 1 complete	414
Beef Dinner (Banquet), 11 oz.	295
Beef Dinner (Swanson), 3 course 1 complete dinner	602
Beef, sliced, gravy (Banquet), 5 oz.	158

Calories

Beef, sliced, gravy (Banquet Buffet Supper) 32 oz.	956
Beef, sliced, BBQ Sauce (Banquet), 5 oz.	174
Beef, macaroni, TV Brand (Swanson), 1 dinner	302
Beef, macaroni (Banquet Buffet Supper), 32 oz.	1027
Beef, macaroni in tomato sauce, EfficienC (Swanson), 1 complete entree	231
Beef, braised short ribs, EfficienC (Swanson), 1 complete entree	445
Beef, chopped (Banquet), 9 oz.	386
Beef, corned beef hash, TV Brand (Swanson), 1 dinner	511
Beef, creamed chipped (Banquet), 5 oz.	127
Beef, enchilada dinner (Patio), 12 oz.	757
Beef Goulash (Seabrook Farms), ½ cup	112
Beef Pie (Stouffer's), 10 oz.	554
Beef Pot Pie (Morton), 8¼ oz.	429
Beef, Deep Dish Meat Pie (Swanson), 1 lb.	631
Beef, Meat Pie (Swanson), 8 oz.	443
Beef Pot Pie (Banquet), 8 oz.	411
Beef Meat Pie (Banquet), 36 oz.	1311
Beef Ragout Specialty (Swanson), 1 complete dinner	177
Beef Stew (Seabrook Farms), ½ cup	116
Beef Stew (Banquet Buffet Supper), 32 oz.	720
Beef Stew, EfficienC (Swanson), 1 complete dinner	202
Beef Stroganoff Specialty (Swanson), 1 complete dinner	213
Chicken à la King, EfficienC (Swanson), 1 complete dinner	166
Chicken à la King (Banquet), cook-in bag, 5 oz.	140
Chicken, White Wine Cream Sauce Specialty (Swanson), 1 complete dinner	243
Chicken, Dumplings (Banquet Buffet Dinner), 32 oz.	1306

Calories

Chicken, Noodles (Banquet Buffet Supper), 32 oz.	736
Chicken, Noodles, TV Brand (Swanson), 1 complete dinner	370
Chicken, Noodles Specialty (Swanson), 1 complete dinner	285
Chicken, Noodles, EfficienC (Swanson), 1 complete dinner	202
Chicken, Creamed (Stouffer's), 11½ oz.	614
Chicken Dinner (Banquet), 11 oz.	542
Chicken, Escalloped, Noodles (Stouffer's), 11½ oz.	587
Chicken, Fried, Dinner (Morton), 11 oz.	435
Chicken, Fried (Banquet, 10 pieces), 32 oz.	2195
Chicken, Fried (Banquet, 5 pieces), 14 oz.	960
Chicken, Fried, TV Brand (Swanson), 1 dinner	600
Chicken, Fried, (Swanson), 3-course dinner	652
Chicken, Fried, TV Brand (Swanson), entree	483
Chicken Pot Pie (Banquet), 8 oz.	412
Chicken Pie (Stouffer's), 10 oz.	561
Chicken Pot Pie (Morton), 8¼ oz.	460
Chicken, Meat Pie (Swanson), 8 oz.	503
Chicken, Deep Dish Meat Pie (Swanson), 1 lb.	731
Ham Dinner (Banquet), 10 oz.	352
Ham Dinner (Banquet), 1 0oz.	352
Ham Dinner, TV Brand (Swanson), 1 dinner	366
Macaroni and Beef Dinner (Morton), 11 oz.	414
Macaroni and Beef with Tomatoes (Stouffer's), 11½ oz.	413
Meatballs and Brown Gravy, EfficienC (Swanson), 1 entree	140
Meat Loaf Dinner (Swanson), 3-course dinner	495
Meat Loaf Dinner, TV Brand (Swanson), 1 dinner	419
Meat Loaf Dinner (Banquet), cook-in bag, 5 oz.	281
Meat Loaf Dinner (Banquet), 11 oz.	420

Calories

Meat Loaf Dinner (Morton), 11 oz.	437
Meat Loaf Dinner with Tomato Sauce, EfficienC (Swanson), 1 entree	233
Pork, Loin, TV Brand (Swanson), 1 dinner	460
Pork, Loin with Gravy and Dressing, EfficienC (Swanson), 1 entree	271
Roast Beef Hash (Stouffer's) 11½ oz.	471
Salisbury Steak Dinner (Morton), 11 oz.	394
Salisbury Steak, TV Brand (Swanson), 1 entree	329
Salisbury Steak Dinner (Swanson), 3-course dinner	520
Salisbury Steak (Banquet Buffet Supper), 32 oz.	1524
Salisbury Steak (Banquet), 11 oz.	335
Salisbury Steak with gravy (Banquet), 5 oz.	239
Salisbury Steak with Mushroom Gravy, EfficienC (Swanson), 1 entree	208
Sirloin, Chopped, TV Brand (Swanson), 1 dinner	447
Swiss Steak (Stouffer's), 10 oz.	583
Swiss Steak with Gravy, EfficienC (Swanson), 1 entree	197
Swiss Steak, TV Brand (Swanson), 1 dinner	361
Turkey, Roast (Checkerboard Farms) 1 oz. roast, 1 oz. gravy	82
Turkey, White, Honeysuckle (Ralston Purina), 3½ oz.	200
Turkey Dinner (Morton), 11 oz.	334
Turkey Dinner (Banquet), 11.50 oz.	280
Turkey Dinner, TV Brand (Swanson), 1 complete dinner	314
Turkey Dinner (Swanson), 3-course dinner	557
Turkey Dinner, TV Brand (Swanson), 1 complete dinner	401
Turkey Pot Pie (Morton), 8¼ oz.	441
Turkey Pot Pie (Banquet), 8 oz.	398
Turkey Meat Pie (Banquet), 36 oz.	1529

Calories

Turkey Meat Pie (Swanson), 8 oz.	442
Turkey, Deep Dish Pie (Swanson), 1 lb.	608
Turkey, Sliced and Giblet Gravy (Checkerboard Farms), 6 oz.	222
Turkey, Sliced with Giblet Gravy (Banquet Buffet Supper), 32 oz.	677
Turkey, Sliced and Giblet Gravy (Banquet) 5 oz.	129
Turkey, Sliced with Dressing and Gravy, EfficienC (Swanson), 1 entree	258
Veal Parmigiana, Breaded, EfficienC (Swanson), 1 entree	244
Veal Parmigiana, TV Brand (Swanson), 1 dinner	492
German Style International Dinner (Swanson), 1 dinner	405
Stuffed Green Pepper with Tomato Sauce, EfficienC (Swanson), 1 entree	228
Sloppy Joe (Banquet), 5 oz.	251

FISH AND SEAFOOD, Canned

Calories

Anchovy Paste (Crosse & Blackwell), 1 tbsp.	20
Brislings, Norwegian (Reese), 3¾ oz.	330
Clams, minced (Doxsee), ½ cup	98
Clams, minced (Snow), 1 lb.	230
Clams, steamed, New England Style (Lord Mott's), 6 clams	35
Crab, Alaska King (Del Monte), ½ cup flakes	86
Crab (Bumble Bee), 7½ oz.	221
Crab (Icy Point), 7½ oz.	221
Gefilte Fish (Manischewitz), 1 piece	110
Gefilte Fish, jumbo, in jars (Manischewitz), 1 piece	64
Gefilte Fish, whitefish and pike, in jars (Manischewitz), 1 piece	40
Herring, in sour cream (Vita), 8 oz.	484

	Calories
Herring, Pickled (Vita), 5 oz.	128
Oysters, Smoked (Reese) 3¾ oz.	259
Salmon, Blueback (Icy Point), 7¾ oz.	395
Salmon, Chinook (Bumble Bee), 7¾ oz.	467
Salmon, Red Sockeye (Del Monte), ⅖ cup	171
Salmon, pink (Bumble Bee), 7¾ oz.	320
Salmon, pink (Icy Point), 7¼ oz.	308
Salmon, pink (Del Monte), ⅖ cup	141
Salmon, smoked (Vita), 4 oz.	280
Salmon (S & W Blue Label), ¼ tin	84
Sardines, Norwegian, in oil (Underwood), 3 oz. drained	167
Sardines, Norwegian, in mustard sauce (Underwood), 3 oz. plus 1 oz. sauce	134
Sardines, Norwegian, in mustard sauce (Del Monte), 1½ large	196
Sardines, Norwegian, in tomato sauce (Underwood), 3 oz. plus 1 oz. sauce	124
Sardines, in tomato sauce (Del Monte), 1½ large	197
Sardines, Portuguese (Reese), 3¾ oz.	330
Shrimp, (Bumble Bee), 4½ oz. drained	151
Tuna Fish, light, in oil, chunk-pack (Bumble Bee), 6½ oz.	285
Tuna Fish, light, packed in oil, chunk-pack (Chicken of the Sea), 6½ oz.	447
Tuna Fish, light, packed in oil, chunk-pack (Icy Point), 6½ oz.	322
Tuna Fish, light, packed in oil, chunk-pack (Star-Kist), 6½ oz.	309
Tuna Fish, white, in oil, solid-pack (Bumble Bee), 7 oz.	297
Tuna Fish, white, in oil, solid-pack (Chicken of the Sea), 7 oz.	507
Tuna Fish, white, in oil, solid-pack (Star-Kist), 7 oz.	333
Tuna Fish, white, in oil (Del Monte), ¾ cup	288

FISH AND SEAFOOD, Frozen *Calories*

Clam Sticks, precooked (Mrs. Paul's) , 8 oz.	568
Cod Fillets, uncooked (Gorton's) , approx. 5-oz. serving	117
Cod Sticks, precooked (Birds Eye) , 8 oz.	552
Cod Sticks, precooked (Gorton's) , 16 oz.	830
Crab, Alaska King Newburg (Stouffer's) , 12 oz.	557
Crab, Deviled (Mrs. Paul's) , 6 oz.	372
Fish and Chips (Gorton's, 16-oz. package) , 8-oz. serving	395
Fish 'n' French Fries, TV Brand (Swanson) , 1 dinner	429
Fish Balls, precooked (Gorton's) , 7 oz.	395
Fish Bites, precooked (Birds Eye) , 8 oz.	552
Fish Cakes, precooked (Gorton's) , 8 oz.	463
Fish Cakes, precooked (Mrs. Paul's) , 8 oz.	488
Fish Dinner (Morton's) , 8¾ oz.	333
Fish Fillet Crisps (Gorton's, 8-oz. package) , 4-oz. serving	240
Fish Puffs (Gorton's, 8 oz. package) , 4-oz. serving	265
Fish Sticks, precooked (Mrs. Paul's) , 9 oz.	495
Fish Sticks, (Gorton's, 8-oz. package) , 4-oz. serving	200
Flounder Fillets, uncooked (Gorton's, 16-oz. package) , approx. 5-oz. serving	120
Flounder, precooked (Gorton's) , 9½ oz.	517
Haddock, Filet, TV Brand (Swanson) , 1 dinner	397
Haddock (Banquet) , 8.8 oz.	424
Haddock, Filets, uncooked (Gorton's) , approx. 5-oz. serving	120
Lobster Newburg (Stouffer's) , 11½ oz.	674
Perch, Ocean (Banquet) , 8.8 oz.	472
Perch, Ocean, Filets (Gorton's,16-oz. package) , approx. 5-oz. serving	133
Perch, Ocean, Breaded (Gorton's, 11-oz. package) , approx. 4-oz. serving	113

	Calories
Scallops, uncooked (Gorton's), 12 oz.	252
Scallop Crisps (Gorton's, 7-oz package), approx. 3½-oz. serving	155
Scallops, precooked (Birds Eye), 7 oz.	420
Scallops, precooked (Gorton's), 7 oz.	304
Scallops, precooked (Mrs. Paul's), 7 oz.	301
Shrimp (Ralston Purina), 3-oz. serving	100
Shrimp, Breaded (Ralston Purina), 3-oz. serving	193
Shrimp, Breaded (Gorton's), 4-oz. serving	158
Shrimp, Fried, TV Brand (Swanson), 1 complete dinner	358
Shrimp, Breaded, Fried (Mrs. Paul's), 6 oz.	348
Shrimp Dinner (Morton), 7¾ oz.	367
Shrimp Scampi, (Gorton's), approx. 4-oz. serving	285
Sole Filets (Gorton's, 16-oz. package), approx. 5-oz. serving	120
Sole, Filet, Bonne Femme, EfficienC (Swanson), 1 entree	214
Sole, in Lemon Butter (Gorton's), 3-oz. serving	147
Tuna, Noodle Casserole (Stouffer's), 11½ oz.	448
Tuna, Pot Pie (Banquet), 8 oz.	479
Tuna, Meat Pie (Swanson), 8 oz.	453
Tuna, and Noodles, EfficienC (Swanson), 1 entree	264

DAIRY PRODUCTS

CHEESE, 1 oz., except as noted	Calories
American:	
American Dairy Association	105
Borden's	104
Kraft	105
Kraft Old English	105
"Vera Sharp"	104
Pasteurized, Process (Sealtest)	105
Process Cheese Food (American Dairy Association), 1 slice	105

Calories

Blue, Blue Moon (Foremost)	105
Blue, Domestic (American Dairy Association)	104
Blue, Danish (Borden's)	105
Blue (Gerber), 1 tbsp.	49
Blue (Kraft)	99
Bonbel Brand-Round	94
Brick (American Dairy Association)	105
Brick, Natural (Kraft)	104
Brick, Processed (Kraft)	102
Camembert, Domestic (American Dairy Association)	84
Camembert (Borden's)	86
Camembert (Kraft)	85
Caraway (Kraft)	111
Cheddar (Sealtest)	115
Cheddar, American (American Dairy Association)	113
Cheddar (Borden's)	113
Cheddar, Sharp (Gerber), 1 tbsp.	50
Cheddar (Kraft)	113
Edam (Kraft)	105
Farmer, Midget (Breakstone), 4 oz.	155
Gorgonzola (Kraft)	112
Gouda (Kraft)	108
Gruyere (Borden's)	101
Gruyere (Gerber), 1 tbsp.	101
Gruyere (Kraft)	110
Gruyere (Swiss Knight)	101
Liederkranz Brand	86
Limburger (American Dairy Association)	98
Limburger (Kraft)	98
Muenster, Natural (Borden's)	85
Muenster, Natural (Dorman's Endeco)	90
Muenster, Natural (Kraft)	100
Muenster, Processed (Kraft)	102
Parmesan (Kraft)	107
Pimento (Borden's)	104

	Calories
Pimento-American (Kraft)	104
Port Du Salut (Kraft)	100
Provolone (Borden's)	93
Provolone (Kraft)	99
Ricotta (Breakstone), 4 oz.	205
Roquefort (Kraft)	105

Swiss:

	Calories
Domestic (American Dairy Association)	105
Domestic (Sealtest)	105
Natural (Borden's)	105
Natural (Dorman's Endeco)	90
Natural (Kraft)	104
Processed (Borden's)	100

GRATED CHEESE, 1 tbsp.

	Calories
American (Borden's)	30
Parmesan (Buitoni)	23
Parmesan (Kraft)	27
Parmesan (La Rosa)	34
Parmesan-Romano (Borden's)	30
Romano (Buitoni)	21
Romano (Kraft)	29

CREAM CHEESE,
foil wrapped and/or in jars, 1 oz.

	Calories
American Dairy Association	106
Plain (Borden's)	96
Plain (Breakstone)	86
Plain (Kraft)	98
Plain (Sealtest)	98
With Bacon and Horseradish (Kraft)	91
With Chive (Borden's)	96
With Chive (Kraft)	84
With Dates and Nuts (Borden's)	96
With Olive and Pimento (Kraft)	85
With Pimento (Borden's)	74

	Calories
With Pimento (Kraft)	85
With Pineapple (Kraft)	87
With Relish (Kraft)	88
With Roquefort (Kraft)	80

CREAM CHEESE, Whipped, in foil dishes, 1 oz.

Plain, Temp-Tee (Breakstone)	86
Plain (Kraft)	101
With Blue (Kraft)	99
With Chive (Kraft)	92
With Onion (Kraft)	93
With Pimento (Kraft)	91
With Roquefort (Kraft)	99
Neufchatel (Kraft)	69

CHEESE SPREAD *Calories*

Snack Mate Pasteurized Process, American, 1 tsp.	15
Snack Mate Pasteurized Process, Cheddar, 1 tsp.	15
Snack Mate Pasteurized Process with Pimiento, 1 tsp.	15
Pimiento (Sealtest), 1 oz.	77

COTTAGE CHEESE, 1/2 cup, except where noted *Calories*

California Style (Breakstone)	115
Chive (Breakstone)	115
Creamed, Chive (Sealtest)	106
Creamed, Chive-Pepper (Sealtest)	102
Creamed, Peach-Pineapple (Sealtest)	115
Creamed, Pineapple (Sealtest)	111
Creamed, Spring Garden (Sealtest)	105
Creamed (American Dairy Association), 1 oz.	30
Creamed (Borden's)	120
Creamed (Foremost)	106

	Calories
Creamed (Deans)	110
Creamed (Sealtest)	106
Diet (Pet)	103
Dry, uncreamed (Sealtest)	89
Light n' Lively (Sealtest)	77
Low Fat (So-Lo)	94
Low Fat, 2% Fat (Sealtest)	93
Low Fat (Breakstone)	90
Pineapple (Breakstone)	132
Pot Style	85
Regular, 4% Fat (Pet)	127
Regular (Breakstone)	115
Skim Milk (Breakstone)	88
Tiny Soft Curd (Breakstone)	115
Uncreamed (Borden's)	98
Uncreamed (Kraft)	103
Uncreamed (Sealtest)	90
Uncreamed (American Dairy Association), 1 oz.	24

YOGURT,
8-oz. container, except when noted

	Calories
Bokoo (Dannon), 4 oz. cuplet	150
Danny, pre-stirred (Dannon), 4 oz.	130
Flavors: Red Raspberry, Strawberry, Cherry Fruit	
Apple, Spiced (Borden's Swiss Style)	270
Apple, Spiced (Sealtest)	245
Apricot (Dannon)	260
Apricot (Borden's Swiss Style)	270
Apricot (Breakstone Regular)	286
Banana (Dannon)	260
Black Cherry (Breakstone Swiss Parfait), 5 oz.	186
Blueberry (Borden's Swiss Style)	270
Blueberry (Breakstone Regular)	284
Blueberry (Dannon)	260

Calories

Blueberry (Sealtest)	257
Blueberry (Breakstone Swiss Parfait)	303
Boysenberry (Borden's Swiss Style)	270
Boysenberry (Dannon)	260
Cherry (Borden's Swiss Style)	270
Cinnamon Apple (Breakstone Regular)	284
Coffee (Dannon)	200
Coffee (Borden's Swiss Style)	270
Lemon (Sealtest)	229
Mandarin Orange (Breakstone Swiss Parfait), 8 oz.	303
Mandarin Orange (Breakstone Swiss Parfait), 5 oz.	189
Natural, Low Fat (Yami)	140
Peach (Breakstone Swiss Parfait)	290
Peach (Sealtest)	252
Peach Melba (Breakstone Swiss Parfait), 5 oz.	195
Pineapple-Orange (Dannon)	260
Pineapple (Breakstone Regular)	286
Plain (Borden's Swiss Style)	167
Plain (Pet)	157
Plain (Dannon)	130
Plain (Sealtest)	134
Plain (Breakstone Regular)	144
Prune (Borden's Swiss Style)	270
Prune (Sealtest)	257
Prune Whip (Dannon)	260
Prune Whip (Breakstone Regular)	284
Raspberry (Borden's Swiss Style)	270
Raspberry (Breakstone Regular)	284
Red Raspberry (Breakstone Swiss Parfait)	293
Red Raspberry (Dannon)	270
Red Raspberry (Sealtest)	225
Royale, Low Fat (Yami)	240
Strawberry (Borden's Swiss Style)	270
Strawberry (Dannon)	260

	Calories
Strawberry (Sealtest)	234
Strawberry (Breakstone Regular)	286
Strawberry (Breakstone Swiss Parfait), 5 oz.	181
Strawberry (Breakstone Swiss Parfait), 8 oz.	291
Vanilla (Borden's Swiss Style)	270
Vanilla (Breakstone Regular)	208
Vanilla (Sealtest)	195
Vanilla (Dannon)	200
Vanilla, Low Fat (Yami)	188
Yogurt, from partially skimmed milk (American Dairy Association)	113

MILK, CREAM, CREAM SUBSTITUTES, 8 oz., except as noted

	Calories
Buttermilk, Cultured, Skimmilk (American Dairy Association)	81
Buttermilk, 0.1% fat (Pet)	83
Buttermilk (Dean)	95
Buttermilk (Golden Nugget)	92
Buttermilk (Light n' Lively)	95
Buttermilk, Bulgarian (Sealtest)	152
Buttermilk, Cultured, 1.5% fat (Foremost)	110
Buttermilk, Lowfat (Sealtest)	114
Buttermilk, Skimmilk (Sealtest)	71
Condensed, Sweetened (American Dairy Association)	728
Egg Nog (Dean)	332
Egg Nog, Dairy Packed, 6% fat (Foremost)	412
Egg Nog, (Sealtest), ½ cup	174
Evaporated Milk (American Dairy Association)	310
Evaporated Milk (Carnation)	348
Evaporated Milk (Sealtest), 4 oz.	172
Evaporated Milk (Sego)	352
Evaporated Milk (Golden Key)	352

Calories

Evaporated Milk (Pet)	352
Evaporated Skim Milk (Pet 99)	180

Whole Milk:

3.25% fat (Sealtest)	144
3.3% fat (American Dairy Association)	147
3.5% fat (American Dairy Association)	147
3.5% fat (Sealtest)	151
3.5% fat (Pet)	149
3.7% fat (Sealtest)	157
3.7% fat (Pet)	153
3.7% fat (Dean)	154

Chocolate Milk:

3.3% fat (Foremost)	218
3.3% fat (American Dairy Association)	198
3.3% fat (Dean)	213
0.5% fat (Sealtest)	146
1.0% fat (Sealtest)	158
2.0% fat (Sealtest)	178
3.4% fat (Sealtest)	207

Chocolate, Ready Shake (Dean), ½ pint	330
Lowfat Milk (Light n' Lively)	114
So-Lo Fortified Low Fat Milk (Foremost), 2% fat	133
Multivitamin (Sealtest)	151
Profile Nonfat (Foremost), 0.1% fat	91
Sweetened Condensed (Sealtest)	65
Skim Milk, 0.1% fat (Pet)	83
Skim Milk, Profile, 0.5% fat (Foremost)	99
Skim Milk (Sealtest)	79
Skim Milk (American Dairy Association)	147
Skim Milk, Partially skimmed, 2% non-fat solids added (American Dairy Association)	134
Skim Milk, Chocolate (Dean)	156
Skim Milk, Diet (Sealtest)	103

Calories

Skim, part, Chocolate Drink (American
    Dairy Association)   172
Value 3 (Sealtest)   141
Vita-lure, 2% fat (Sealtest)   137

INSTANT MILK, CREAM, CREAM SUBSTITUTES, 8 oz., except as noted

8 oz., except as noted	Calories
Milk (Carnation), reconstituted	82
Milk, Dry (Milkman), 1 quart reconstituted	383
Milk, Dry nonfat (Pet), reconstituted	81
Milk, Dry nonfat (Sealtest), ¼ cup	101
Milk, Dry whole (Sealtest), ¼ cup	141
Great Shakes Mix, All Flavors (Birds Eye), made with whole milk	260
Great Shakes Mix, All Flavors (Birds Eye), made with nonfat milk	189
Chocolate Drink (Chiradelli), 1 tbsp.	46
Instant Breakfast, prepared with 8 oz. whole milk:	
Chocolate, Strawberry, Vanilla (Carnation)	290
Milk Chocolate, Dutch Chocolate, Chocolate Fudge, Coffee, Cherry Vanilla, Vanilla, Strawberry (Foremost)	290
Breakfast Plus, Chocolate, Chocolate Fudge, Chocolate Malt Milk, Strawberry, Vanilla (Pet), made with whole milk	290
made with skim milk	210
Chocolate, Chocolate Malt, Vanilla, (Pillsbury), 1 oz.	101
Strawberry (Pillsbury), 1 oz.	104
Malted Milk Powder, Plain (Sealtest) 3 tbsp.	117
Malted Milk Powder, Chocolate (Sealtest) 3 tbsp.	115

CREAM:

Half and Half (American Dairy Association)   38

Calories

Half and Half, 10.5% fat (Foremost), 1 tbsp.	19
Half and Half, 10.5% fat (Sealtest), ½ cup	148
Half and Half, 12.0% fat (Foremost), 1 tbsp.	21
Half and Half, 12.0% fat (Sealtest), ½ cup	161
Half and Half, 12.0% fat (Pet), 1 tbsp.	20
Half and Half (Dean), 2 tbsp.	43
Heavy or Whipping Cream (American Dairy Association), 1 oz.	100
Heavy Cream (Dean), 2 tbsp.	102
Heavy Cream, 30% fat (Sealtest), 1 tbsp.	44
Heavy Cream, 36% fat (Sealtest), 1 tbsp.	52
Light Cream (American Dairy Association), 1 oz.	28
Light Cream (Sealtest), 1 tbsp.	28
Light Cream (Foremost), 1 tbsp.	28
Light Cream, 20% fat (Foremost), 1 tbsp.	31
Light Cream, 16% fat (Sealtest), 1 tbsp.	26
Light Cream, 25% fat (Sealtest), 1 tbsp.	38
Sour Cream (American Dairy Association), 1 oz.	57
Sour Cream (Pet), 1 tbsp.	31
Sour Cream, 18% fat (Foremost), 1 tbsp.	19
Sour Cream, 20% fat (Foremost), 1 tbsp.	21
Sour Cream (Dean), 2 tbsp.	56
Sour Cream (Sealtest), 2 tbsp.	57
Sour Cream-imitation-canned (Pet), 1 tbsp.	27
Sour Cream, non-dairy (Sealtest), 2 tbsp.	60
Sour Half and Half, 10.5% fat (Foremost), 1 tbsp.	19
Sour Half and Half, 12.0% fat (Foremost), 1 tbsp.	21
Sour Half and Half (Sealtest), 2 tbsp.	41
Coffee Twin, frozen (Sealtest), ½ oz.	25
Coffee Creamer, non-dairy (Pet), 1 tbsp.	33
Coffee Creamer, non-dairy, frozen (Pet), 100 grams	149

ICE CREAM, ICE MILK, SHERBET, AND RELATED PRODUCTS

Because ice cream is produced in so many different regions and has so many small variations, the calorie and gram counts of the American Dairy Association, which represents the entire American Dairy Industry, have been included.

	Calories
Ice Cream, Plain, 10% fat (American Dairy Association), 1 pint	437-450
Vanilla, 10.2% fat (Sealtest), ¼ pint	133
Vanilla, 12.1% fat (Sealtest), ¼ pint	144
Vanilla, Party Slice (Sealtest), ¼ pint	133
Vanilla, French, Prestige (Sealtest), ¼ pint	183
Vanilla, Fudge Royal (Sealtest), ¼ pint	132
Vanilla (Dean), ½ pint	338
Vanilla, Dutch Pride, Imitation, 10.65% fat (Foremost), ½ pint	270
Vanilla, 10.35% fat (Foremost), ½ pint	265
Vanilla (Carnation), ⅓ pint	174
Vanilla, 4.20% fat, Big Dip (Sealtest), ½ pint	219
Ice Cream Plain, 12% fat (American Dairy Association), 1 pint	465-500
Chocolate (Carnation), ⅓ pint	169
Chocolate Chip (Carnation), ⅓ pint	169
Chocolate, Prestige (Sealtest), ¼ pint	182
Chocolate (Sealtest), ¼ pint	136
Chocolate, 9.15% fat (Foremost), ½ pint	262
Chocolate, Dutch Pride, Imitation, 10.71% fat (Foremost), ½ pint	266
Strawberry (Carnation), ⅓ pint	169
Strawberry (Sealtest), ¼ pint	133
Strawberry, 8.65% fat (Foremost), ½ pint	242
Strawberry, Dutch Pride, Imitation, 10.11% fat (Foremost)	263

ICE MILK *Calories*

Ice Milk (American Dairy Association), 1 pint	350-378
Ice Milk, 3% fat (Pet), ½ pint	170
Ice Milk, 4% fat (Pet), ½ pint	208
Vanilla (Light n' Lively), ¼ pint	95
Vanilla, Dutch Pride, Imitation, 7% fat (Foremost), ½ pint	213
Vanilla-Chocolate-Strawberry (Light n' Lively), ¼ pint	96
Vanilla Fudge (Light n' Lively), ¼ pint	103
Almond, Buttered (Light n' Lively), ¼ pint	108
Chocolate, Big Dip, 4.40% fat (Foremost), ½ pint	216
Chocolate (Light n' Lively), ¼ pint	98
Chocolate, Dutch Pride, Imitation, 7% fat (Foremost), ½ pint	216
Orange Pineapple (Light n' Lively), ¼ pint	94
Peach (Light n' Lively), ¼ pint	98
Strawberry (Light n' Lively), ¼ pint	93
Strawberry, Dutch Pride, Imitation, 6.65% fat (Foremost), ½ pint	208
Strawberry, Big Dip, 3.75% fat (Foremost), ½ pint	211

SHERBET *Calories*

Lemon, 1.20% fat (Foremost), ½ pint	227
Lime, 1.20% fat (Foremost), ½ pint	227
Orange, 1.20% fat (Foremost), ½ pint	227
Orange (Sealtest), ¼ pint	120
Pineapple, 1.02% fat (Foremost), ½ pint	221
Raspberry, 1.05% fat (Foremost), ½ pint	223
Orange Ice (Sealtest), ¼ pint	130

NOVELTIES

Good Humor Products, 1 piece:	
Chocolate Malt Good Humor	200
Strawberry Good Humor	240

	Calories
Toasted Almond Good Humor	215
Vanilla Good Humor	197
Chocolate Eclair Super Humor	235
Chocolate Fudge Cake Super Humor	234
Grape Bon Joy	99
Orange Vanilla Humorette	100
Orange Ice Stick	85
Bittersweet Sundae	233
Vanilla Cup, Regular	108
Vanilla Cup, Large	290
Vanilla Ice Milk Sandwich	189

Popsicle Industries Products:

Creamsicle, 3 fl. oz.	96
Fudgsicle, 2½ fl. oz.	110
Popsicle, 3 fl. oz.	70

Sealtest Ice Cream Novelties, 2½ fl. oz., except as noted:

Chocolate Coated Ice Cream Bar	149
Chocolate Coated Ice Milk Bar	132
Choco-Nut Sundae Cone	186
Fudge Bar	91
Ice Cream Sandwich, 3 fl. oz.	173
Orange Creame Bar	103
Toffee Krunch Bar, 3 fl. oz.	149

MARGARINE, 1 pat, 1 tbsp.

	Calories
Blue Bonnet	50
Blue Bonnet Soft	50
Blue Bonnet Whipped	35
Fleischmann's, Salted	50
Fleischmann's, Unsalted	50
Fleischmann's, Soft	50
Fleischmann's, Diet	25
Good Luck	101
Golden Glow	89
Imperial	101

	Calories
Imperial Sof-Spread	89
Mazola	100
Mazola, Unsalted	100
Nucoa	100
Parkay	100
Pet	100
Sealtest	73

OILS AND SHORTENINGS,*
1 tbsp.

	Calories
Crisco Oil	121
Mazola Corn Oil	125
Planters Oil	125
Snowdrift	114
Wesson Buttery Flavor Oil	125
Crisco, Vegetable	126
Wesson, Vegetable	125
Crisco Shortening	103
Saff-O-Life	124
Spry Shortening	97

*Note: Products of this nature contain no carbohydrate grams.

VEGETABLES,
Canned and Jarred

	Calories
Asparagus (Diet Delight), ½ cup	12
Asparagus (Musselman), ½ cup	21
Asparagus, All Green Tips (Stokely's), ½ cup with liquid	18
Asparagus, All Green Tips (Stokely's), 1 cup with liquid	35
Asparagus, Green (Del Monte), 6 spears	24
Asparagus, White (Del Monte), 6 spears	47
Asparagus, All Green Cut Spears (Stokely's), ½ cup without liquid	22
Asparagus, All Green Cut Spears (Stokely's), 1 cup with liquid	74

Calories

Asparagus, Whole Spears (Green Giant), ½ cup	18
Asparagus, All Green (S & W Blue Label), 5 whole	16
Beans, Baked with Pork, in Molasses Sauce (Green Giant), ½ cup	144
Beans, Baked, New England Style Sauce (B & M), 1 cup	360
Beans, Oven Baked (Morton House), 11 oz.	460
Beans, Barbecue (Campbell's), ⅓-½ cup	126
Beans, Campside (Heinz), 1 cup	350
Beans 'N Beef in Tomato Sauce (Campbell's), ⅓-½ cups	114
Beans and Franks (Heinz), 1 can	399
Beans and Franks in Tomato Sauce (Campbell's), ⅓-½ cup	160
Beans in Molasses Sauce (Heinz), 1 cup	283
Beans in Tomato Sauce, Vegetarian (Heinz), 1 cup	267
Beans in Tomato Sauce, Vegetarian (Van Camp), ½ cup	136
Kidney Beans (Hunt Wesson), ½ cup	118
Pork 'N Beans and Tomato Sauce (Heinz), 1 cup	293
Pork and Beans (Hunt Wesson), ½ cup	144
Pork and Beans and Molasses Sauce, Boston Style (Heinz), 1 cup	303
Pork and Beans (Van Camp), ½ cup	138
Red Beans (Van Camp), ½ cup	100
Red Beans (Van Camp), 1 cup	204
Red Beans (Hunt Wesson), ½ cup	110
Beans, Chili, Western Style Sauce (Morton House), 15 oz.	545
Beans, Chili (Hunt Wesson), ½ cup	117
Beans, Green (Stokely's), ½ cup	20
Beans, Green (Stokely's), 1 cup	41
Beans, Green (Lord Mott's), ½ cup	22

Calories

Beans, Green, Cut (Diet Delight), ½ cup	15
Beans, Green, Diagonal Cut (Green Giant), ½ cup	17
Beans, Cut Green (S & W Blue Label), ½ cup	16
Beans, Green in Brine (Comstock), 1 lb.	82
Beans, Green in Brine (Del Monte), 1 cup without liquid	34
Beans, Dilly (Lord Mott's), 1 oz.	7
Beans, Shellie (Stokely's), ½ cup	40
Beans, Shellie (Stokely's), 1 cup	81
Beans, Lima (Stokely's), ½ cup	80
Beans, Lima (Stokely's), 1 cup	161
Beans, Lima (Del Monte), 1 cup without liquid	167
Beans, Wax, Whole (Green Giant), ½ cup	13
Beans, Wax, (Stokely's), ½ cup	21
Beans, Wax in Brine (Comstock), 1 lb.	86
Beans, Wax (Del Monte), 1 cup, cut, without liquid	34
Beets (Comstock), 1 lb.	154
Beets, Sliced (S & W Blue Label), ½ cup	28
Beets (Lord Mott's), ½ cup	25
Beets (Stokely's), ½ cup	38
Beets (Del Monte), diced, 1 cup	60
Beets (Del Monte), sliced, 1 cup	65
Beets (Del Monte), whole, 1 cup	58
Beets, Harvard (Greenwood), 1 lb.	208
Beets, Harvard (Lord Mott's), ½ cup	40
Beets, Pickled (Greenwood), 1 lb.	224
Beets, Pickled (Lord Mott's), ½ cup	63
Cabbage, Sweet Sour Red (Greenwood), 1 lb.	280
Cabbage, Sweet 'n Sour Red (Lord Mott's), ½ cup	60
Carrots (Del Monte), 1 cup without liquid	47
Carrots (Stokely's), ½ cup	31
Carrots (Stokely's), 1 cup	63
Carrots (Lord Mott's), ½ cup	23

	Calories
Carrots, Sliced (S & W Blue Label), ½ cup	22
Carrots in Brine (Comstock), 1 lb.	122
Corn, Cream Style (Green Giant), ½ cup	94
Corn, Cream Style (Del Monte), 1 cup solid and liquid	205
Corn, Cream Style (S & W Blue Label), ½ cup	84
Corn, Whole Kernel (Libby, McNeill & Libby), ½ cup	75
Corn, Family Style (Del Monte), 1 cup without liquid	145
Corn, Whole Kernel (S & W Blue Label), ½ cup	52
Corn, Whole Kernel (Stokely's), ½ cup	76
Corn, Whole Kernel (Diet Delight), ½ cup	55
Corn, Whole Kernel, Brine Pack (Green Giant), ½ cup	66
Corn, Vacuum Packed (Stokely's), ½ cup	94
Corn, Vacuum Packed (Del Monte), 1 cup	176
Corn, Vacuum Packed (Green Giant), ½ cup	101
Mixed Vegetables (Del Monte), 1 cup without liquid	89
Mushrooms in Brine (Brandywine), 4 oz.	19
Mushrooms, Button (Reese), 4 oz.	25
Mushroom, Broiled-in-Butter (Grocery Store Products Co.), 1 can including broth	20
Onions, in Cream Style Sauce (Lord Mott's), ½ cup	64
Onions, Whole Boiled (Lord Mott's), ½ cup	25
Onions with Cream Sauce (Durkee), 15 oz.	352
Peas (Del Monte), 1 cup	138
Peas, Early, Alaska (Stokely's), ½ cup	75
Peas, Early June (Le Sueur), ½ cup	50
Peas (Lord Mott's), ½ cup	83
Peas (Diet Delight), ½ cup	36
Peas, Sweet (Libby, McNeill & Libby), ½ cup	65
Peas, Sweet, Hone Pod, Mixed Sizes (Stokely's), ½ cup	64

Calories

Peas, Sweet, Hone Pod, Mixed Sizes (Stokely's) , 1 cup	129
Peas, Sweet (S & W Blue Label) , ½ cup	35
Peas, Sweets (Green Giant) , ½ cup	46
Peas, Blackeyed (Lord Mott's) , ½ cup	87
Peas and Carrots (Stokely's) , ½ cup	52
Peas and Carrots (Stokely's) , 1 cup	103
Peas and Carrots (S & W Blue Label) , ½ cup	32
Peas and Carrots (Del Monte) , 1 cup without liquid	73
Peas and Carrots (Diet Delight) , ½ cup	34
Peas and Carrots (Lord Mott's) , ½ cup	54
Pimientos (Stokely's) , 1 cup	61
Potatoes, Whole White (Lord Mott's) , ½ cup	59
Potatoes, Whole (Hunt Wesson) , ½ cup	49
Potatoes, Small Whole White (Stokely's) , ½ cup	54
Potatoes, Small Whole White (Stokely's) , 1 cup	109
Potatoes (Del Monte) , ⅖ cup	44
Sauerkraut, Chopped or Shredded (Stokely's) , ½ cup	20
Sauerkraut, Chopped or Shredded (Stokely's) , 1 cup	41
Sauerkraut (Del Monte) , ⅔ cup	18
Sauerkraut, Bavarian Style (Stokely's) , ½ cup	24
Spinach (Del Monte) , 1 cup without liquid	54
Spinach (Hunt Wesson) , ½ cup	20
Spinach, Regular and Chopped (Stokely's) , ½ cup	20
Spinach, Chopped (Lord Mott's) , ½ cup	22
Spinach, in Cream Style Sauce (Lord Mott's) , ½ cup	39
Spinach, Leaf (Lord Mott's) , ½ cup	22
Succotash, Cream Style, Corn and Limas (Stokely's) , ½ cup	91

Calories

Succotash, Whole Kernel Corn and Limas (Stokely's), ½ cup	77
Sweet Potatoes (Del Monte), 1 cup with liquid	287
Sweet Potatoes, (Lord Mott's), ½ cup	117
Tomatoes, Solid Pack (Sacramento), 1 lb.	95
Tomatoes (Del Monte), 1 cup solids and liquid	50
Totmatoes, Pureed (Lord Mott's), ½ cup	44
Tomatoes, Whole (Hunt Wesson), ½ cup	22
Tomatoes, Whole (Stokely's), ½ cup	22
Tomatoes, Whole (S & W Blue Label), ½ cup	21
Tomatoes, Stewed (Hunt Wesson), ½ cup	22
Turnip Greens, Chopped and Regular (Stokely's), ½ cup	20
Zucchini (Del Monte), 1 cup	42

POTATO MIXES

Calories

Au Gratin (French's), 5½ oz.	672
Mashed, Country Style (French's), 1⅓ cup	267
Mashed, Instant (French's), 3¼ oz.	324
Pancakes (French's), 3 oz.	284
Scalloped (French's), 5⅝ oz.	552
Scalloped (Pillsbury), 1 oz.	97

VEGETABLES, Frozen
1/2 cup, except as noted

Calories

Artichoke Hearts (Birds Eye Deluxe), 5 or 6 hearts	22
Asparagus Cuts (Birds Eye)	21
Asparagus, Cuts and Tips (Seabrook Farms)	16
Asparagus, Cuts and Tips in Hollandaise Sauce (Seabrook Farms)	84
Asparagus Spears (Birds Eye), ⅓ package	23
Asparagus Spears (Seabrook Farms), 5 spears	19
Asparagus, Whole Cuts, in Butter Sauce (Green Giant)	71
Beans, Baby Butter (Birds Eye), 1 package	313

Calories

Beans, Green, Cut (Birds Eye)	22
Beans, Whole Green (Birds Eye Deluxe)	23
Beans, Green, Cut (Seabrook Farms)	18
Beans, Green, Diagonal Cut in Butter Sauce (Green Giant)	95
Beans, Green, Diagonal Cut, in Mushroom Sauce (Green Giant)	67
Beans, Green, French-Style (Birds Eye)	23
Beans, Green, Italian (Birds Eye)	23
Beans, Green, French-Style (Seabrook Farms)	20
Beans, Green, French-Style, with Toasted Almonds (Birds Eye)	52
Beans, Green French-Style, with Sauteed Mushrooms (Birds Eye)	33
Beans, Green, French-Style, in Butter Sauce (Birds Eye Deluxe)	48
Beans, Green, French-Style, in Mushroom Sauce (Seabrook Farms)	100
Beans, Lima, Baby (Birds Eye)	111
Beans, Lima, Baby (Seabrook Farms)	95
Beans, Lima, Fordhook (Birds Eye)	94
Beans, Lima, Fordhook (Seabrook Farms)	85
Beans, Lima, Fordhook, in Butter Sauce (Birds Eye)	117
Beans, Lima, Baby in Butter Sauce (Green Giant)	135
Beans, Lima, in Cheese Sauce (Seabrook Farms)	140
Beans, Wax, Cut (Seabrook Farms)	20
Beans, Wax (Birds Eye)	24
Beets, Sliced in Orange-Flavor Glaze (Birds Eye)	53
Broccoli, Chopped (Birds Eye)	27
Broccoli, Chopped (Seabrook Farms)	23
Broccoli, Chopped, in Cream Sauce (Birds Eye)	118
Broccoli, Spears, in Butter Sauce (Green Giant)	59
Broccoli, Cut, in Cheese Sauce (Green Giant)	67
Broccoli, Spears (Birds Eye)	26

Calories

Broccoli, Spears, Baby (Birds Eye Deluxe)	26
Broccoli, Spears, in Deluxe Butter Sauce (Birds Eye)	58
Broccoli, Spears, with Hollandaise Sauce (Birds Eye)	100
Brussels Sprouts (Seabrook Farms)	38
Brussels Sprouts (Birds Eye)	34
Brussels Sprouts, Baby (Birds Eye Deluxe)	34
Brussels Sprouts, in Butter Sauce (Green Giant)	69
Butterbeans (Birds Eye), 1 package	313
Butterbeans (Seabrook Farms)	102
Carrots, Nuggets, in Butter Sauce (Green Giant)	54
Carrots, Sliced, in Deluxe Butter Sauce (Birds Eye)	70
Carrots, with Brown Sugar Glaze (Birds Eye)	78
Cauliflower (Seabrook Farms)	17
Cauliflower (Birds Eye)	21
Cauliflower, Cut, Young, in Butter Sauce (Green Giant)	45
Cauliflower, Cut, Young, in Cheese Sauce (Green Giant)	83
Cauliflower Au Gratin (Stouffer's), 10 oz. package	318
Collard Greens (Seabrook Farms)	22
Collard Greens, Chopped (Birds Eye), 1/3 cup	29
Corn on the Cob (Birds Eye), 1 ear	98
Corn, Whole Kernel, in Butter Sauce (Green Giant)	97
Corn, Whole Kernel, with Peppers and Butter Sauce (Green Giant)	107
Corn, Whole Kernel, White, in Butter Sauce (Green Giant)	106
Corn, Sweet Whole Kernel (Birds Eye)	77
Corn, Sweet, White (Birds Eye Deluxe)	77
Corn, Cut (Seabrook Farms)	70

Calories

Corn, in Deluxe Butter Sauce (Birds Eye)	101
Corn, Cream Style (Birds Eye)	79
Corn and Peas, with Tomatoes (Birds Eye)	68
Corn and Carrots and Pearl Onions, in Cream Sauce (Birds Eye)	120
Corn Souffle (Stouffer's), 12 oz. package	492
Kale, Chopped Leaf (Seabrook Farms)	30
Kale, Chopped (Birds Eye)	29
Mushrooms, Whole, in Butter Sauce (Green Giant)	65
Mushrooms, Whole (Birds Eye)	25
Mustard Greens, Chopped (Birds Eye)	19
Mustard Greens, Leaf, Chopped (Seabrook Farms)	21
Okra, Cut (Birds Eye)	36
Okra, Cut and Whole (Seabrook Farms)	26
Okra, Whole (Birds Eye)	36
Onions, Chopped (Birds Eye), ¼ cup	14
Onions, Cream Sauce (Birds Eye)	127
Onions in Cream Sauce (Seabrook Farms)	116
Onions, Small, in Cream Sauce (Green Giant)	54
Onion Rings, French Fried (Birds Eye)	168
Onion Rings, French Fried (Mrs. Paul's), 5 oz. package	202
Onions, Small Whole (Birds Eye), ⅙ package	42
Peas, Blackeye (Birds Eye)	92
Peas, Blackeye (Seabrook Farms)	100
Peas, Green Sweet (Seabrook Farms)	52
Peas, Green (Birds Eye)	70
Peas, Petite (Seabrook Farms)	74
Peas, Tender, Tiny (Birds Eye Deluxe)	70
Peas, Green, with Mushrooms (Birds Eye)	66
Peas, Green in Deluxe Butter Sauce (Birds Eye)	90
Peas, Green, Early June, in Butter Sauce (Le Sueur)	87
Peas, Sweet, in Butter Sauce (Green Giant)	91

Calories

Peas, Green, in Butter Sauce (Seabrook Farms)	100
Peas, Green, with Cream Sauce (Birds Eye)	129
Peas, Green, with Sauteed Mushrooms (Birds Eye)	67
Peas, Green, in Onion Sauce (Seabrook Farms)	96
Peas, Sweet, with Onions in Butter Sauce (Green Giant)	97
Peas and Carrots (Seabrook Farms)	41
Peas and Carrots (Birds Eye)	55
Peas, Green and Celery (Birds Eye)	56
Peas, Green and Pearl Onions (Birds Eye)	67
Peas, Green, and Rice with Mushrooms (Birds Eye)	49
Peas, Green, and Potatoes with Cream Sauce (Birds Eye)	136
Potatoes, Buttered Parsley (Seabrook Farms)	104
Potatoes, Whole, Boiled (Seabrook Farms)	76
Potatoes Au Gratin Specialty (Swanson)	241
Potatoes Au Gratin (Stouffer's), 11½ oz.	301
Potatoes Au Gratin (General Mills)	160
Potato Buds (General Mills)	134
Potatoes, Creamed with Peas (Stouffer's), 10 oz.	325
Potatoes, French Fried (Birds Eye), 17 pieces	145
Potatoes, French Fried (Seabrook Farms), 17 pieces	153
Potatoes, French Fried, Tiny Taters (Birds Eye), 1 lb.	822
Potatoes, French Fried, Crinkle Cut (Birds Eye), 17 pieces	145
Potatoes, French Fried, Puffs (Birds Eye), 8 oz.	483
Potatoes, Patties (Birds Eye), 1 patty	180
Potatoes, Scalloped Specialty (Swanson)	257
Potatoes, Scalloped (Stouffer's), 12 oz.	389
Potatoes, Scalloped (General Mills)	150
Potatoes, Sweet, Candied (Birds Eye)	215

Calories

Potatoes, Sweet, with Brown Sugar, Pineapple Glaze	135
Rice and Peas with Mushrooms (Birds Eye)	37
Spinach, Leaf (Birds Eye), ⅓ package	23
Spinach, Leaf, in Butter Sauce (Green Giant)	24
Spinach, Leaf (Seabrook Farms)	24
Spinach, Chopped (Seabrook Farms)	25
Spinach, Chopped (Birds Eye)	23
Spinach, Chopped, in Deluxe Butter Sauce (Birds Eye)	55
Spinach, Chopped, Creamed (Seabrook Farms)	104
Spinach, Creamed (Birds Eye)	62
Spinach, Creamed (Green Giant)	119
Spinach Souffle (Stouffer's), 12 oz.	484
Spinach Souffle (Swanson)	260
Squash, Cooked (Birds Eye)	43
Squash, Cooked, Sliced Summer (Birds Eye)	20
Squash, Cooked (Seabrook Farms)	46
Squash, Summer (Birds Eye)	20
Succotash (Seabrook Farms)	87
Succotash (Birds Eye)	88
Turnip Greens (Birds Eye)	22
Vegetable Jubilee (Birds Eye)	138
Vegetables, Mixed (Birds Eye)	60
Vegetables, Mixed (Seabrook Farms)	50
Vegetables, Mixed, in Butter Sauce (Green Giant)	67
Vegetables, Mixed in Deluxe Butter Sauce (Birds Eye)	83
Vegetables, Mixed, in Onion Sauce (Birds Eye)	120

FRUITS, Canned and Dried
1/2 cup, except as noted

Calories

Apples, dried, uncooked (Del Monte), 1 cup	237
Apples sliced (Musselman), ½ cup	112
Apples and Apricots, mixed, in jars (Mott's Fruit Treats)	104

Calories

Apples and Cherries, mixed, in jars (Mott's Fruit Treats)	109
Apples and Pineapples, mixed, in jars (Mott's Fruit Treats)	127
Apples and Raspberries, mixed, in jars (Mott's Fruit Treats)	111
Apples and Strawberries, mixed, in jars (Mott's Fruit Treats)	104
Apple Rings, Spiced (Musselman), 1 ring	21
Apple Sauce (Musselman)	112
Apple Sauce Dietetic (Musselman)	55
Apple Sauce (Diet Delight)	44
Apple Sauce with Cinnamon, Country Style (Mott's)	105
Apple Sauce, Golden Delicious (Mott's)	105
Apple Sauce, McIntosh (Mott's)	105
Applesauce (S & W Blue Label)	48
Applesauce (S & W Red Label)	48
Applesauce (S.P.)	67
Applesauce (Del Monte), 1 cup	238
Applesauce, in jars (Mott's)	105
Apricots (Del Monte), Juice Pack, 1 cup with liquid	130
Apricots (Del Monte), Light Syrup, 1 cup with liquid	163
Apricots (Del Monte), Heavy Syrup, 1 cup with liquid	217
Apricots (Hunt Wesson)	103
Apricots, Halves (S & W Blue Label), 4 halves	38
Apricots, Halves (Diet Delight)	35
Apricots, Halves (S & W Red Label), 4 halves	40
Apricots, dried (Sunsweet)	224
Apricots, dried, uncooked (Del Monte), 1 cup	330
Apricots, (Stokely's)	92
Apricots, Whole, peeled (Diet Delight)	28

Calories

Blackberries (S & W Red Label)	36
Blackberries (Musselman)	107
Blueberries (Musselman)	119
Boysenberries (S & W Red Label)	32
Boysenberries (Del Monte), Juice Pack, 1 cup with liquid	130
Boysenberries (Del Monte), Light Syrup, 1 cup with liquid	163
Boysenberries (Del Monte), Heavy Syrup, 1 cup with liquid	217
Cherries, Sweet (Musselman)	96
Cherries, Water-pack (Musselman)	60
Cherries (Del Monte), 1 cup light syrup	163
Cherries, Royal Anne (S & W Blue Label), 14 whole cherries	47
Cherries, Royal Anne (S & W Red Label), 14 whole cherries	49
Cherries, Royal Anne (Diet Delight)	47
Cherries, Light & Dark Sweet, Unpitted (Stokely's)	88
Cherries, Dark, Sweet (S & W Red Label)	53
Citrus Salad (Del Monte), 1 cup with liquid	174
Crabapples (Musselman), 1 crabapple	36
Cranberry Sauce, jellied, canned (Ocean Spray), 100 grams	162
Cranberry Sauce, jellied, canned (Ocean Spray), 1 oz.	46
Cranberry Sauce, whole, canned (Ocean Spray), 100 grams	168
Cranberry Sauce, whole, canned (Ocean Spray), 1 oz.	48
Dates, Chopped (Dromedary), 1 cup	493
Dates, Pitted, (Dromedary), 4 oz.	376
Figs (Del Monte), Light Syrup, 1 cup	158

Calories

Figs (Del Monte), Heavy Syrup, 1 cup	208
Figs (Del Monte), Extra Heavy Syrup, 1 cup	261
Figs, Kadota (Diet Delight)	47
Figs, Whole (S & W Blue Label), 6 whole figs	52
Figs, Whole (S & W Red Label)	49
Fruit Cocktail (Stokely's)	88
Fruit Cocktail (Diet Delight)	32
Fruit Cocktail (Del Monte), Light Syrup, 1 cup	145
Fruit Cocktail (Del Monte), Heavy Syrup, 1 cup	187
Fruit Cocktail (S & W Blue Label)	35
Fruit Cocktail (S & W Red Label)	36
Fruit Cocktail (Dole), 1 lb., 1 oz.	288
Fruit Cocktail (Hunt Wesson)	89
Fruit Cocktail (Libby, McNeill & Libby)	86
Fruit Cocktail (S. P.)	98
Fruit Cocktail, low calorie (Dole), 1 lb.	144
Fruit for Salad (Diet Delight)	25
Fruits for Salad (Del Monte), Light Syrup, 1 cup	143
Fruits for Salad (Del Monte), Heavy Syrup, 1 cup	185
Grapefruit Sections (S & W Red Label)	35
Grapefruit Sections (Diet Delight)	30
Oranges, Mandarin (Del Monte), 1 cup with light syrup	163
Oranges, Mandarin-Segments (Diet Delight)	26
Peaches (Del Monte), Juice Pack, 1 cup	113
Peaches (Del Monte), Light Syrup, 1 cup	147
Peaches (Del Monte), Heavy Syrup, 1 cup	203
Peaches, Cling Slices (S & W Blue Label)	24
Peaches, Cling Slices (S & W Red Label)	25
Peaches, Freestone Halves (Diet Delight)	26

Calories

Peaches, Freestone Halves (S & W Red Label)	26
Peaches, Cling Halves (Diet Delight)	25
Peaches, Freestone Slices (Diet Delight)	25
Peaches, Freestone Slices (S & W Red Label	24
Peaches, Cling Slices (Diet Delight)	27
Peaches (Hunt Wesson)	96
Peaches (Libby, McNeill & Libby)	89
Peaches (S.P.)	98
Peaches, dried (Sunsweet)	216
Peaches, dried, uncooked (Del Monte), 1 cup	461
Pears, Halves (S & W Blue Label), 2 halves	30
Pears, Halves & Quarters (Diet Delight)	32
Pears, Halves (S & W Red Label), 2 halves	28
Pears, Quartered (S & W Red Label)	26
Pears (Hunt Wesson)	90
Pears, dried (Sunsweet)	208
Pears, Bartlett (Stokely's)	86
Pears, Low calorie (Dole), 1 lb.	145
Pears, Quartered (S & W Blue Label)	27
Pears (Del Monte), Juice Pack, 1 cup	104
Pears (Del Monte), Light Syrup, 1 cup	139
Pears (Del Monte), Heavy Syrup, 1 cup	177

Pineapple:

Chunks (Diet Delight)	48
Chunks, in pure Pineapple Juice (Dole), 1 lb., 4 oz.	320
Chunks (S & W Red Label)	
Chunks, in heavy syrup (Dole), 1 lb., 4½ oz.	420
Chunks, sliced, low calorie (Dole), 1 lb., 4 oz.	272
Chunks, extra heavy syrup (Stokely's)	84
Crushed, in pure Pineapple Juice (Dole), 1 lb., 4 oz.	320

	Calories
Crushed (Diet Delight)	48
Crushed, in heavy syrup (Dole), 1 lb., 4½ oz.	420
Crushed, in heavy Syrup (Stokely's)	52
Sliced, in pure Pineapple Juice (Dole), 1 lb., 4 oz.	320
Slices (Diet Delight)	36
Sliced (S & W Blue Label), 2½ slices	69
Sliced (S & W Red Label), 2½ slices	56
Sliced, dietetic (Dole), 1 lb., 4 oz.	320
Sliced (Del Monte), Juice Pack, 1 cup	161
Sliced (Del Monte), Light Syrup, 1 cup	164
Sliced (Del Monte), Heavy Syrup, 1 cup	209
Sliced, Heavy Syrup (Stokely's)	52
Sliced, Rings, in heavy syrup (Dole), 1 lb., 4½ oz.	420
Spears (Dole), 1 lb., 4½ oz.	420
Tidbits (Dole), 1 lb., 4½ oz.	420
Tidbits (Diet Delight)	40
Tidbits (S & W Blue Label)	69
Tidbits (S & W Red Label)	49
Tidbits, Dietetic (Dole), 8½ oz.	154
Plums, Purple (S & W Red Label)	50
Plums, Purple (Del Monte), 1 cup in heavy syrup	194
Plums, Purple (Diet Delight)	51
Plums (Musselman)	103
Prunes, dried (Sunsweet)	272
Prunes, dried, uncooked (Del Monte), ready to eat, 1 cup	477
Prunes, Stewed, (Sunsweet)	195
Prunes, Cooked (Del Monte), 1 cup	317
Raspberries, Black (Musselman)	109
Raisins, Seedless (Sun Maid)	214

	Calories
Raisins, dried, uncooked (Del Monte), 1 cup	413
Salad Fruits (S & W Blue Label)	38
Salad Fruits (S & W Red Label)	35
Snack Pack Fruit Cup (Hunt Wesson), 5½ oz.	112
Snack Pack Peaches (Hunt Wesson), 5 oz.	106
Snack Pack Applesauce (Hunt Wesson), 5 oz.	94
Strawberries (S & W Red Label)	20

FRUITS, Frozen
1/2 cup, except as noted

	Calories
Apples, Escalloped (Stouffer's), 12 oz.	414
Blueberries (Birds Eye)	121
Blueberries, unsweetened (Seabrook Farms)	45
Cherries, Bing (Birds Eye)	122
Melon Balls (Birds Eye), ½ package	72
Mixed Fruit (Birds Eye)	111
Peaches (Birds Eye)	87
Peaches, Sliced, Sweetened (Seabrook Farms)	106
Peaches and Strawberries (Birds Eye)	81
Pineapple Chunks (Dole), 13½ oz.	275
Raspberries (Birds Eye)	129
Raspberries, Sweetened (Seabrook Farms)	120
Rhubarb (Birds Eys), ¼ package	138
Strawberries, Whole, Unsweetened (Seabrook Farms)	42
Strawberries, Halves (Birds Eye)	152
Strawberries, Sliced (Seabrook Farms)	140
Strawberries, Whole (Birds Eye)	122

FRUIT JUICES, Frozen
reconstituted, 6-oz. glass, except as noted

	Calories
Grape (Minute Maid)	99
Grape (Snow Crop)	99

	Calories
Grape (Welch's)	90
Grapefruit (Birds Eye)	72
Grapefruit (Minute Maid)	75
Grapefruit (Snow Crop)	75
Lemon (Minute Maid), 2 tbsp.	7
Lemon (Snow Crop), 2 tbsp.	7
Orange (Birds Eye), ½ cup	51
Orange (Minute Maid)	90
Orange (Snow Crop)	90
Orange-Grapefruit (Birds Eye)	72
Orange-Grapefruit (Minute Maid)	84
Orange-Grapefruit (Snow Crop)	84
Pineapple (Dole)	101
Pineapple-Grapefruit (Dole)	77
Pineapple-Orange (Dole)	77
Tangerine (Minute Maid)	85
Tangerine (Snow Crop)	85

FRUIT JUICES, Canned or Bottled *Calories*

Apple (Musselman), 6 oz.	78
Apple (Heinz), 5½ oz.	69
Apple (Mott's), 6 oz.	84
Apple (Sealtest), 4 oz.	61
Apple-Apricot-Prunes (Sunsweet), 6 oz.	95
AM-PM (Mott's), 6 oz.	91
Apricot Nectar (Diet Delight), ½ cup	24
Apricot Nectar (S & W Red Label), ½ cup	31
Apricot Nectar (Heinz), 5½ oz.	81
Apricot Nectar (Del Monte), 1 cup	140
Apricot Nectar (Mott's), 6 oz.	105
Apricot and Pineapple Nectar (S & W Blue Label), ½ cup	31
Cider, Sweet (Mott's), 6 oz.	84

Calories

Cranberry Cocktail, Low Calorie, 4 oz.	24
Cranberry Cocktail (Ocean Spray), 6 oz.	124
Cranberry-Apple, Low Calorie (Cranapple), 6 oz.	28
Cranberry-Apple (Cranapple), 6 oz.	141
Cranberry-Grape (Grapeberry), 6 oz.	122
Cranberry-Prune (Cranprune), 6 oz.	123
Apple Cranberry (Mott's), 6 oz.	84
Cranberry Flavored Juice (Mott's), 6 oz.	84
Grape (Welch's), 6 oz.	128
Grape (S & W Blue Label), ½ cup	60
Grape (Heinz), 5½ oz.	112
Grapefruit, Unsweetened (Diet Delight), ½ cup	41
Grapefruit, Sweetened (Del Monte), 1 cup	129
Grapefruit, Unsweetened (Del Monte), 1 cup	100
Grapefruit (Sealtest), ½ cup	51
Grapefruit and Orange (Del Monte), 1 cup	123
Orange, Fresh (Pet), 6 oz.	76
Orange (Heinz), 5½ oz.	69
Orange, Sweetened (Del Monte), 1 cup	127
Orange, Unsweetened (Del Monte), 1 cup	118
Orange (Sealtest), ½ cup	58
Orange (Sealtest), 6 oz.	97
Peach Nectar (Del Monte), 1 cup	118
Pear Nectar (S & W Red Label), ½ cup	30
Pear Nectar (Del Monte), 1 cup	128
Pineapple (S & W Blue Label), ½ cup	59
Pineapple (Heinz), 5½ oz.	86
Pineapple (Stokely's), ½ cup	61
Pineapple Unsweetened (Del Monte), 1 cup	135
Pineapple Unsweetened (Dole), 1 pint, 2 oz.	330
Pineapple-Grapefruit (Dole), 1 pint, 2 oz.	279
Pineapple-Pink Grapefruit (Dole), 12 oz.	186

Calories

Prune (Sunsweet), 6 oz.	128
Prune (Del Monte), 1 cup	189
Prune (Heinz), 5½ oz.	119
Prune (Sealtest), 4 oz.	95
Prune with Lemon (Sunsweet), 6 oz.	128
Juices with Tomato:	
Beef-a-mato (Mott's), 6 oz.	86
Clamato (Mott's), 6 oz.	73
Tomato (S & W Blue Label), ½ cup	22
Tomato (Campbell's), ⅓-½ cup	20
Tomato (Diet Delight), ½ cup	20
Tomato (Heinz), 5½ oz.	36
Tomato (Hunt's), 1 cup	46
Tomato (Libby, McNeill & Libby), ½ cup	25
Tomato (Musselman), 6 oz.	39
Tomato (Sacramento), 6 oz.	86
Tomato (Del Monte), 1 cup	47
Tomato (Sealtest), ½ cup	23
Vegetable (V-8), ⅓-½ cup	19
Vegetable Juice Cocktail (S & W Blue Label), ½ cup	21

PASTA, Dry

Calories

EGG NOODLES, COOKED, 1 CUP:

Goodman's*	177
La Rosa, except spinach*	189
Pennsylvania Dutch*	200
Prince*	192
Ronzoni*	200

MACARONI, COOKED, 1 CUP:

Goodman's**	150
Goodman's*	185

*7-9 minutes
**15-20 minutes

Calories

	Calories
La Rosa**	170
La Rosa*	190
Prince**	162
Prince*	182
Ronzoni**	155
Ronzoni*	192

SPAGHETTI, COOKED, 1 CUP:

Buitoni**	163
Buitoni*	204
Goodman's**	150
Goodman's*	185
La Rosa**	161
La Rosa*	174
Prince**	152
Prince*	193
Ronzoni**	155
Ronzoni*	192

*7-9 minutes
**15-20 minutes

PASTA, Canned and Mixes

	Calories
Macaroni 'n Beef in Tomato Sauce (Franco-American), 1/3-1/2 cup	99
Mac-A-Roni and Cheddar (Golden Grain), 3/4 cup	141
Macaroni and Cheddar (General Mills), 3/4 cup	244
Macaroni and Cheese (Franco-American), 1/3-1/2 cup	97
Macaroni and Cheese, Stir 'n Serve (Golden Grain) 1/2 cup	183
Macaroni with Cheese Sauce (Heinz), 8 oz.	231

	Calories
Macaroni Creole (Heinz), 1 can	169
Mac-A-Roni, Fiesta (Golden Grain), ½ cup	135
Macaroni O's with Cheese Sauce (Franco-American), ⅓-½ cup	75
Macaroni Monte Bello (General Mills), 1 cup	350
Scallop A-Roni (Golden Grain), ⅔ cup	118
Twist A-Roni (Golden Grain), ½ cup	125
Noodles, Almondine (General Mills), ½ cup	213
Noodles, Italiano (General Mills), ½ cup	207
Noodles Romanoff (General Mills), ½ cup	241
Noodle Canton Dinner (General Mills), 1 cup	403
Noodles Stroganoff (General Mills), 1 cup	500
Noodles with Beef (Heinz), 1 can	171
Noodle Roni Almondine (Golden Grain), ½ cup	125
Noodle Roni Au Gratin (Golden Grain), ⅔ cup	127
Noodle Roni Casserole (Golden Grain), ⅔ cup	128
Noodle Roni Parmesano (Golden Grain), ¾ cup	195
Noodle Roni Romanoff (Golden Grain), ½ cup	181
Noodle Roni Stroganoff (Golden Grain), ½ cup	120
Beef Rice-A-Roni (Golden Grain), ½ cup	161
Cheese Rice-A-Roni (Golden Grain), ½ cup	145
Chicken Rice-A-Roni (Golden Grain), ½ cup	157
Drumstick (Minute), ½ cup	153
Fried Rice-A-Roni (Golden Grain), ½ cup	187
Ham Rice-A-Roni (Golden Grain), ½ cup	102
Rice Teriyaki (General Mills), 1 cup	412
Rib Roast (Minute), ½ cup	149
Spanish Rice (Heinz), 1 can	122

	Calories
Spanish Rice (Minute), ½ cup	149
Spanish Rice A-Roni (Golden Grain), ½ cup	118
Spanish Rice (El Paso), ½ cup	97
Turkey Rice-A-Roni (Golden Grain), ½ cup	186
Wild Rice-A-Roni (Golden Grain), ½ cup	141
Spaghetti 'n Beef in Tomato Sauce (Franco-American), ⅓-½ cup	119
Spaghetti and Franks in Tomato Sauce (Heinz), 1 can	308
Spaghetti, Italian Style (Franco-American), ⅓-½ cup	77
Spaghetti, Italiano (Golden Grain), ½ cup	137
Spaghetti with Meatballs (Franco-American), ⅓-½ cup	116
Spaghetti with Meat Sauce (Heinz), 1 can	174
Spaghetti and Meatballs in Tomato Sauce (Morton House), 12¾-oz. can	920
Spaghetti in Tomato Sauce with Cheese (Heinz), 8 oz.	178
Spaghetti with Tomato Sauce (Van Camp), ½ cup	105
Spaghetti O's with Sliced Franks (Franco-American), ⅓-½ cup	111
Spaghetti O's with Meatballs (Franco-American), ⅓-½ cup	94
Spaghetti O's in Tomato and Cheese Sauce (Franco-American), ⅓-½ cup	81

PASTA, Frozen

	Calories
Macaroni and Beef Dinner (Morton), 11 oz.	414
Macaroni and Beef with Tomatoes (Stouffer's), 11½ oz.	413
Macaroni and Cheese, TV Brand (Swanson), 1 complete dinner	367

	Calories
Macaroni and Cheese, EfficienC (Swanson), 1 entree	196
Macaroni and Cheese (Stouffer's), 12 oz.	480
Macaroni and Cheese (Banquet), 12 oz.	342
Macaroni and Cheese (Banquet), 8 oz.	279
Macaroni and Cheese (Banquet), 20 oz.	742
Macaroni and Cheese (Banquet), cook-in bag, 8 oz.	280
Macaroni and Cheese Dinner (Morton), 12¾ oz.	445
Macaroni and Cheese Specialty (Swanson), 1 complete dinner	367
Macaroni and Cheese Casserole (Morton), 8 oz.	227
Spaghetti with Meat Sauce (Banquet), 8 oz.	310

PASTA, Packaged Dinners (Kraft), 1/2 cup, prepared according to package directions

	Calories
Italian Macaroni Style	133
Macaroni and Cheese	175
Macaroni and Cheese Deluxe	162
Mexican Macaroni Style	151
Noodles and Cheese	232
Noodles with Chicken	149
Noodles Romanoff	239
Spaghetti, Mild American Style	146
Spaghetti with Meat Sauce, Deluxe	180
Spaghetti, Tangy Italian Style	138

RICE
Cooked, 1 cup, except as noted

	Calories
For canned rice products see Pasta section.	
Canadian, Wild (Reese), 1 oz.	100
Carolina, Brown	200

	Calories
Carolina, Long Grain, White	184
Carolina, Precooked, White	184
Minute Rice, Precooked, White, 2/3 cup	122
River, Brown	200
River, Medium Grain, White	184
Uncle Ben's Quick, Precooked, White	194
Village Inn Seasoned Rices, 6 oz. package	approx. 750

RICE, Frozen, 1/2 cup

	Calories
Medley, with Peas and Mushrooms (Green Giant)	109
Pilaf, with Mushrooms and Onions (Green Giant)	120
Spanish (Green Giant)	80
Verdi, with Bell Peppers and Parsley (Green Giant)	135
White and Wild (Green Giant)	114

ITALIAN FOODS, Frozen

	Calories
Chicken Cacciatore (Seabrook Farms), 1/2 cup	140
Lasagna with Meat Sauce, EfficienC (Swanson), 1 entree	325
Italian Style (Banquet), 11 oz.	414
Italian Style International Dinner (Swanson), 1 complete dinner	448
Spaghetti & Meatballs (Banquet), 11.5 oz.	423
Spaghetti & Meatballs (Banquet Buffet Supper), 32 oz.	1324
Spaghetti and Meatballs, EfficienC (Swanson), 1 entree	285
Spaghetti and Meatballs, TV Brand (Swanson), 1 complete dinner	323

	Calories
Spaghetti with Meat Balls Dinner (Morton), 11 oz.	530
Spaghetti with Meat Sauce (Banquet), cook-in bag, 8 oz.	323
Spaghetti with Meat Sauce Specialty (Swanson), 1 complete dinner	233
Spaghetti and Meat Sauce, EfficienC (Swanson), 1 entree	184
Turkey Tetrazzini (Stouffer's), 12 oz.	713

LATIN AMERICAN FOODS

	Calories
Chili Con Carne (El Paso), 8 oz.	376
Chili Con Carne without Beans (Van Camp), ½ cup	255
Chili Con Carne without Beans (Morton House), 15 oz.	1065
Chili without Beans (Armour), 15½ oz.	629
Chili with Beans (Armour), 15½ oz.	534
Chili with Beans (El Paso), 8 oz.	392
Chili Con Carne with Beans (Bounty), ⅓-½ cup	119
Chili Con Carne with Beans (Heinz), 1 can	352
Chili Con Carne with Beans (Morton House), 15 oz.	925
Chili Con Carne with Beans (Van Camp), ½ cup	176
Chili Con Carne with Beans (Van Camp), 1 cup	335
Chili, Green, with Meat and Beans (El Paso), 8 oz.	184
Chili Con Carne with Beans (Banquet), 8 oz.	310
Chili Con Carne with Beans, TV Brand (Swanson), 1 complete dinner	459
Enchilada in Chili Gravy (Patio), 1 piece	185

Calories

Enchilada, Beef (Banquet), 12.5 oz.	467
Enchilada, Beef, with Sauce (Banquet), cook-in bag, 6 oz.	259
Enchilada Dinner, Beef (Patio), 12 oz.	757
Enchilada Dinner, Cheese (Patio), 12 oz.	591
Enchilada, Cheese (Banquet), 12.5 oz.	482
Mexican Style Dinner (Banquet), 16.25 oz.	569
Mexican Style Dinner (Patio), 15 oz.	722
Mexican Style Combination Dinner (Patio), 12 oz.	683
Mexican Style International Dinner (Swanson), 1 complete dinner	658
Tacos (Patio), 1 piece	179
Tamales (El Paso), 1 piece	81
Tamales and Beef Chili Gravy (Patio), 1 piece	175
Tamales with Sauce (Banquet), cook-in bag, 6 oz.	219
Tortillas (Patio), 1 piece	22
Tortillas (El Paso), 1 piece	66

ORIENTAL FOODS, Canned
1 cup, except as noted

Calories

Bamboo Shoots, sliced (La Choy), ½ cup	6
Bamboo Shoots, (Chun King)	64
Bamboo Sprouts (La Choy)	15
Bean Sprouts (Chun King)	38
Beef Chow Mein (La Choy)	77
Beef Chow Mein (Chun King)	149
Beef Chow Mein, Bi-Pack (La Choy)	90
Beef Chow Mein, Divider-Pak (Chun King)	59
Chicken Chow Mein-303 (La Choy)	74
Chicken Chow Mein (Chun King)	100
Chicken Chow Mein, 2-can package (La Choy)	118

	Calories
Chicken Chow Mein, Divider-Pak (Chun King)	107
Mixed Chinese Vegetables (La Choy)	22
Chinese Vegetables (Chun King)	20
Mushroom Chow Mein, Bi-Pack (La Choy)	81
Mushroom Chow Mein, Divider-Pak (Chun King)	49
Chop Suey Vegetable (La Choy)	30
Chow Mein Noodles (Chun King)	211
Chow Mein Noodles (La Choy), ½ cup	129
Chow Mein Vegetables (Chun King)	23
Meatless Chow Mein-303 (La Choy)	49
Meatless Chow Mein (Chun King)	83
Pork Chow Mein, Divider-Pak (Chun King)	107
Fried Rice (La Choy), ½ cup	137
Meatless Fried Rice (Chun King)	185
Fried Rice with Chicken (La Choy), ½ cup	137
Chicken Fried Rice (Chun King)	256
Pork Fried Rice (Chun King)	243
Shrimp Fried Rice (Chun King)	229
Shrimp Chow Mein-303 (La Choy)	75
Shrimp Chow Mein, Bi-Pack (La Choy)	110
Shrimp Chow Mein, Divider-Pak (Chun King)	188
Water Chestnuts (La Choy), ½ cup	20
Water Chestnuts (Chun King)	46

ORIENTAL FOODS, Frozen

	Calories
Egg Rolls, Meat and Shrimp (Chun King), 1 roll	29
Egg Rolls, Shrimp (Chun King), 1 roll	24
Egg Rolls, Chicken (Chun King), 1 roll	28
Egg Rolls, Lobster and Meat (Chun King), 1 roll	26
Egg Foo Young (Chun King), 6 oz.	120

	Calories
Egg Foo Young Premium Dinner (Chun King), 11 oz.	403
Chow Mein, Beef Premium Dinner (Chun King), 11 oz.	389
Chow Mein, Beef (Chun King), 1 cup	134
Chow Mein, Chicken (Chun King), 1 cup	163
Chow Mein, Chicken (Stouffer's), 11½ oz.	528
Chow Mein, Chicken, Premium Dinner (Chun King), 11 oz.	352
Chow Mein, Chicken, EfficienC (Swanson), 1 entree	124
Chow Mein, Chicken (Banquet), 7 oz.	123
Chow Mein, Chicken (Banquet), 11 oz.	291
Chow Mein, Chicken (Banquet), 32 oz.	563
Chow Mein, Shrimp (Chun King), 1 cup	95
Chow Mein, Shrimp Premium Dinner (Chun King), 11 oz.	378
Chow Mein, Vegetable, EfficienC (Swanson), 1 entree	92
Chop Suey, Beef (Banquet), 7 oz.	121
Chop Suey, Beef (Banquet), 11 oz.	287
Chop Suey, Beef (Banquet), 32 oz.	554
Rice, Fried with Chicken (Chun King), 1 cup	309
Rice, Fried with Meat (Chun King), 1 cup	317
Pork, Sweet and Sour (Chun King), 1 cup	338
Chinese Style International Dinner (Swanson), 1 complete dinner	356

TOMATO PRODUCTS

Calories

TOMATO PASTE & PUREE

Paste, canned (Contadina), 6 oz.	182
Paste, canned (Del Monte), 1 cup	212
Paste, canned (Hunt's), ½ cup	108
Puree, canned (Contadina), ½ cup	46
Puree, canned (Hunt's), ½ cup	46

TOMATO SAUCE, 1 cup, except as noted *Calories*

Tomato Sauce (Contadina), ½ cup	52
Tomato Sauce (Hunt's)	78
Tomato Sauce (Del Monte)	85
Tomato Sauce with Cheese (Hunt's)	97
Tomato Sauce with Mushrooms (Hunt's)	76
Tomato Sauce with Onions (Hunt's)	93
Tomato Sauce with Tomato Bits (Hunt's)	75
Tomato Sauce (Stokely's)	342

TOMATOES *Calories*

Tomatoes, Sliced Baby (Contadina), ½ cup	24
Tomatoes, Round, Peeled (Contadina), ½ cup	17
Tomatoes, Whole, Peeled (Diet Delight), ½ cup	20

SAUCES, GRAVIES, CONDIMENTS, AND SEASONINGS

Calories

A La King Sauce without chicken (Durkee), 1⅛ cups prepared	297
All Purpose Soy Sauce (Chun King), 1 tbsp.	6
Au Jus Gravy (McCormick), 1 oz.	90
Au Jus Gravy Mix (French), ¼ cup	5
Bar-B-Q Flavor (Lawry's), 4.5 oz.	394
Barbecue Sauce-Open Pit (Good Seasons), 1½ tbsp.	39
Barbecue Sauce Mix (Kraft), ½ cup	147
Barbecue, Chicken (Compliment), ½ cup	122
Beef Goulash, Mix (Lawry's), 1.66 oz.	127
Beef Gravy (Franco-American), ⅓-½ cup	78
Beef Stew (Lawry's), 1.64 oz.	131
Beef Stew Seasoning (French), 1.78 oz.	133
Beef Stew Seasoning Mix (McCormick), 1½ oz.	90
Beef Stroganoff Mix (Lawry's), 1.5 oz.	118

Calories

Bordelaise (General Mills), ¼ cup	33
Brown Gravy (McCormick), ⅞ oz.	103
Brown Gravy (Lawry's), 1.25 oz.	136
Brown Gravy Mix (Durkee), 1 cup prepared	96
Brown Gravy Mix (French's), ¼ cup	18
Brown Gravy Mix (Kraft), ½ cup	45
Butter Flavored Salt, Imitation (Durkee), 1 tsp.	88
Cheddar Cheese Sauce Mix (Kraft), ½ cup	212
Cheese Sauce (General Mills), ¼ cup	87
Cheese Mix for Macaroni (French's) per ½ cup macaroni and cheese	172
Cheese Omelet Seasoning Mix (McCormick), 1¼ oz.	128
Cheese Sauce Mix (McCormick), 1 package	170
Cheese Sauce Mix (French's), 1 cup	340
Cheese Sauce Mix (Durkee's), 1 cup prepared	264
Chicken Gravy (Franco-American), ⅓-½ cup	88
Chicken Gravy (Lawry's), 1 oz.	110
Chicken Gravy (McCormick), ⅞ oz.	81
Chicken Gravy Mix (Kraft), ½ cup	60
Chicken Gravy Mix (French's), ¼ cup	32
Chicken Gravy Mix (Durkee), 1 cup prepared	96
Chicken Supreme (Compliment), ½ cup	118
Chili Con Carne Mix, without Meat & Beans (Durkee), 1¼ cups prepared	196
Chili Con Carne Mix with Meat and Beans (Durkee), 2½ cups prepared	1720
Chili Dog Sauce Mix (McCormick), 25 grams	250
Chili-O (French), 1.75 oz.	123
Chili Seasoning Mix (Lawry's), 1.62 oz.	137
Chili Seasoning Mix (McCormick), 1¼ oz. including tomato sauce	78

Calories

Chop Suey Sauce Mix (Durkee), 1¼ cups prepared	128
Enchilada Sauce, Hot (El Paso), 1 oz.	9
Enchilada Sauce, Mild (El Paso), 1 oz.	9
Enchilada Sauce Mix (Lawry's), 1.63 oz.	144
Enchilada Seasoning Mix (McCormick), 1½ oz.	113
Famous Sauce (Durkee), 6½ oz. or 13 tbsp.	690
Famous Sauce (Durkee), 10 oz. or 20 tbsp.	1062
Garlic Salt (Lawry's), 2.80 oz.	116
Garlic Spread (Lawry's), 4 oz.	626
Giblet Gravy (Franco-American), ⅓-½ cup	48
Gravy for Pork (French), ¼ cup	19
Gravy for Turkey (French), ¼ cup	23
Ground Beef Seasoning with Garlic (French's), 1 oz.	83
Hamburger and Meat Loaf Seasoning Mix (McCormick), 1½ oz.	119
Hawaiian Barbecue Sauce (Chun King), 1 tbsp.	16
Herb Gravy (McCormick), ¼ cup	82
Hollandaise (Lord Mott's), ½ cup	56
Hollandaise (General Mills), ¼ cup	84
Hollandaise Sauce (McCormick), 2 oz.	73
Hollandaise Sauce Mix (Durkee), ⅔ cup prepared	297
Hollandaise Sauce Mix (French's), ¾ cup	192
Hollandaise Sauce Mix (Kraft),	217
Horseradish Dressing (Reese), 1 tbsp.	54
Italian Sauce (Cookbook), ½ cup	72
Maggi Seasoning, 1 tbsp.	17
Meat Loaf Seasoning Mix (Lawry's), 3.5 oz.	333
Meat Loaf (Compliment), ½ cup	109
Meat Loaf (Cookbook), ½ cup	64

Calories

Meat Marinade, Instant (McCormick), including vegetable oil, 1⅛ oz.	69
Meat Marinade, 15 Minute (Adolph's), 0.8 oz.	26
Meat Tenderizer, Seasoned, Instant (Adolph's)	trace
Mushroom Gravy (McCormick), ¾ oz.	72
Mushroom Gravy (Lawry's), 1.3 oz.	145
Mushroom Gravy (Franco-American), ⅓-½ cup	50
Mushroom Gravy Mix (Durkee), 1 cup prepared	64
Mushroom Gravy Mix (French's), ¼ cup	16
Mushroom Omelet Seasoning Mix (McCormick), 1¼ oz.	108
Mushroom Sauce (Cookbook), ½ cup	88
Mushroom Sauce (General Mills), ¼ cup	36
Newburg (General Mills), ¼ cup	68
Onion Burger (McCormick), 1 oz.	86
Onion Gravy (McCormick), ⅞ oz.	101
Onion Gravy Mix (Kraft), ½ cup	46
Onion Gravy Mix (French's), ¼ cup	18
Onion Gravy Mix (Durkee), 1 cup prepared	96
Onion Juice Bottled (McCormick), 1 tsp.	1
Onion Salt, (Lawry's), 3 oz.	105
Oven Barbecue (Cookbook), ½ cup	112
Oven Barbecue Seasonings, Sweet 'n Sour (Lawry's), 4.5 oz.	408
Pepper, Lemon (Durkee), 1 tsp.	3
Pepper, Lemon, Marinade (Lawry's), 2.69 oz.	159
Pepper, Seasoned (Lawry's), 1.63 oz.	158
Pinch of Herbs (Lawry's), 2.19 oz.	212
Pizza Sauce (Hunt Wesson), ½ cup	98
Pizza Sauce (French's), 12 servings	218
Pork Barbecue Sauce (Compliment), ½ cup	104

Calories

Salt, Seasoned (Lawry's), 3 oz.	21
Sauces, Cooking (Compliment), ½ cup	30
Savory Pork Chop Sauce (Compliment), ½ cup	120
Seafood Cocktail Sauce (Reese), 1 tbsp.	16
Seafood Cocktail Sauce Mix (Lawry's), 0.56 oz.	43
Sloppy Joe Sauce Mix with Meat and Tomato Sauce (McCormick), 3 oz. per serving	200
Sloppy Joe Seasoning (French's), 1.5 oz.	117
Sloppy Joe Seasoning Mix (McCormick), 1 5/16 oz.	102
Sloppy Joe Seasoning Mix (Lawry's), 1.5 oz.	139
Sloppy Joe, with Meat and Tomato Paste (Durkee), 3 cups prepared	1639
Sour Cream Sauce (French's), ⅔ cup	280
Sour Cream Sauce (McCormick), 2 oz.	40
Sour Cream Sauce Mix (Durkee), prepared with whole milk, ⅔ cup	216
Sour Cream Sauce Mix (Durkee), prepared with skim milk, ⅔ cup	186
Sour Cream Sauce Mix (Kraft), ½ cup	242
Spaghetti Sauce Mix (Kraft), ½ cup	66
Spaghetti Sauce Mix without Meat (Durkee), 1½ cups	132
Spaghetti Sauce without Meat (McCormick), 4 oz.	80
Spaghetti Sauce, Italian (French's), 2½ cups	448
Spaghetti Sauce with Meat (Franco-American), ⅓-½ cup	96
Spaghetti Sauce with Meat (Heinz), 8 oz.	220
Spaghetti Sauce Mix, Meatless (Heinz), 8 oz.	195
Spaghetti Sauce Mix with Mushrooms (Lawry's), 1.5 oz.	147
Spaghetti Sauce Mix with Mushrooms (Lawry's), 2 cups, prepared	466

Calories

Spaghetti Sauce with Mushrooms (French's) , 5 oz.	96
Spaghetti Sauce with Mushrooms (Heinz), 8 oz.	184
Spaghetti Sauce with Mushrooms (Franco-American) , 1/3-1/2 cup	77
Spaghetti Sauce with Mushrooms (French's) , 2 1/2 cups	362
Spaghetti Sauce Mix with Mushrooms and Tomato Paste (Durkee) , 3 cups	367
Spaghetti Sauce with Mushrooms and Meat (Heinz) , 8 oz.	213
Spanish Rice Seasoning Mix (Lawry's) , 1.5 oz.	125
Stroganoff Sauce (French's) , 1 1/3 cup	416
Stroganoff (Cookbook) , 1/2 cup	68
Supreme Sauce (Hunt Wesson) , 1/2 cup	76
Sweet and Sour Sauce (Durkee), 1 1/2 cups	230
Sweet-Sour Sauce (Chun King) , 1 tbsp.	51.8
Swiss Steak Seasoning Mix (McCormick) , 1 oz.	44
Swiss Steak Sauce (Cookbook) , 1/2 cup	44
Taco Seasoning (French's) , 1.75 oz.	123
Tacos Sauce (El Paso) , 1 oz.	8
Taco Seasoning Mix (McCormick) , 1 1/4 oz.	61
Taco Seasoning Mix (Lawry's) , 2 cups prepared	1016
Tartar (Reese) , 1 tbsp.	72
Teriyaki Sauce (Chun King) , 1 tbsp.	11
Tomato Swiss Steak (Compliment) , 1/2 cup	34
Turkey Gravy (McCormick) , 7/8 oz.	82
Western Style Omelet Seasoning Mix (McCormick) , 1 1/4 oz.	113

	Calories
White Roquefort Dressing (Reese), 1 tbsp.	27
White Sauce Mix (Kraft), ½ cup	197
White Sauce Supreme (McCormick), 2 oz.	22

SALAD DRESSINGS

	Calories
Bacon Dressing Mix (Lawry's), 7 oz.	69
Bleu Cheese, Cheese Garlic (Good Seasons), 1 tbsp.	85
Bleu Cheese, French Style (Wish-Bone), 1 tsp.	21
Blue Cheese (Diet Delight), ½ cup	46
Blue Cheese, Bottled (Kraft), ½ oz.	73
Blue Cheese, Bottled (Kraft Roka Brand), ½ oz.	53
Blue Cheese (Lawry's), 8 oz.	995
Blue Cheese Dressing Mix (Lawry's), 7 oz.	79
Caesar (Lawry's), 8 oz.	1116
Caesar Garlic Cheese Mix (Lawry's), 8 oz.	1333
Canadian (Lawry's), 8 oz.	1147
Cheddar-Blue Cheese Dressing (Hellmann's/ Best Foods), 1 tbsp.	70
French (Heinz), 1 tbsp.	78
French (Hellmann's/Best Foods Family), 1 tbsp.	65
French (Kraft Casino), ½ oz.	60
French (Kraft Catalina), ½ oz.	60
French (Kraft Miracle), 1 tbsp.	66
French, Classic (Wish-Bone), 1 tsp.	21
French, Deluxe (Wish-Bone), 1 tsp.	20
French, Low Cal (Wish-Bone), 1 tsp.	9
French, Old Fashioned Mix (Lawry's), .84 oz.	72
French, Old Fashioned Mix (Lawry's), 8 oz.	1334

French, Old-Fashioned Mix (Good Seasons), 1 tbsp.	84
French, San Francisco (Lawry's), 8 oz.	854
Garlic (Good Seasons), 1 tbsp.	84
Garlic French (Wish-Bone), 1 tsp.	23
Garlic French, Low Cal (Wish-Bone), 1 tsp.	6
Green Goddess (Lawry's), 8 oz.	948
Green Goddess (Wish-Bone), 1 tsp.	20
Green Goddess Dressing Mix (Lawry's), 9 oz.	1671
Hawaiian (Lawry's), 8 oz.	1234
Hickory Bits (Wish-Bone), 1 tsp.	26
Italian (Good Seasons), 1 tbsp.	84
Italian, True (Hellmann's/Best Foods), 1 tbsp.	85
Italian (Kraft), ½ oz.	78
Italian (Kraft Imperial), ½ oz.	62
Italian (Lawry's), 8 oz.	1270
Italian Mix (Lawry's), 8 oz.	1306
Italian, Golden (Wish-Bone), 1 tsp.	15
Italian, Swiss (Hellmann's/Best Foods), 1 tbsp.	75
Italian, Low Cal (Wish-Bone), 1 tsp.	3
Italian (Diet Delight), ½ cup	130
Italian Rosé (Wish-Bone), 1 tsp.	21
Italian with Cheese (Lawry's), 8 oz.	961
Italian with Cheese Mix (Lawry's), 8 oz.	1331
Mayonnaise (Best Foods), 1 tbsp.	100
Mayonnaise (Hellmann's), 1 tbsp.	100
Mayonnaise (Kraft), 1 tbsp.	108
Mayonnaise (Wesson), 1 tbsp.	60
Onion, Dressing, California (Wish-Bone), 1 tsp.	78
Onion, Creamy (Wish-Bone), 1 tsp.	24
Russian (Wish-Bone), 1 tsp.	19
Russian, Low Cal (Wish-Bone), 1 tsp.	9
Salad Dressing (Heinz), 1 tbsp.	63

Calories

Salad Dressing (Durkee), 1 tsp.	4
Salad Seasoning with Cheese (Durkee), 1 tsp.	10
Salad Supreme (McCormick), 1 oz.	80
Sherry (Lawry's), 8 oz.	881
Snowdrift (Hunt Wesson), 1 tbsp.	110
Tahitian Isle (Wish-Bone), 1 tsp.	19
Thousand Island (Good Seasons), 1 tbsp.	85
Thousand Island (Kraft), ½ oz.	73
Thousand Island (Lawry's), 8 oz.	1104
Thousand Island (Wish-Bone), 1 tsp.	24
Whipped Dressing (Diet Delight), ½ cup	112

CEREALS, Ready to Cook

Calories

Barley, Pearled (Quaker Scotch Brand), ¼ cup, uncooked	171
Barley, Quick Pearled (Quaker Scotch Brand), ¼ cup, uncooked	171
Corn Meal (Quaker or Aunt Jemima), ⅙ cup, uncooked	85
Cream of Wheat, Instant, 1 oz.	99
Cream of Wheat, Quick, 1 oz.	99
Cream of Wheat, Regular, 1 oz.	101
Cream of Wheat, Mix 'n Eat, 1 oz.	99
Hominy Grits (Quaker or Aunt Jemima), ⅙ cup, uncooked	103
Hominy, White and Golden (Van Camp), ½ cup	61
Farina, Enriched (Quaker), ⅙ cup, uncooked	100
Farina, Creamed (H-O), 1 cup	635
Masa Farina (Quaker), 2-6 tortillas	136
Oatmeal, Instant (H-O), ½ cup, uncooked	125
Oatmeal, Instant (Quaker), 1 oz. packet	107
Oatmeal, Instant, with Apples and Cinnamon (Quaker), 1⅛ oz. packet	119

Calories

Oatmeal, Instant, with Raisins and Spice (Quaker), 1½ oz. packet	154
Oats (H-0), Quick, ½ cup, uncooked	125
Oats, Old Fashioned (H-O), ½ cup, uncooked	125
Oats, Quick or Old Fashioned (Quaker Oats), ⅓ cup, uncooked	107
Oats (Ralston), 5 tbsp., uncooked	107
Ralston, Hot Instant (Ralston Purina), 4 tbsp., uncooked	97
Ralston, Hot Regular (Ralston Purina), 3⅓ tbsp., uncooked	97
Rice, Cream of (Grocery Store Products), ½ cup	72
Wheat Oata (Ralston-Purina), ¼ cup, uncooked	104
Whole Wheat, Rolled (Quaker Pettijohns), ⅓ cup, uncooked	96
Whole Wheat, Cook-in-a-Bowl (Ralston), 1 packet	112
Whole Wheat, Cook-in-a-Bowl (Ralston), 1 packet	125

CEREALS, Ready to Eat

Calories

General Mills:

Cheerios, 1¼ cups	112
Clackers, 1 cup	111
Cocoa Puffs, 1 cup	107
Corn Bursts, 1 cup	110
Corn Flakes, 1⅓ cups	111
Frost O's, ¾ cup	111
Kix, 1⅓ cups	112
Lucky Charms, 1¼ cups	110
Stax, 1 cup	109
Sugar Jets, ⅞ cup	111

	Calories
Total, 1 cup	101
Trix, 1 cup	110
Twinkles, 7/8 cup	112
Wheaties, 1 cup	101

Kellogg's:

Apple Jacks, 1 cup	112
All-Bran, 1/2 cup	96
Bran Buds, 1/2 cup	98
40% Bran Flakes, 3/4 cup	104
Bran, Raisin, 2/3 cup	100
Cocoa Krispies, 1 cup	113
Concentrate, 1/3 cup	106
Corn Flakes, 1 1/3 cups	105
Froot Loops, 1 cup	114
Frosted Flakes, Sugar, 3/4 cup	107
Krumbles, 3/4 cup	105
Pep Wheat Flakes, 1 cup	106
Product 19, 1 cup	106
Puffa Puffa Rice, 1 cup	120
Rice Krispies, 1 cup	106
Shredded Wheat, 2 biscuits	139
Special K, 1 1/2 cups	109
Stars, 1 cup	110
Sugar Smacks, 1 cup	110
Sugar Pops, 1 cup	110

Nabisco:

100% Bran, 1 oz.	97
Rice Honeys, 1 oz.	114
Shredded Wheat Biscuit, 1 biscuit	86
Shredded Wheat, spoon size, 1 oz.	107
Team Flakes, 1 oz.	107
Wheat Honeys, 1 oz.	115

Calories

Quaker Oats:

Cap'n Crunch, ¾ cup	122
Life, ⅔ cup	107
Puffed Rice, 1¼ cups	56
Puffed Wheat, 1⅓ cups	51
Quake, 1 cup	118
Quisp, 1¹⁄₁₆ cups	120
Rice Puffs, Diet Frosted, 1 cup	56
Shredded Wheat, 2 biscuits	132
Wheat Puffs, Diet Frosted, 1⅓ cups	51

Post:

Alpha Bits Sugar Frosted Oats, 1 cup	100
Bran and Prime Flakes, ¾ cup	89
40% Bran Flakes, ⅔ cup	89
Crispy Critters Oat, 1 cup	110
Grape Nuts Brand, ¼ cup	100
Grape Nuts Flakes, ⅔ cup	100
Honeycomb Sweet Crisp Corn, 1⅓ cups	110
Fortified Oat, ⅔ cup	110
Post Toasties Corn Flakes, 1 cup	89
Super Sugar Crisp Puffed Wheat, ¾ cup	111
Sugar Rice Krinkles, ⅔ cup	110

Ralston Purina:

Bran Chex, Raisin, ⅔ cup	92
Corn Chex, 1¼ cups	111
Corn Flakes, 1 cup	111
Rice Chex, 1⅙ cup	112
Sugar Frosted Chex, ⅞ cup	130
Wheat Chex, ⅔ cup	102

Sunshine:

Shredded Wheat, 1 biscuit	104

BREAKFAST TARTS

	Calories
Animals, all flavors (Toast 'Em), 1 tart	181
Brown Sugar-Cinnamon, Plain, or Frosted (Kellogg's Pop Tarts), 1.8 oz.	209
Danka Toaster Danish (Toast 'Em), 1 tart	210
Frosted Pop Ups, all flavors (Toast 'Em), 1 tart	198
Fruit Filled (Kellogg's Pop Tarts), 1.8 oz.	203
Fruit Filled, Frosted (Kellogg's Pop Tarts), 1.8 oz.	207
Toastettes, Apple, (Nabisco), 1 piece	190

BREAD, 1 slice, as packaged, except as noted

	Calories
Brown, with Raisins, canned (B & M), ½″	90
Cheese Bread (Van de Kamp)	61
Cinnamon Cake Loaf (Van de Kamp)	85
Cinnamon Raisin (Monk's)	86
Corn, Mix, Prepared * (Aunt Jemima), 2¾″ x 2⅝″ x 1¼″ slice	224
Date and Nut (Crosse & Blackwell), ½″ slice	65
Date Nut (Thomas')	100
Dutch Crunch (Van de Kamp)	63
Egg Sesame Bread (Van de Kamp)	77
English Muffin Loaf (Van de Kamp)	65
French (Van de Kamp)	51
Giraffe Soft Sandwich Loaf (Arnold)	67
Gluten (Thomas' Glutogen)	35
Honey Bran Bread (Van de Kamp)	77
Irish Oatmeal Bread (Van de Kamp)	69
Low Sodium Enriched Bread (Van de Kamp)	66
Melba Thin Diet Slice (Arnold)	43
Oatmeal Bread (Arnold)	64
100% Milk 'n Butter Bread (Van de Kamp)	71
Panettone (Van de Kamp)	91

Calories

Profile Bread	52
Protein (Thomas')	45
Pumpernickel (Van de Kamp)	48
Raisin Bread (Thomas' English)	66
Raisin Bread (Van de Kamp)	70
Raisin, Cinnamon (Thomas')	63
Raisin Tea Loaf (Arnold)	67
Rye (Arnold)	61
Rye, Dutch (Van de Kamp)	46
Rye, Melba Thin (Arnold)	41
Salt Rising Bread (Van de Kamp)	67
Stone Ground Wheat Bread (Monks')	77
Wheat Bread, thin sliced (Van de Kamp)	62

White Bread:

Arnold Brick Oven	64
Arnold Brick Oven, large slice	84
Arnold Brick Oven, long loaf	79
Arnold, Hearthstone	72
Daffodil	51
Monks'	80
Thomas'	64
Van de Kamp	77
Van de Kamp, thin sliced	62
Van de Kamp, extra thin sliced	53
Wonder	66

Whole Wheat Bread:

Arnold, Brick Oven	64
Arnold, Melba Thin	42
Thomas'	65
Van de Kamp, Krinko 100%	63

*According to package directions.

BREADSTICKS, 1 piece, as packaged   *Calories*

Plain (Stella D'oro)	40
Onion flavored (Stella D'oro)	36
Sesame (Stella D'oro)	38

BISCUITS, MUFFINS, ROLLS
1 piece, as packaged, except as noted *Calories*

Biscuits, refrigerator, baked (Bordens Big 10 Flaky)	83
Biscuits, Baking Powder (Van de Kamp)	87
Biscuits, Shortcake (Van de Kamp)	173
Buns, Barbecue (Arnold)	111
Buns, Hamburger, Sliced (Van de Kamp)	256
Buns, Hot Dog (Arnold)	104

Muffins:

Bran (Van de Kamp)	168
Corn, Mix, Prepared* (Flako), 2½" diameter	135
Corn (Thomas')	140
Egg Toasting (Arnold)	156
English (Cain's)	145
English (Di Carolo)	145
English (Hostess)	145
English (Thomas')	140
English (Van de Kamp)	148
English (Wonder)	145

Popovers, Mix, Prepared* (Flako), 1 popover, 3" diameter	166

Rolls:

Brown 'n Serve (Wonder)	80
Butter (Van de Kamp)	105
Dinner (Arnold)	59
Finger (Sara Lee), 1 oz.	84
French (Van de Kamp)	130

*According to package directions.

	Calories
Parkerhouse (Sara Lee), 1 oz.	83
Sesame Seed (Sara Lee), 1 oz.	84
Twist, Large Delicatessen (Arnold)	109
Scones (Hostess)	188

BREADS, Refrigerated

Biscuits, 1 oz.	*Calories*
Baking Powder (Tenderflake)	94
Butter Tastin' (Hungry Jack)	101
Buttermilk (Pillsbury)	72
Buttermilk, Flaky (Hungry Jack)	97
Buttermilk (Hungry Jack)	77
Buttermilk, Baking Powder (Tenderflake)	94
Buttermilk (Tenderflake)	94
Buttermilk, Extra Light (Pillsbury)	75
Country Style (Pillsbury)	72
Flaky (Hungry Jack)	97
Ovenready (Ballard)	72
Tenderburst (Pillsbury)	95

Rolls, 1 oz.	*Calories*
Butterflake Dinner (Pillsbury)	80
Cinnamon with Icing (Pillsbury)	100
Crescent Dinner (Pillsbury)	94
Parkerhouse Dinner (Pillsbury)	76
Snowflake Dinner (Pillsbury)	84

CRUMBS, MEAL, AND STUFFINGS

	Calories
Bread Crumbs (Wonder), 1 cup	94
Bread Crumbs, Flavored (La Rosa), 1 cup	435
Cracker Meal (Keebler), 1 cup	449
Graham Cracker Meal (Keebler), 1 cup	470
Graham Cracker Crumbs (Nabisco), 1 9″ pie shell	535

Calories

Shake 'n Bake Seasoned Coating:

Chicken, 1 envelope, approx. 4 servings	277
Fish, 1 envelope, approx. 4 servings	226
Pork, 1 envelope, approx. 4 servings	260

PANCAKES, WAFFLES, Etc., Mixes

Calories

Pancake, prepared (Aunt Jemima), 3 4″ pancakes	183
Pancake, prepared (Hungry Jack), 1 oz.	97
Pancake, prepared, Deluxe Easy Pour (Aunt Jemima), 3 4″ pancakes	237
Pancake, prepared, Extra Light (Hungry Jack), 1 oz.	97
Pancake, Blueberry (Hungry Jack), 1 oz.	98
Pancake, Buckwheat, prepared (Aunt Jemima), 3 4″ pancakes	192
Pancake, Buckwheat, prepared (Hungry Jack), 1 oz.	95
Pancake, Buttermilk, prepared (Aunt Jemima), 3 4″ pancakes	213
Pancake, Buttermilk, prepared (Hungry Jack), 1 oz.	98
Pancake and Muffin Mix, Buttermilk (Duncan Hines), 1 lb.	1380
Pancake, Sweet Cream (Hungry Jack), 1 oz.	101
Waffle, prepared (Aunt Jemima), 3 4″ waffles	183
Waffle Mix, prepared, Deluxe Easy Pour (Aunt Jemima), 3 4″ waffles	237
Waffle, Buckwheat, prepared (Aunt Jemima), 3 4″ waffles	192
Waffle, Buttermilk, prepared (Aunt Jemima), 3 4″ waffles	213

PANCAKES, WAFFLES, Etc., Frozen

	Calories
Corn Sticks (Aunt Jemima), 3 sticks	171
Country Waffles (Aunt Jemima), 2 waffle sections	116
French Toast (Downy Flake), 1 oz.	72
Pancakes (Downy Flake), 1 oz.	55
Waffles (Downy Flake), 1 oz.	66

CRACKERS, Packaged, 1 piece, as packaged, except as noted

	Calories
Bacon Flavored Thins (Nabisco)	10
Butter flavored:	
Butter thins (Keebler)	17
Butter thins (Nabisco)	15
Hi-Ho (Sunshine)	17
Club (Keebler)	15
Townhouse (Keebler)	19
Tam-Tams (Manischewitz)	13
Cheese Flavored:	
Cheddar Krisp (Ralston Purina)	6
Cheez-it (Sunshine)	6
Cheese Nips	5
Cheese Snacks (Sunshine)	16
Cheese Tid-Bits	4
Cheese Wafers (Keebler)	11
Shapies, Cheese Flavored Dip Delights (Nabisco)	9
Chicken in a Biskit (Nabisco)	10
Chipsters, Potato Snacks, 100 grams	471
Matzo, (Manischewitz Products), 1 sheet, as packaged:	
Diet thins	109
Egg	136
Egg 'N Onion	112

	Calories
Regular, daily and Passover	121
Testeas	139
Thin Tea, daily and Passover	109
Whole Wheat, Passover	120
Meal Mates Sesame Bread Wafers (Nabisco)	22
Oyster:	
Dandy	3
Keebler	3
Oysterettes	3
Sunshine	4
Onion, French (Nabisco)	11
Saltines, Soda and Water Crackers:	
Krispy (Sunshine)	12
Premium	12
Royal Lunch	55
Saltines (Keebler)	14
Sip 'n Chips Snacks (Nabisco)	8
Sociables (Nabisco)	10
Ry-Krisp, Pizza (Ralston Purina)	8
Ry-Krisp, Seasoned (Ralston Purina)	25
Ry-Krisp, traditional (Ralston Purina)	21
Smack Wafers (Sunshine)	10
Toasts and Toasted Crackers:	
Barbecue Snack Wafers (Sunshine)	17
Dutch Rusk	61
Holland Rusk	33
Keebler Party Toasts	15
Nabisco Zweiback	31
Old London Melba Toast Rounds	9
Old London Garlic Melba Toast Rounds	9
Old London Pumpernickel Melba Toast	16
Old London Rye Melba Toast	16

	Calories
Old London Salty Rye Melba Toast Rounds	8
Old London Sesame Melba Toast Rounds	11
Old London Wheat Melba Toast	16
Old London White Melba Toast	16
Old London White Melba Toast Rounds	9
Sunshine Zweiback	30
Sunshine Toasted Wafers	10
Uneeda Biscuit	22
Tomato Onion (Sunshine)	15
Waverly Wafers (Nabisco)	18
Wheat (Keebler Wheat Toast)	15
Wheat (Nabisco Wheat Thins)	9
Wheat, Shredded (Triscuit Wafers)	20

COOKIES, Packaged, 1 cookie, as packaged except as noted

	Calories
Burry, Grocery Products:	
Butter Flavored	23
Best Chocolate Chip	85
Best Sugar	68
Best Sugar Fudge	63
Best Pecan	70
Crunchy Grahams	46
Euphrates	22
Fiddle Flakes, Original	65
Fiddle Flakes, Fudge & Peanut	65
Fudge Town	67
Gaucho	72
Lemon Punch	62
Milk Lunch	36
Mr. Chips	42
Scooter Pies	162
Sierra Eclairs	62

Calories

Burry, Vending Products, 6 cookies:

Chocolate-Vanilla Creme, 1⅝ oz.	226
Chocolate-Vanilla Creme, 2⅜ oz.	330
Lemon Sandwich Creme, 1⅝ oz.	225
Lemon Sandwich Creme, 2⅜ oz.	329
Mr. Chips, Chocolate, 1¼ oz.	176
Mr. Chips, Chocolate, 1¾ oz.	247
Peanut Butter & Cheese, 1½ oz.	217
Peanut Butter & Cheese, 2 oz.	289
Peanut Butter & Jelly (Imitation) 1⅝ oz.	226

Keebler:

Almond, Jan Hagel	47
Almond-Spice, Dutch Almond	51
Animal Crackers	8
Animal Crackers, Iced Party	60
Apple Flavored, Dutch Apple	34
Cashew, Bavarian Fudge Creme	79
Cashew, Nut Fudge Drops	31
Cashew, Pecan Fudgies	66
Chocolate Chip	49
Chocolate Chip Coconut Flavored	80

Creme Sandwiches:

Butterscotch	85
Chocolate, Dutch	96
Chocolate, Opera	84
Chocolate Fudge	97
Lemon	85
Vanilla, French	95
Vanilla, Opera	85
Ginger Snaps	23

Calories

Graham Crackers:
Honey	17
Thin	17
Very Thin	14
Chocolate Covered, Deluxe	44
Lemon, Old Fashioned	83

Marshmallow:
Chocolate Covered, Chocolate Dainties	68
Chocolate Covered, Chocolate Treasures	83
Chocolate Covered, Galaxies	82
Chocolate Covered, Tulips	83
Sandwich, Mellow	81
Oatmeal, Old Fashioned	78
Oatmeal, Iced	82
Peanut Butter, Chocolate Covered, Penguin	117
Raisin, Iced, Bars	81
Shortbread, Buttercup	27
Shortbread, Coconut, Iced	65
Shortbread, Pecan, Sandies	84
Sugar, Giant	70
Sugar, Old Fashioned	81

Sugar Wafers:
14-oz. package, all flavors	31
7-oz. package, Chocolate	26
7-oz. package, Strawberry	25
7-oz. package, Vanilla	25
Vanilla, Wafers	19

Nabisco:
Animal Crackers, Barnum's	12
Apple Flavored, Apple Strudel	48
Arrowroot, National	22
Brown Edge, Wafers	28
Brown Sugar, Family Favorite	25

	Calories
Butter Flavored	37
Cashew	57
Cashew, Famous Wafers	28
Chocolate and Chocolate Fudge, Snaps	18
Chocolate Almond	55
Chocolate Cakes, Pinwheels	138
Chocolate Chip	51
Chocolate Chip, Family Favorite	33
Chocolate Chip, Snacks	21
Chocolate Chip, Coconut Flavored	76
Chocolate Wafers	27
Cinnamon Almond	53
Creme Sandwich, Chocolate, Oreo	50
Creme Sandwich, Coconut, Oasis	53
Creme Sandwich, Swiss	43
Creme Sandwich, Social Tea	51
Devil's Food Cake	58
Fancy Crests	54
Fig Newton Cakes	57
Fruit, Iced	70
Ginger Snaps, Old Fashioned	29
Graham Crackers	30
Graham Crackers, Honeymaid	26
Grahams Crackers, Chocolate Covered	55
Graham Crackers, Chocolate Covered, Fancy	68
Lemon, Snaps	17
Macaroons, Sandwich	71
Marshmallow, Chocolate Covered, Puffs	94
Marshmallow, Chocolate Covered, Twirls	133
Marshmallow, Sandwich	32
Oatmeal, Family Favorites	24
Oatmeal, Home Style	61
Peanut Cream, Patties	34

	Calories
Raisin, Fruit Biscuit	56
Shortbread, Cashew, Home Style	50
Shortbread, Pecan	77
Social Tea Biscuits	21
Sugar, Snaps	17
Sugar Rings	68
Sugar Wafer, Chocolate Covered	76
Sugar Wafer, Chocolate Covered, Stix	53
Sugar Wafer, Spiced	33
Vanilla, Snaps	13
Vanilla, Wafers	18

Sunshine:

Animal Crackers	10
Applesauce	33
Applecauce, Iced	104
Arrowroot	15
Butter Flavored	24
Chocolate Wafers	13
Chocolate Ice Box Wafers	30
Chocolate Chip	37
Chocolate Chip, Nuggets	23
Chocolate Chip, Coconut	76
Cinnamon Wafers	20
Clover Leaves	25
Coconut Bars	47
Creme Sandwich, Chocolate Fudge	74
Creme Sandwich, Coconut, Orbit	51
Creme Sandwich, Vanilla, Cup Custard	79
Date and Nut	82
Delito Grahams	41
Devil's Cake	55
Dutch Rusk	61
Fig Bars	42
Frosted Cakes	68

	Calories
Ginger Snaps, large	32
Ginger Snaps, small	14
Golden Fruit	73
Graham Crackers	17
Graham Crackers, Sugar Honey	46
Hydrox	46
Kreenalined Wafers	45
Macaroons	85
Macaroons, Butter-flavored	85
Macaroons, Coconut	81
Marshmallow, Chocolate Covered Chocolate Puffs	63
Marshmallow, Chocolate Covered Kings	135
Marshmallow Nut Sundae	74
Marshmallow with Chocolate Sprinkles	71
Mallo Puffs with Coconut	70
Milco Dandees	91
Milco Sugar Wafers	80
Oatmeal	60
Peanut	33
Peanut Butter, Crunch	68
Peanut Butter, Patties	30
Pecan, Krunch	78
Raisin, Golden Fruit	73
Shortbread, Scottie	39
Sugar Wafers	47
Sugar Wafers, Regent	23
Sugar Wafers, Chocolate Covered, Ice Box	30
Toy Cookies	13
Vanilla Wafers	14
Vienna Finger Sandwich	69
Yum Yums	83
Zweiback	30

Van de Kamp:

	Calories
Almond Ice Box	63
Cherry Nut Shortbread	59
Chocolate	79
Chocolate Chip	66
Coconut Macaroon	89
Maple Pecan	58
Molasses, Old Fashioned	82
Oatmeal	59
Peanut Butter	44
Sugar	79

COOKIES, Refrigerated, 1 oz.

	Calories
Butterscotch Nut (Pillsbury)	128
Chocolate Chip (Pillsbury)	116
Fudge Nut (Pillsbury	119
Oatmeal Raisin (Pillsbury)	116
Peanut Butter (Pillsbury)	129
Sugar (Pillsbury)	125

CAKES, COOKIES, BREADS, Etc.
Mixes

CAKES

	Calories
Angel Food, Deluxe (Duncan Hines), 1 cake	1750
Angel Food, Traditional (General Mills), 1/16	100
Angel Food (General Mills), 1/16	111
Angel Food, Confetti (General Mills), 1/16	114
Angel Food, Lemon Custard (General Mills), 1/16	111
Angel Food, Raspberry Swirl (Pillsbury), 1 oz.	102
Angel Food, Strawberry (General Mills), 1/16	115
Angel Food, White (Pillsbury), 1 oz.	102
Applesauce Raisin (Duncan Hines), 1 cake	1693
Applesauce, Spice (Pillsbury), 1 oz.	117

Calories

Apple Cinnamon (Duncan Hines), 1 cake	2368
Banana, Chiquita (General Mills), $\frac{1}{12}$	205
Banana Flavor (Pillsbury), 1 oz.	120
Banana Flavor Loaf (Pillsbury), 1 oz.	117
Black Walnut (General Mills), $\frac{1}{12}$	202
Butter Flavor (Pillsbury), 1 oz.	122
Butter Brickel (General Mills), $\frac{1}{12}$	203
Caramel Apple (General Mills), $\frac{1}{12}$	203
Caramel Supreme (Duncan Hines), 1 cake	2351
Cheese Cake (Royal No-Bake Products), 10$\frac{1}{2}$ oz.	235
Cherry Chip (General Mills), $\frac{1}{12}$	198
Cherry Fudge (General Mills), $\frac{1}{12}$	199
Cherry Supreme (Duncan Hines), 1 cake	2222
Chocolate, German (General Mills), $\frac{1}{12}$	200
Chocolate, German (Pillsbury), 1 oz.	121
Chocolate, Loaf (Pillsbury), 1 oz.	120
Chocolate, Malt (General Mills), $\frac{1}{12}$	200
Chocolate, Milk (General Mills), $\frac{1}{12}$	199
Chocolate, Sour Cream, Fudge (General Mills), $\frac{1}{12}$	195
Coconut Surprise (Duncan Hines), 1 cake	2367
Coffee Cake (Aunt Jemima Easy Mix), 1 piece	181
Deep Chocolate (Duncan Hines), 1 cake	2222
Dessert, Boston Cream Pie (General Mills), $\frac{1}{8}$	265
Dessert, Gingerbread (General Mills), $\frac{1}{9}$	171
Devil's Food (Duncan Hines), 1 cake	2337
Devil's Food (General Mills), $\frac{1}{12}$	199
Devil's Food, Butter Recipe (General Mills), $\frac{1}{12}$	269
Dutch Chocolate Pie (Royal No-Bake Products), package (2)	255
Fudge (Duncan Hines), 1 cake	3248
Fudge, Chocolate (Pillsbury), 1 oz.	120

Calories

Fudge, Dark Chocolate (General Mills), 1/12	198
Fudge, Macaroon (Pillsbury), 1 oz.	124
Fudge, Marble (Duncan Hines), 1 cake	2313
Fudge, Sour Cream Flavored (Pillsbury), 1 oz.	118
Fudge, Toffee (Pillsbury), 1 oz.	119
Gingerbread (Pillsbury), 1 oz.	110
Golden Cake (Duncan Hines), 1 cake	3287
Honey Spice (General Mills), 1/12	202
Lemon Chiffon, Sunkist (General Mills), 1/12	151
Lemon, Sunkist (General Mills), 1/12	202
Lemon Supreme (Duncan Hines), 1 cake	2368
Lemon, Cream Moist (Pillsbury), 1 oz.	122
Marble (General Mills), 1/12	206
Orange (Pillsbury), 1 oz.	120
Orange Chiffon, Sunkist (General Mills), 1/12	135
Orange, Sunkist (General Mills), 1/12	201
Orange Supreme (Duncan Hines), 1 cake	2369
Pineapple (Pillsbury), 1 oz.	122
Pineapple Chiffon, Dole (General Mills), 1/12	150
Pineapple, Dole (General Mills), 1/12	199
Pineapple Supreme (Duncan Hines), 1 cake	2369
Pound Cake (Dromedary), 1 slice	278
Pound Cake, Golden (General Mills), 1/12	210
Pudding, Apple Cinnamon (General Mills), 1/6	223
Pudding, Caramel (General Mills), 1/6	225
Pudding, Chocolate (General Mills), 1/6	221
Pudding, Sunkist Lemon (General Mills), 1/6	227
Red Devil's Food (Pillsbury), 1 oz.	119
Spice (Duncan Hines), 1 cake	2317
Spice 'N Apple with Raisins (General Mills), 1/12	206
Swiss Chocolate (Duncan Hines), 1 cake	2334
Upside Down, Apple Cinnamon (General Mills), 1/9	269

Calories

Upside Down, Cherry (General Mills), 1/9	282
Upside Down, Pineapple (General Mills), 1/9	270
White (Pillsbury), 1 oz.	121
White (Duncan Hines), 1 cake	2222
White Cake (General Mills), 1/12	190
White, Loaf (Pillsbury), 1 oz.	122
White, Sour Cream (General Mills), 1/12	191
White, Whipping Cream (Pillsbury), 1 oz.	127
Yellow (Duncan Hines), 1 cake	2386
Yellow (General Mills), 1/12	202
Yellow (Pillsbury), 1 oz.	122
Yellow, Butter Recipes (General Mills), 1/12	278
Yellow, Loaf, (Pillsbury), 1 oz.	120

COOKIES

Coconut Macaroon (General Mills), 1	73
Cookie Mix with Morsels (Nestle's), 1 with egg	52
Cookie Mix without Morsels (Nestle's), 1 with egg	43
Date Bar (General Mills), 1	58
Vienna Dream Bar (General Mills), 1	87

BREADS

Corn (Aunt Jemima Easy Mix), 1 piece	225
Corn (Ballard), 1 oz.	103
Rolls (Pillsbury), 1 oz.	113
Muffins, 1 muffin, except as noted	
Apple Cinnamon (General Mills)	159
Chiquita Banana Nut (General Mills)	167
Blueberry (General Mills)	118
Butter Pecan (General Mills)	159
Corn (Dromedary)	144
Corn (General Mills)	156
Corn (Flako)	134

	Calories
Golden Corn (Pillsbury), 1 oz.	112
Date Nut (General Mills)	152
Honey Bran (General Mills)	154
Sunkist Lemon (General Mills)	149
Oatmeal (General Mills)	166
Sunkist Orange (General Mills)	153
Spice (General Mills)	151

BROWNIES

	Calories
Butterscotch, (General Mills), 1½″ square	59
Fudge, (General Mills), 1½″ square	58
Fudge, (Pillsbury), 1 oz.	125
Fudge Supreme, (General Mills), 1½″ square	59
German Chocolate, (General Mills), 1½″ square	70
Walnut, (General Millls), 1½″ square	63
Walnut, (Pillsbury), 1 oz.	129
Pillsbury Brand, (refrigerated), 1 oz.	110

FROSTINGS (General Mills)
1/12 portion, except as noted

	Calories
Butter Brickle	140
Caramel Apple	130
Cherry Fluff	59
Cherry Fudge	132
Chiquita Banana	139
Chocolate Flavor Walnut	131
Chocolate Fudge	134
Chocolate Malt	136
Coconut Pecan	102
Creamy Cherry	139
Creamy Spice	139
Creamy White	140

	Calories
Dark Chocolate Fudge	130
Dole Pineapple	134
Fluffy Chocolate	70
Fluffy White	58
Fudge Nugget	133
Golden Caramel	139
Milk Chocolate	130
Sour Cream Chocolate Flavor Fudge	129
Sour Cream White	130
Sunkist Lemon	134
Sunkist Lemon Fluff	58
Sunkist Orange	134
Toasted Coconut	141
Ready-to-Spread, 1/12 portion:	
Butterscotch	164
Cherry	167
Chocolate	162
Dark Dutch Fudge	153
Sunkist Lemon	166
Milk Chocolate	164
Vanilla	166
Canned (Pillsbury) , 1 oz.:	
Pink, Red, Yellow, Green	110

TOPPINGS, SYRUPS, AND RELATED PRODUCTS

	Calories
Baking Chocolate (Hershey) , 1 oz.	169
Bosco Milk Amplifier, 1 tbsp.	45
Choco-Bake, Pre-melted Chocolate (Nestle's) , 1 oz.	172
Chocolate Chips (Ghiradelli) , 1/3 cup	293
Chocolate Chips, Semi-Sweet (Baker's) , 1/6 cup	127
Chocolate Flavored Syrup (Hershey), 1 oz.	69
Chocolate Topping (Diet Delight) , 1/2 cup	36

Calories

Cocoa (Hershey), 1 oz.	111
Cocoa Mix, Instant (Hershey), 1 oz.	105
Coconut, Angel Flake (Baker's), 1/4 cup	135
Coconut Crunchies (Baker's), 1/4 cup	170
Coconut, Premium Shred & Cookie (Baker's), 1/4 cup	140
Cool n' Creamy (Birds Eye), 1/2 cup	202
Eagle Bar (Ghiradelli), 1 square	149
Ground Chocolate (Ghiradelli), 1/4 cup	38
Milk Block (Ghiradelli), 1 square	178
Milk Chocolate Fudge Topping (Hershey), 1 oz.	96
Syrup (Mrs. Butterworth's), 1 tbsp.	54
Syrup (Brer Rabbit), Light Gold Label, 1 tbsp.	60
Syrup (Brer Rabbit), Dark Green Label, 1 tbsp.	53
Syrup (Aunt Jemima), 1/4 cup	212
Syrup (Log Cabin), 1 tbsp.	50
Syrup (Old Manse), 1 tbsp.	54
Syrup, Buttered (Log Cabin), 1 tbsp.	54
Syrup, Corn, Dark (Karo), 1 tbsp.	60
Syrup, Corn, Light (Karo), 1 tbsp.	60
Syrup, Maple Imitation (Karo), 1 tbsp.	60
Syrup, Pancake and Waffle (Log Cabin), 1 tbsp.	50
Syrup, Pancake and Waffle (Karo), 1 tbsp.	60
Syrup, Pancake and Waffle (Diet Deight), 1/2 cup	30
Syrup (Vermont Maid), 1 tbsp.	49
Hard Sauce (Crosse & Blackwell), 1 tbsp.	64
Whipped Topping (D-Zerta), 1 tbsp.	7
Whipped Topping (Dream Whip), 1 tbsp.	14
Lucky Whip Dessert Topping (Imperial Lever), 1 tbsp.	12
Lucky Whip Dessert Topping Mix (Imperial Lever), 1 tbsp.	11

	Calories
Frozen Non-dairy Whipped Topping (Pet), 100 grams	330
Zip Whipt Aerosol, Real Cream Topping, 1.5 oz.	26

PIES, CAKES, PASTRIES, AND RELATED PRODUCTS
Packaged

	Calories
Angel Food Cake (Van de Kamp), 1 cake	1661
Angel Food Cake, Iced Chocolate (Van de Kamp), 1 cake	2528
Angel Food Loaf Cake (Van de Kamp), 1 cake	1006
Apple Puffs (Van de Kamp), 1 puff	304
Apricot-Pineapple Coffee Cake (Van de Kamp), 1 cake	357
Banana Nut Loaf Cake (Van de Kamp), 1 cake	1288
Bear Claw Coffee Cake (Van de Kamp), 1 cake	124
Butter Horn Coffee Cake (Van de Kamp), 1 cake	287
Butter Loaf Cake (Van de Kamp), 1 cake	1284
Butterfly Coffee Cake (Van de Kamp), 1 cake	187
Chocolate Cake, Dutch German (Van de Kamp), 1 cake	3984
Chocolate Cake, Milk Chocolate (Van de Kamp), 1 cake	2825
Chocolate and Pecan Cake (Van de Kamp), 1 cake	3336
Cinnamon Rolls (Van de Kamp), 1 roll	127
Coconut Cake (Van de Kamp), 1 cake	2472
Cruller, Old Fashioned (Hostess), 1 cruller	100
Cupcake, Chocolate (Hostess), 1 cupcake	205
Cupcake, Chocolate (Van de Kamp), 1 cupcake	175
Cupcake, Cherry (Van de Kamp), 1 cupcake	173
Cupcake, Orange (Hostess), 1 cupcake	185
Cupcake, Pineapple (Van de Kamp), 1 cupcake	170
Danish Go-Rounds (Kellogg's), 2 oz.	236

Calories

Ding Dong (Hostess), 1 cake	173
Dinky Twinky (Hostess), 1 cake	152
Doughnuts, 1 doughnut:	
(Van de Kamp)	174
Chocolate (Hostess)	280
Chocolate (Van de Kamp)	224
Chocolate Coated Gems (Hostess)	110
Chocolate, Long Johns (Van de Kamp)	179
Crumb (Van de Kamp)	167
Crumb Dunkettes (Van de Kamp)	105
Maple, Long Johns (Van de Kamp)	197
Orange (Van de Kamp)	212
Sugared (Hostess)	223
Sugared Mini-Gems (Hostess)	95
Sugared, Dainty Dozen (Van de Kamp)	53
Powdered Sugar (Van de Kamp)	165
Sugared Dunkettes (Van de Kamp)	90
Sugar Gems, Chocolate Inside (Hostess)	100
Fruit Pie, Individual (Hostess), 1 pie	435
Ho-Ho (Hostess), 1 cake	120
Jam Tarts, English (Van de Kamp), 8¾ oz. package, 1 tart	236
Jam Tarts, English (Van de Kamp), 8½ oz. package, 1 tart	238
Jelly Roll, Lemon (Van de Kamp), 1 roll	879
Jelly Roll, Raspberry (Van de Kamp), 1 roll	589
Lemon Pies, Individual (Van de Kamp), 1 pie	236
Orange Roll (Van de Kamp), 1 coffee cake	95
Pecan Pies (Van de Kamp), 1 pie	233
Pecan Spice Cake (Van de Kamp), 1 cake	3268
Pound Cake (Van de Kamp), 1 cake	1204
Sno Balls (Hostess), 1 cake	200
Suzy Q (Hostess), 1 cake	260
Twinkie (Hostess), 1 cake	187

PIES, CAKES, PASTRIES
AND RELATED PRODUCTS
Frozen

Apple Danish (Sara Lee), 1 oz.	84
Apple Nut Kuchen (Durkee), 1 piece	56
Apple Pie (Banquet), 20 oz.	1404
Apple Pie (Banquet), 46 oz.	3229
Apple Pie (Morton), 1 pie	1530
Banana Pie (Banquet), 14 oz.	1036
Blackberry Pie (Banquet), 20 oz.	1504
Blackberry Pie (Banquet), 46 oz.	3459
Blueberry Pie (Banquet), 20 oz.	1464
Blueberry Pie (Banquet), 46 oz.	3367
Blueberry Rings (Sara Lee), 1 oz.	108
Boysenberry Pie (Banquet), 20 oz.	1376
Butterscotch Pie (Banquet), 14 oz.	1086
Caramel Nut Roll (Durkee), 1 piece	103
Cherry Danish (Sara Lee), 1 oz.	75
Cherry Pie (Morton), 1 pie	1546
Cherry Pie (Banquet), 20 oz.	1408
Cherry Pie (Banquet), 46 oz.	3238
Chocolate Cake (Sara Lee), 1 oz.	102
Chocolate Cream Pie (Morton), 1 pie	1160
Chocolate Pie (Banquet), 14 oz.	1131
Cinnamon Whirl (Durkee), 1 piece	78
Cinnamon Sticks (Aunt Jemima), 3 sticks	148
Coconut Pie (Banquet), 14 oz.	1170
Custard Pie (Banquet), 20 oz.	1096
Custard Pie (Banquet), 46 oz.	2521
Custard, Coconut Pie (Banquet), 20 oz.	1176
Custard, Coconut Pie (Banquet), 46 oz.	2705
Doughnuts, Powdered (Morton), 1 doughnut	95
Doughnuts, Sugar and Spice (Morton), 1 doughnut	97
German Chocolate Cake (Sara Lee), 1 oz.	91

	Calories
Key Lime Pie (Banquet), 14 oz.	1142
Lemon Pie (Banquet), 14 oz.	1002
Lemon Puffs, Sweet (Durkee), 1 piece	90
Mincemeat Pie (Banquet), 20 oz.	1604
Mincemeat Pie (Banquet), 46 oz.	3689
Neapolitan Pie (Banquet), 14 oz.	1053
Orange Cake (Sara Lee), 1 oz.	103
Peach Pie (Banquet), 20 oz.	1280
Peach Pie (Banquet), 46 oz.	2944
Pound Cake (Sara Lee), 1 oz.	110
Pumpkin Pie (Banquet), 20 oz.	1224
Pumpkin Pie (Banquet), 46 oz.	2815
Raspberry Rings (Sara Lee), 1 oz.	109
Strawberry Pie (Banquet), 14 oz.	1047
Strawberry Cream Pie (Morton), 1 pie	939

GELATIN, PIE FILLINGS, PUDDINGS, CUSTARDS

	Calories

GELATIN, 1/2 cup

All Flavors (Jell-O)	81
All Flavors (Jell's Best)	76
All Flavors (Royal)	80
All Flavors (D-Zerta)	9

PIE FILLING

Apple (Musselman), 4 oz.	113
Apple (Motts), 25 oz.	851
Apple, French (Comstock), 21 oz.	693
Apple (Comstock), 21 oz.	695
Apricot (Comstock), 21 oz.	612
Blackberry (Comstock), 21 oz.	855
Blueberry (Comstock), 21 oz.	649
Blueberry (Musselman), 4 oz.	113

	Calories
Blueberry (Mott's), 25 oz.	800
Boysenberry (Comstock), 21 oz.	724
Cherry (Comstock), 21 oz.	652
Cherry (Musselman), 4 oz.	113
Cherry (Mott's), 25 oz.	964
Key Lime (Royal Pudding), 2 packages	450
Lemon (Comstock), 22 oz.	713
Lemon (Royal Pudding), 2 packages	450
Mincemeat (Comstock), 22 oz.	885
Mincemeat (None Such Rum & Brandy), 18 oz.	1057
Mincemeat (None Such), 28 oz.	1511
Peach (Comstock), 22 oz.	715
Peach (Musselman), 4 oz.	113
Pineapple (Comstock), 21 oz.	547
Pumpkin (Comstock), 29.4 oz.	872
Pumpkin (Del Monte), 1 cup	261
Raisin (Comstock), 22 oz.	744
Red Raspberry (Comstock), 21 oz.	832
Strawberry (Comstock), 21 oz.	620

PUDDINGS AND CUSTARDS
1/2 cup, except where noted

Banana, Regular (Royal)	165
Banana Cream (Jell-O)	178
Banana Cream (My-T-Fine)	175
Banana Cream, Instant (Jell-O)	178
Banana Cream, Instant (Royal)	175
Bavarian Cream (My-T-Fine)	175
Bavarian Custard Rice-A-Roni (Golden Grain), 1 cup	248
Butterscotch (Hunt Wesson), Snack Pack, 5 oz.	238
Butterscotch (Jell-O), whole milk	173
Butterscotch (Jell-O), nonfat milk	138
Butterscotch (My-T-Fine)	175

Calories

Butterscotch (D-Zerta), whole milk	107
Butterscotch (D-Zerta), nonfat milk	71
Butterscotch (Sealtest)	124
Butterscotch (Royal)	190
Butterscotch (Del Monte), 5 oz.	176
Butterscotch, Instant (Jell-O)	178
Butterscotch, Instant (My-T-Fine), 1 cup	310
Butterscotch (Mott's Snack Pack), 4¾ oz.	225
Butterscotch, Instant (Royal)	185
Butter Pecan (My-T-Fine)	176
Caramel Nut, Instant (Royal)	195
Caramel Rich 'n Ready (My-T-Fine)	184
Cherry Vanilla (Mott's), Snack Pack, 4¾ oz.	225
Chocolate, Dutch (Bounty), ⅓-½ cup	152
Chocolate (Hunt Wesson), Snack Pack, 5 oz.	234
Chocolate (Jell-O), whole milk	175
Chocolate (Jell-O), nonfat milk	140
Chocolate (My-T-Fine)	187
Chocolate (Sealtest)	136
Chocolate (Royal)	190
Chocolate (Mott's), Snack Pack, 4¾ oz.	225
Chocolate, Instant (Jell-O)	191
Chocolate, Instant (My-T-Fine), 1 cup	362
Chocolate Rich 'n Ready (My-T-Fine)	191
Chocolate, Instant (Royal)	200
Chocolate (Royal Shake-a-Pudd'n)	200
Chocolate Malt (Royal Shake-a-Pudd'n)	200
Chocolate with Nuts (My-T-Fine)	195
Chocolate with Nuts, Instant (My-T-Fine)	366
Chocolate Fudge, Rich 'n Ready (My-T-Fine)	186
Chocolate Fudge (Jell-O), 1 cup	336
Chocolate Fudge (My-T-Fine)	190
Chocolate Fudge, Instant (Jell-O)	370
Chocolate Fudge (Mott's), Snack Pack, 4¾ oz.	225

	Calories
Chocolate Fudge (Del Monte), 5 oz.	175
Coconut, Toasted, Instant (Royal)	185
Coconut Cream (Jell-O), whole milk	175
Coconut Cream (Jell-O), nonfat milk	140
Coconut Cream, Instant (Jell-O)	189
Custard (Royal)	145
Custard, Egg (Jell-O)	165
Custard, Egg (Sealtest)	149
Custard, Egg, Caramel (My-T-Fine), 1 cup	290
Custard, Egg, Coconut (My-T-Fine), 1 cup	322
Dark 'N' Sweet (Royal)	195
Dark 'N' Sweet, Instant (Royal)	200
Lemon (Hunt-Wesson), Snack Pack, 5 oz.	175
Lemon (Jell-O)	178
Lemon (Mott's), Snack Pack, 4¾ oz.	225
Lemon (My-T-Fine)	178
Lemon, Instant (Jell-O)	178
Lemon, Instant (My-T-Fine), 1 cup	352
Lemon (Royal), 1 cup	360
Mince Meat (Crosse & Blackwell), 1 tbsp.	60
Mocha Nut, Instant (Royal)	170
New England Indian Pudding (B & M), 1 cup	300
Pistachio Nut, Instant (Royal)	185
Plum Pudding (Crosse & Blackwell), 4 oz.	340
Rice Pudding (Bounty), ⅓-½ cup	151
Strawberry (Royal Shake-a-Pudd'n)	160
Tapioca, Chocolate (Jell-O)	165
Tapioca, Chocolate (Royal)	185
Tapioca, Lemon (Jell-O)	165
Tapioca (Minute)	150
Tapioca, Orange (Jell-O)	165
Tapioca, Vanilla (Sealtest)	130
Tapioca, Vanilla (Jell-O)	165
Tapioca, Vanilla (Royal)	170

	Calories
Tapioca, Vanilla (My-T-Fine)	143
Vanilla (Bounty French), 1/3-1/2 cup	112
Vanilla (Hunt Wesson), Snack Pack	238
Vanilla (Jell-O), 1 cup	336
Vanilla Pudding (Del Monte), 5 oz.	176
Vanilla (My-T-Fine)	175
Vanilla, Rich 'n 'Ready (My-T-Fine)	192
Vanilla (Royal)	165
Vanilla (Sealtest)	125
Vanilla (Royal Shake-a-Pudd'n)	165
Vanilla (Mott's), Snack Pack, 4¾ oz.	225
Vanilla, Instant (Jell-O), 1 cup	370
Vanilla, Instant (My-T-Fine), 1 cup	332
Vanilla, Instant (Royal)	185
Whip and Chill, made with whole milk:	
Chocolate	138
Lemon	138
Strawberry	134
Vanilla	138
1-2-3-Dessert, all flavors, 2/3 cup average	135
Ready-To-Serve (General Mills):	
Butterscotch	171
Chocolate	175
Chocolate Fudge	175
Lemon	198
Rice	154
Vanilla	170

JAMS, JELLIES, PRESERVES, HONEY, SPREADS, 1 tbsp., except as noted

	Calories
Apple Butter (Musselman)	33
Honey (Sioux Honey Association)	65
Jam, Strawberry (Musselman)	54

	Calories
Jelly, All Flavors (Crosse & Blackwell)	51
Jelly, All Flavors (Musselman)	53
Jelly, All Flavors (Smucker's)	43
Jelly, Mint with Leaves (Reese)	58
Marmalade (Crosse & Blackwell)	60
Marmalade, Orange (Musselman)	51
Peanut Butter (Big Top)	72
Peanut Butter (Jif)	72
Peanut Butter (Planter's), 1 jar	100
Peanut Butter, Chunk Style (Skippy)	100
Peanut Butter, Creamy Style (Skippy)	100
Preserves, All Flavors (Crosse & Blackwell)	59
Preserves, All Flavors (Smucker's)	45
Preserves (Reese):	
Wild Strawberry	55
Wild Blueberry	55
Quince	55
Low Calorie Artificially Sweetened Diet Delight Products ½ cup:	
Apple Jelly	35
Apricot Pineapple Preserves	35
Blackberry Jam	29
Concord Grape Jelly	37
Raspberry Jam	32
Strawberry Jam	25

RELISHES, GARNISHES, COCKTAIL ACCOMPANIMENTS, AND RELATED PRODUCTS

	Calories
Barbecue Sauce with Bits of Onion (Heinz), Regular, 1 tbsp.	19
Barbecue Sauce with Bits of Onion (Heinz), Hickory Smoked, 1 tbsp.	18
Brown Sauce (La Choy), ¼ cup	321

Calories

Capers (Crosse & Blackwell), 1 tbsp.	6
Cauliflower, Sweet (Heinz), 1 bud	9
Chili Sauce (Hunt Wesson), ½ cup	149
Chili Sauce (Del Monte), 1 cup	257
Chili Sauce (Hunt's), 1 cup	149
Chow Chow (Crosse & Blackwell), 1 tbsp.	6
Cocktail Sauce (Hunt Wesson), ½ cup	108
57 Sauce (Heinz), 1 tbsp.	14
Mint Sauce (Crosse & Blackwell), 1 tbsp.	16
Mustard, Brown (Heinz), 1 tsp.	8
Mustard, Cream Style (French), 1 tbsp.	11
Mustard with Horseradish (Best Foods), 1 tbsp.	10
Mustard, Yellow (Heinz), 1 tsp.	5
Olives, Green, Manzanilla, Stuffed (Durkee), 1 olive	4
Olives, Green, Manzanilla, Stuffed (Grandee), 1 olive	4
Olives, Green, Queen, Stuffed (Durkee), 1 olive	14
Olives, Ripe, Pitted (Durkee), 1 olive	7
Onions, Cocktail (Crosse & Blackwell), 1 tbsp.	1
Onions, Cocktail (Heinz), 1 onion	trace
Pickles, Bread & Butter (Fannings), 3 slices	15
Pickles, Dill (Aunt Jane), 1 lb.	50
Pickles, Dill (Del Monte), 1 large	11
Pickles, Dill (Heinz), 1, 4″ long	7
Pickles, Dill, Processed (Heinz), 1, 3″ long	1
Pickles, Dill Hamburger Slices (Crosse & Blackwell), 1 slice	2
Pickles, Dill Hamburger Slices (Heinz), 3 slices	1
Pickles, Fresh Cucumber (Del Monte), 12 slices	73
Pickles, Kosher Dill Slices (Crosse & Blackwell), 1 tbsp.	2
Pickles, Sour (Del Monte), 1 large	11
Pickles, Sour (Heinz), 1, 2″ long	9

Calories

Pickles, Sweet (Aunt Jane), 1 lb.	662
Pickles, Sweet Chips (Crosse & Blackwell), 1 tbsp.	17
Pickles, Sweet Cucumber Slices (Crosse & Blackwell), 1 tbsp.	15
Pickles, Sweet (Del Monte), 1 large	146
Pickles, Sweet Cucumber Slices (Heinz), 3 slices	20
Pickles, Sweet Gherkins (Heinz), 1, 2″ long	16
Pickles, Kosher Dill Gherkins (Crosse & Blackwell), 1 tbsp.	2
Pickles, Sweet Mixed (Heinz), 3 slices	23
Pickles, Sweet Mustard (Heinz), 1 tbsp.	30
Relish, Barbecue (Heinz), 1 tbsp.	35
Relish, Corn (Crosse & Blackwell), 1 tbsp.	15
Relish, Hamburger (Cross & Blackwell), 1 tbsp.	20
Relish, Hamburger (Heinz), 1 tbsp.	15
Relish, Hot Dog (Heinz), 1 tbsp.	17
Relish, Hot Dog, Barbecue (Crosse & Blackwell), 1 tbsp.	22
Relish, India (Heinz), 1 tbsp.	17
Relish, Piccalilli (Heinz), 1 tbsp.	23
Relish, Piccalilli, India (Crosse & Blackwell), 1 tbsp.	26
Relish, Sweet (Heinz), 1 tbsp.	28
Relish, Sweet (Del Monte), 2 tbsp.	69
Relish, Sour (Del Monte), 2 tbsp.	8
Savory Sauce (Heinz), 1 tbsp.	74
Seafood Cocktail Sauce (Crosse & Blackwell), 1 tbsp.	22
Soy Sauce (La Choy), ½ cup	102
Steak Sauce (Crosse & Blackwell), 1 tbsp.	21
Sweet & Sour Sauce (Contadina), ½ cup	148
Sweet & Sour Sauce (La Choy), ½ cup	244
Tartar Sauce (Best Foods), 1 tbsp.	75
Tartar Sauce (Hellmann's), 1 tbsp.	75

	Calories
Tartar Sauce Mix (Lawry's), .63 oz. package	64
Tomato Catsup (Diet Delight), ½ cup	40
Tomato Catsup (Del Monte), 1 cup	298
Tomato Catsup (Hunt's), ½ cup	146
Tomato Casup (Stokely's), 1 tbsp.	17
Tomato Ketchup (Pride of the Farm), ½ cup	115
Tomato Ketchup (Steakhouse), ½ cup	115
Tomato Ketchup (Heinz), 1 tbsp.	16
Tomato Ketchup (Snider), ½ cup	115
Worcestershire Sauce (Crosse & Blackwell), 1 tbsp.	15
Worcestershire Sauce (Heinz), 1 tbsp.	11
Worcestershire Sauce (French), 5 oz.	62
Watermelon Rind (Crosse & Blackwell), 1 tbsp.	38

SNACKS

	Calories
Bacon Bits, Imitation (Durkee), 1 tsp.	8
Bacon Bits, Imitation (McCormick), 1 tbsp.	20
BakenEts, Fried Pork Rinds (Frito-Lay), 100 grams	533
Bacon Rinds (Wonder), 1 oz.	140
Bows (General Mills), 152 pieces	568
Bows (General Mills), 22 pieces	81
Bugles, General Mills), 104 pieces	568
Bugles (General Mills), 15 pieces	81
Buttons (General Mills), 339 pieces	514
Buttons (General Mills), 48 pieces	73
Cheese Twists (Wonder), 1¾ oz.	263
Chee Tos (Frito-Lay), 100 grams	566
Corn Cheese (Tom Huston), 10 pieces	29
Corn Chips, Regular and King Size (Fritos), 100 grams	579
Corn Chips (Wonder), 1¾ oz.	292

Calories

Corn Chips, Popped, Intermission (Frito-Lay), 100 grams	541
Corn Snacks, Fandangos (Frito-Lay), 100 grams	579
Corn Sticks (Wonder), 1¾ oz.	282
Daisy's (General Mills), 198 pieces	481
Daisy's (General Mills), 28 pieces	68
Danish Salama Sticks (Reese), 1 oz.	128
French Fried Onions (O & C), 2 cups	618
Onion Flavored, Funyuns (Frito-Lay), 100 grams	512
Pop Corn (Wonder), 1¾ oz.	228
Popcorn (Tom Huston), 1 cup	68
Potato Chips, Ruffles (Frito-Lay), 100 grams	569
Potato Crisps, Munchos (Frito-Lay), 100 grams	536
Potato Sticks (O & C), 1½ cups	282
Pretzels, Rold Gold (Frito-Lay), 100 grams	384
Pretzels, Mister Salty (Nabisco), 1 piece	11.7
Tortilla Chips, Doritos (Frito-Lay), 100 grams	505
Space Food Sticks, Peanut Butter Flavor (Pillsbury), 1 oz.	118
Space Food Sticks, Chocolate Flavor (Pillsbury), 1 oz.	118
Space Food Sticks, Caramel Flavor (Pillsbury), 1 oz.	118
Space Food Sticks, Chocolate Malt Flavor (Pillsbury), 1 oz.	118
Whistles (General Mills), 120 pieces	499
Whistles (General Mills), 17 pieces	71

NUTS

Calories

Almonds, Roasted (Funsten), 1 oz.	177
Almonds, Dry Roasted (Planter's), 1 jar	185
Cashews (Tom Huston), 15 nuts	168
Cashews, Dry Roasted (Planter's), 1 jar	180

Calories

Cashews, Dry Roasted (Skippy), 1 oz.	175
Cashews, Oil Roasted (Planter's), 1 can	180
Cashews, Salted (Skippy), 1 oz.	175
English Walnuts (Funsten), 1 oz.	185
Mixed Salted Nuts (Skippy), 1 oz.	180
Mixed, Dry Roasted (Planter's), 1 jar	175
Mixed, Dry Roasted (Skippy), 1 oz.	180
Mixed, Oil Roasted, with Peanuts (Planter's), 1 can	185
Mixed, Oil Roasted, without Peanuts (Planter's), 1 can	180
Peanuts, Dry Roasted, Lay's (Frito-Lay), 100 grams	637
Peanuts, Dry Roasted, Lay's (Frito-Lay), 1 oz.	181
Peanuts, Dry Roasted (Planter's), 1 jar	170
Peanuts, Dry Roasted (Skippy), 1 oz.	175
Peanuts, Oil Roasted, Cocktail (Planter's), 1 bag	130
Peanuts, Oil Roasted, Cocktail (Planter's), 1 can	185
Peanuts, Salted (Skippy), 1 oz.	175
Peanuts, Toasted (Tom Huston), 2 tbsp.	176
Pecans, Dry Roasted (Planter's), 1 jar	205
Pecans (Funsten), 1 oz.	194
Spanish, Dry Roasted (Planter's), 1 jar	175
Spanish Peanuts, Oil Roasted (Planter's), 1 can	180
Walnuts (Diamond), 15 halves	98
Walnuts, Black (Funsten), 1 oz.	178

CANDY AND OTHER CONFECTIONS

Calories

Almond Chocolate Bar (Nestle's), 1 oz.	149
Almond Candy Bar (Ghiradelli), 10¢ size	171
Bit-O-Honey (Chunky), 10¢ bar	200

Calories

Bit-O-Honey (Chunky), 9 oz. bag	1000
Bit-O-Honey (Chunky), per unit	21
Bit-O-Licorice (Chunky), 9 oz. bag	925
Bit-O-Licorice (Chunky), per unit	19
Bit-O-Licorice (Chunky), 10¢ bar	185
Bit-O-Peanut Butter (Chunky), 10¢ bar	225
Bit-O-Peanut Butter (Chunky), 9 oz. bag	1125
Bit-O-Peanut Butter (Chunky), per unit	24
Bonanza Chocolate Bar (Nestle's), 1 oz.	153
Butter Chip Bar (Hershey), 1 oz.	144
Butterscotch Morsels (Nestle's), 6 oz.	900
Caramel Cream Chocolate Bar (Nestle's), 1 oz.	124
Caramels, (Whirligigs), per piece	15
Caramel Pop (Sugar Daddy), per piece	1806
Cashew Crunch (Planter's), 1 can	135
Cheers (Chunky), 10¢ box	195
Chocolate Chips (Ghiradelli), ⅓ cup	292
Crisp and Milk Chocolate Candy Bar (Ghiradelli), 10¢ size	159
Divinity (Stuckey's), 1 piece	115
Eagle Bar (Ghiradelli), 1 square	148
Full Dinner (Tom Huston), 1 bar	194
Fudge (Stuckey's), 1 oz.	121
Fudge, Chocolate (Tom Huston), 1 bar	179
Fudge with Black Walnuts (Stuckey's), 1 oz.	128
Milk Chocolate Bar, Plain (Hershey), 1 oz.	152
Milk Chocolate Bar (Nestle's), 1 oz.	148
Block Milk Chocolate (Hershey), 1 oz.	145
Block Milk Chocolate (Ghiradelli), 1 oz.	178
Milk Chocolate Bar with Almonds (Hershey), 1 oz.	154
Milk Chocolate Covered Candy Coated Almonds (Hershey), 1 oz.	142
Milk Chocolate Chips (Hershey), 1 oz.	152

Milk Chocolate Kisses (Hershey), 1 oz.	152
Milk Chocolate Covered Coated Peanuts (Hershey), 1 oz.	139
Mint Chocolate (Ghiradelli), 1 oz.	169
Peppermint Cream Chocolate Bar (Nestle's), 1 oz.	120
Praline, Coconut (Stuckey's), 1 praline	125
Praline, Maple (Stuckey's), 1 praline	125
Raisin Bar (Ghiradelli), 1 bar	160
Semi-Sweet Chocolate Bar (Hershey), 1 oz.	145
Semi-Sweet Chocolate Bar (Nestle's), 1 oz.	141
Semi-Sweet Chocolate Chips (Hershey), 1 oz.	145
Semi-Sweet Chocolate Morsels (Nestle's), 6 oz.	820
Sweet Chocolate Sprigs (Hershey), 1 oz.	136
Chunky, 10¢ bar	194
Chunky, Family Bar	1028
Chunky, Pecan, 10¢ bar	181
Pecan Log Roll (Stuckey's), 1 oz.	135
Coconut Cream Egg (Hershey), 1 oz.	142
Crunch Chocolate Bar (Nestle's), 1 oz.	140
Fruit 'n Nut Chocolate Bar (Nestle's), 1 oz.	140
Triple Decker Chocolate Bar (Nestle's), 1 oz.	148
Cracker Jack, regular, 1⅜ oz.	193
Cracker Jack, Pass-Around Pack, 6 oz.	750
Cracker Jack, Park Pack, 3 oz.	370
Goobers (Chunky), 10¢ box	188
Candy Coated Hershey-Ets (Hershey), 1 oz.	134
Krackel Bar (Hershey), 1 oz.	148
Marshmallows, Old Fashioned (Campfire), 1 marshmallow	23
Marshmallows, Super Soft (Campfire), 1 marshmallow	19
Marshmallows, Miniature (Campfire), 1 marshmallow	2

	Calories
Milk Morsels (Nestle's), 6 oz.	850
Mint Morsels (Nestle's), 6 oz.	710
Mr. Goodbar (Hershey), 1 oz.	153
$100,000 Chocolate Bar (Nestle's), 1 oz.	121
Jumbo Peanut Block (Planters), 1 bar	140
Peanuts, double coated (Tom Huston), 1 oz.	157
Peanut Brittle (Stuckey's), 1 oz.	122
Peanut Plank (Tom Huston), 1 bar	216
Raisinets (Chunky), 10¢ box	143
Reese's Peanut Butter Cup (Hershey), 1 oz.	143
Reese's Peanut Butter Egg (Hershey), 1 oz.	135
Sno Caps (Chunky), 10¢ box	179
Doublemint Gum (Wrigley), 1 stick	8
Juicy Fruit Gum (Wrigley), 1 stick	9
Spearmint Gum (Wrigley), 1 stick	9
Thin Mints (Nabisco), 1 piece	45
Tootsie Rolls, Midgies, and 1¢ piece, per piece	26
Tootsie Rolls, 2¢, per piece	43
Tootsie Rolls, 5¢, per piece	116
Tootsie Rolls, 10¢, per piece	202
Tootsie Roll Pop Sucker	55
Tootsie Roll Pop Drop, per piece	18

BEVERAGES, Canned and Bottled
1 cup, except as noted

	Calories
Apple Drink (Del Monte)	105
Apricot Apple (Betty Crocker)	128
Cherry Apple (Betty Crocker)	136
Cider (Mott's), 6 oz.	84
Cider, Cherry Flavored (Mott's), 6 oz.	84
Coffee, Ground (Yuban, Maxwell House, Sanka)	2
Fruit Punch (Del Monte)	137
Grape Ade (Sealtest)	130
Grape Apple (Betty Crocker)	144

	Calories
Grape Drink (Del Monte)	132
Hawaiian Punch:	
Apple Red	110
Fruit Juicy Red, Canned	110.5
Great Grape	110
Lemon Pink	110
Sunshine Orange	111
Pineapple	110
Very Berry	110
Lemon Drink (Sealtest)	121
Lemonade (Sealtest)	110
Orange Ade (Sealtest)	128
Orange Drink (Del Monte)	120
Orange Drink (Sealtest)	115
Orange Drink Deluxe	
(Sealtest), 50% Orange Juice	113
Orange Apricot (Betty Crocker)	120
Orange Apricot Juice Drink (Del Monte)	105
Orange Banana (Betty Crocker)	120
Orange Grapefruit (Betty Crocker)	120
Orange Pineapple (Betty Crocker)	128
Pineapple-Apricot Juice (Del Monte)	115
Merry Pineapple Cherry (Del Monte)	120
Pineapple Grapefruit Juice Drink (Del Monte)	130
Pineapple Orange Juice Drink (Del Monte)	103
Pineapple-Pear Juice Drink (Del Monte)	103
Pink Pineapple-Grapefruit (Del Monte)	118
Tropical Fruit (Mott's), 6 oz.	90

BEVERAGES, Instant

	Calories
Coffee, (Maxwell House, Yuban, Sanka), 1 cup	3
Coffee, Freeze Dried (Maxim), 1 cup	3
Coffee, Freeze Dried (Sanka), 1 cup	4
Nescafé (Nestles), 1 slightly rounded tsp.	4

	Calories
Decaf (Nestles), 1 tsp.	4
Kool-Aid Soft Drink Mix, average all flavors, 1 cup	98
Nestea (Nestles), 1 level tsp.	.5
Nestea, Iced (Nestles), All Flavors, sweetened with sugar, 3 tsp.	58
Nestea, Iced (Nestles), All Flavors, sweetened without sugar, 2 tsp.	11
Postum, 1 cup	9
Replay, Orange, 1 cup	88
Replay, Citrus, 1 cup	89
Start, ½ cup	60
Tang, ½ cup	66
Twist, Sugar Sweetened Imitation Lemonade Mix, 1 cup	81

BEVERAGES, Frozen
1 cup, except as noted

	Calories
Awake, for Imitation Orange Juice (Birds Eye), ½ cup	51
Fruit Juicy Red, prepared as directed (Hawaiian Punch)	110
Great Grape, prepared as directed (Hawaiian Punch)	110
Lemonade (Birds Eye)	98
Lemonade (Minute Maid)	98
Lemonade (Snow Crop)	98
Lemonade, Pink (Birds Eye)	102
Limeade (Birds Eye)	102
Limeade (Minute Maid)	100
Orange Plus, Imitation Orange Juice (Birds Eye), ½ cup	67

SODA Calories

Birch Beer (Canada Dry), 6 oz.	71
Bitter Lemon (Canada Dry), 6 oz.	78
Bitter Lemon (Schweppes), 1 oz.	16
Bitter Orange (Schweppes), 1 oz.	15
Black Cherry (Shasta), sugar sweetened, 8 oz.	128
Black Cherry (Canada Dry), 6 oz.	93
Black Cherry (Shasta), diet, 8 oz.	1
Citrus (Gatorade), 1 oz.	5
Cherry (Canada Dry), 6 oz.	85
Cherry Cola (Shasta), sugar sweetened, 8 oz.	102
Cherry Crush (Crush International), 1 oz.	16
Cherry Crush (Crush International), 10 oz.	163
Cherry Cola (Shasta), diet, 8 oz.	1
Club Soda (Canada Dry), 6 oz.	trace
Cola (Gatorade), 1 oz.	5
Cola (Royal Crown), 1 oz.	13
Cola (Shasta), sugar sweetened, 8 oz.	102
Cola, New Cyclamate Free, Diet-Rite (Royal Crown), 6 oz.	6
Cola (Canada Dry), 6 oz.	77
Cola (Shasta), diet, 8 oz.	1
Collins (Shasta), 8 oz.	87
Collins Mixer (Canada Dry), 6 oz.	64
Cream Soda (Shasta), sugar sweetened, 8 oz.	112
Cream Soda (Canada Dry), 8 oz.	93
Cream Soda (Shasta), diet, 8 oz.	1
Dr. Pepper, regular, 1 oz.	11
Dr. Pepper, New Diet, 1 oz.	2
Ginger Ale (Shasta), sugar sweetened, 8 oz.	97
Ginger Ale (Canada Dry), 6 oz.	64
Ginger Ale (Shasta), diet, 8 oz.	1
Ginger Ale (Schweppes), 1 oz.	11
Ginger Beer (Schweppes), 1 oz.	12
Grape Soda (Shasta), sugar sweetened, 8 oz.	117

Calories

Grape (Nehi), 1 oz.	15
Grape (Canada Dry), 6 oz.	93
Grape Soda (Shasta), diet, 8 oz.	1
Grape Crush (Crush International), 1 oz.	17
Grape Crush (Crush International), 10 oz.	170
Grape Drink (Sierra Valley), 8 oz.	122
Grapefruit Crush (Crush International), 1 oz.	12
Grapefruit Crush (Crush International), 10 oz.	128
Hi-Spot (Canada Dry), 6 oz.	73
Lemon Juice (Rose's), 1 oz.	11
Lemon-Lime (Shasta), sugar sweetened, 8 oz.	97
Lemon-Lime (Canada Dry), green, 6 oz.	89
Lemon-Lime (Shasta), diet, 8 oz.	1
Lime Juice (Rose's), 1 oz.	49
No-Cal, 1 oz.	trace
Orange (Shasta), sugar sweetened, 8 oz.	128
Orange (Canada Dry), 6 oz.	100
Orange (Nehi), 1 oz.	16
Orange (Shasta), diet, 8 oz.	1
Orange Crush (Crush International), 1 oz.	15
Orange Crush (Crush International), 10 oz.	158
Orange Drink (Sierra Valley), 8 oz.	122
Quinine (Shasta), sugar sweetened, 8 oz.	75
Quinine (Shasta), diet, 8 oz.	1
Raspberry (Shasta), diet, 8 oz.	1
Root Beer (Hires), 1 oz.	12
Root Beer (Hires), 10 oz.	124
Root Beer (Hires), diet, 10 oz.	1
Root Beer (Nehi), 1 oz.	15
Root Beer (Shasta), sugar sweetened, 8 oz.	112
Rooti Root Beer (Canada Dry), 6 oz.	78
Root Beer (Shasta), diet, 8 oz.	1
Sun-drop (Crush International), 1 oz.	14
Sun-drop (Crush International), 10 oz.	148

	Calories
Sport Cola (Canada Dry), 6 oz.	77
Strawberry (Shasta), sugar sweetened, 8 oz.	107
Strawberry (Canada Dry), 6 oz.	89
Strawberry (Shasta), diet, 9 oz.	1
Strawberry Crush (Crush International), 1 oz.	16
Strawberry Crush (Crush International), 10 oz.	163
Swing (Shasta), sugar sweetened, 8 oz.	112
Swing (Shasta), diet, 8 oz.	1
Tahitian Treat (Canada Dry), 6 oz.	89
Tiki (Shasta), sugar sweetened, 8 oz.	112
Tiki (Shasta), diet 8 oz.	1
Tonic Water (Schweppes), 1 oz.	11
Tonic Water (Canada Dry), 6 oz.	71
Whiskey Sour (Canada Dry), 6 oz.	71
Whiskey Sour (Schweppes), 6 oz.	52
Whiskey Sour (Shasta), 8 oz.	87
Wink (Canada Dry), 6 oz.	89

COCKTAILS, LIQUEURS, LIQUORS, WINES

Calories

COCKTAILS

Red Herring, 1 jigger, Cherry Heering, 2 jiggers, Courvoisier	75
Rusty Nail, ½ oz., Drambuie, ½ oz., Scotch	75
Daiquiri (Calvert), 3 oz.	190
Gin Sour (Calvert), 3 oz.	195
Manhattan (Calvert), 3 oz.	161
Margarita (Calvert), 3 oz.	176
Martini (Calvert), 3 oz.	176
Tequila Sour (Calvert), 3 oz.	185
Vodka Martini (Calvert), 3 oz.	188
Whiskey Sour (Calvert), 3 oz.	190

Absinthe (Leroux Liqueurs-American), 3 oz.	262
Anesone (Leroux Liqueurs-American), 3 oz.	259
Anisette (Bois), 50 proof, 1 oz.	111
Anisette, White or Red (Leroux Liqueurs-American), 3 oz.	267
Anisette (Schieffelin), 1 oz. pony	80
Apricot (Leroux Liqueurs-American), 3 oz.	255
Apricot (Leroux Flavored Brandy), 3 oz.	276
Aquavit (Leroux Liqueurs-American), 3 oz.	225
Banana (Leroux Liqueurs-American), 3 oz.	275
Blackberry Brandy and all flavored brandies (Bois), 70 proof, 1 oz.	100
Blackberry Liqueur and all fruit liqueurs (Bois), 60 proof, 1 oz.	96
Blackberry (Leroux Liqueurs-American), 3 oz.	235
Blackberry (Leroux Flavored Brandy), 3 oz.	273
Brandy and Coffee (Leroux Flavored), 3 oz.	273
Casanove, Italy (Leroux Liqueurs-Imported), 3 oz.	313
Chartreuse (Schieffelin), 1 oz. pony	75
Cheri Suisse (Leroux Liqueurs-Imported), 3 oz.	271
Cherry (Leroux Liqueurs-American), 3 oz.	240
Cherry (Leroux Flavored Brandy), 3 oz.	273
Cherry Heering, on the rocks (Ted Worner Associates), 1 oz.	55
Cherry Karise (Leroux Liqueurs-American), 3 oz.	213
Cherry Kijafa (Seagram), 3 oz.	148
Claristin (Leroux Liqueurs-American), 3 oz.	343
Cognac (Schieffelin), 1 oz. pony	75
Creme de Cacao (Bois), 54 proof, 1 oz.	101
Creme de Cacao, Brown (Leroux Liqueurs-American), 3 oz.	304

Calories

Creme de Cacao, White (Leroux Liqueurs-American) , 3 oz.	293
Creme de Cacao (Schieffelin) ,1 oz. pony	90
Creme de Cafe (Leroux Liqueurs-American) , 3 oz.	311
Creme de Cassis (Leroux Liqueurs-American), 3 oz.	264
Creme de Menthe (Bois) , 60 proof, 1 oz.	112
Creme de Menthe, Green (Leroux Liqueurs-American) , 3 oz.	330
Creme de Menthe, White (Leroux Liqueurs-American) , 3 oz.	302
Creme de Menthe (Schieffelin) , 1 oz. pony	90
Creme de Noyaux (Bois) , 60 proof, 1 oz.	115
Creme de Noya (Leroux Liqueurs-American) , 3 oz.	325
Curacao, Blue (Bois), 64 proof, 1 oz.	105
Curacao, Orange (Bois) , 64 proof, 1 oz.	100
Curacao (Leroux Liqueurs-American) , 3 oz.	263
Deluxe Brandy (Leroux) , 3 oz.	202
Five Star Brandy (Leroux) , 3 oz.	218
Ginger (Leroux Flavored Brandy) , 3 oz.	228
Ginger, Sharp (Leroux Flavored Brandy) , 3 oz.	231
Gold-O-Mint (Leroux Liqueurs-American), 3 oz.	330
Grenadine (Leroux Liqueurs-American) , 3 oz.	243
Kirschwasser (Leroux Brandy) , 3 oz.	241
Kummel (Liqueurs-American) , 3 oz.	224
Lechan Ora (Leroux Liqueurs-Imported) , 3 oz.	267
Maraschino (Leroux Liqueurs-American) , 3 oz.	265
Pasha Turkish Coffee (Leroux Liquers-Imported) , 3 oz.	290
Peach (Leroux Liqueurs-American), 3 oz.	255

	Calories
Peach (Leroux Flavored Brandy), 3 oz.	280
Peppermint Schnapps (Leroux Liqueurs-American), 3 oz.	260
Polish Blackberry (Leroux Flavored Brandy), 3 oz.	276
Raspberry (Leroux Liqueurs-American), 3 oz.	223
Rock & Rye (Leroux Liqueurs-American), 3 oz.	274
Rock & Rye, Irish Moss (Leroux Liqueurs-American), 3 oz.	329
Sabra (Leroux Liqueurs-Imported), 3 oz.	273
Strawberry (Leroux Liqueurs-American), 3 oz.	223
Triple Sec (Bois), 78 proof, 1 oz.	113
Triple Sec (Leroux Liqueurs-American), 3 oz.	305
Vandermint (Leroux Liqueurs-Imported), 3 oz.	270

LIQUORS

Canadian-Gold Pennant (Brown-Forman), 86.18 proof, 1 oz.	87
Early Times (Brown-Forman), 86 proof, 1 oz.	86
King Blend (Brown-Forman), 86 proof, 1 oz.	86
Mint Gin (Leroux Flavored), 3 oz.	209
Old Forester (Brown-Forman), 100 proof, 1 oz.	100
Old Forester (Brown-Forman), 86 proof, 1 oz.	86
Orange Gin (Leroux Flavored), 3 oz.	209
Rum, Jamaica (Schieffelin), 1 oz. jigger	125
Scotch Whiskey (Schieffelin), 1 oz. jigger	85
Scotch, Green Stripe (Usher's) 86 proof, 1 oz.	86
Silvertop Dry Gin (Bois), 90 proof, 1 oz.	90
Slo Gin (Bois), 66 proof, 1 oz.	85
Sloe Gin (Leroux Flavored), 3 oz.	221
Vodka (Bois), 100 proof, 1 oz.	100
Vodka (Bois), 80 proof, 1 oz.	80

Beaujolais (Cruse), 1 oz.	24
Beajolais St. Louis, Burgundy Red French (Barton & Guestier), 3 oz.	60
Bolla; Cello; Frescobalki; Vaselli; Asti (Brown-Forman), 1 oz.	42
Bordeaux Rouge (Cruse), 1 oz.	21
Chablis (Barton & Guestier), 3 oz.	60
Chablis (Cruse), 1 oz.	22
Champagne, Brut (Schieffelin), 6 oz.	115
Champagne, Veuve Clicquot (Brown-Forman), 1 oz.	26
Chateau Pontet Canot (Cruse), 1 oz.	24
Chateauneuf du Pape (Barton & Guestier), 3 oz.	70
Chateauneuf du Pape (Cruse), 1 oz.	24
Chiante Classico (Brolio), 3 oz.	66
Chianti Classico (Brown-Forman), 1 oz.	25
Cordon Rouge Brut (Mumm's), 3 oz.	65
Extra Dry Champagne (Mumm's), 3 oz.	82
Govrey Chambertin (Cruse), 1 oz.	24
Graacher Himmelreich, German Moselle (Seagram), 3 oz.	60
Graves (Barton & Guestier), 3 oz.	65
Graves (Cruse), 1 oz.	23
Liebfraumilch, Annheuser (Brown-Forman), 1 oz.	21
Liebfraumilch Glockenspiel (Julius Kayser), 3 oz.	57
Margaux (Barton & Guestier), 3 oz.	62
Medoc (Cruse), 1 oz.	24
Nectarose Vin Rose (Seagram), 3 oz.	70
Niersteiner (Julius Kayser), 3 oz.	54
Nuit St. George (Barton & Guestier), 3 oz.	70

Calories

Piesporter Riesling, German Moselle (Seagram) , 3 oz.	57
Pommard (Barton & Guestier) , 3 oz.	67
Pommard (Cruse) , 1 oz.	24
Pouilly Fuisse (Barton & Guestier) , 3 oz.	64
Pouilly Fuisse (Cruse), 1 oz.	24
Pouilly Fume (Barton & Guestier) , 3 oz.	60
Prince Blanc (Barton & Guestier) , 3 oz.	62
Prince Noir (Barton & Guestier) , 3 oz.	61
Puligny Montrachet (Barton & Guestier) , 3 oz.	61
St. Emilion (Barton & Guestier) , 3 oz.	63
St. Emilion (Cruse) , 1 oz.	23
St. Julien (Cruse), 1 oz.	23
Sancerre (Barton & Guestier) , 3 oz.	61
Sauternes, Bordeaux White French (Barton & Guestier) , 3 oz.	95
Sauternes, Haut, Bordeaux White French (Barton & Guestier) , 3 oz.	99
Sparkling Burgundy, Red French (Barton & Guestier) , 3 oz.	69
Vermouth (Brown-Forman) , Dry, 1 oz.	42
Vermouth (Brown-Forman) , Rosso, 1 oz.	51
Vermouth (Brown-Forman) , Bianco, 1 oz.	44
Vermouth, Dry (Noilly Prat), 3 oz.	101
Vermouth, Sweet (Noilly Prat) , 3 oz.	128
Vin Rose (Cruse) , 1 oz.	24
Wine, Dry (Schieffelin) , 4 oz. glass	95
Wine, Sweet (Schieffelin) , 4 oz. glass	125

TABLE OF CONTENTS
BRAND-NAME CARBOHYDRATE GRAM COUNTER

HORS D'OEUVRE, DIPS, AND SPREADS

	Carbohydrate Grams
Anchovies, Flat (Reese), 2 oz.	0.1
Bacon and Smoke Dip 'n Dressing (Sealtest), 8 oz.	13.9
Beef, Chipped, Dip 'n Dressing (Sealtest), 8 oz.	14.6
Blue Cheese Dip 'n Dressing (Sealtest), 8 oz.	12.1
Blue Tang Dip (Dean), 2 tbsp.	8.2
	per 100 grams
Casino Dip 'n Dressing (Sealtest), 8 oz.	16.7
Caviar (Northland Queen), 1 oz.	0.9
Chicken Livers, Chopped (Reese), 1 oz.	0.9
Chicken Spread (Underwood), 1 tbsp.	3.29
Corned Beef Spread (Underwood), 1 tbsp.	trace
Ham, Deviled (Underwood), 1 tbsp.	trace
French Onion Dip (Dean), 2 tbsp.	7.2
	per 100 grams
French Onion Dip (Sealtest), 8 oz.	17.2
Onion and Garlic Dip 'n Dressing (Sealtest), 8 oz.	17.9
Jalapeño Bean Dip (El Paso), 1 oz.	7.0
Jalapeño Bean Dip, Fritos (Frito-Lay), 100 grams	12.8
Liver Pate (Sell's), 1 tbsp.	9.88
Liverwurst Spread (Underwood), 1 tbsp.	9.88
Sandwich Spread (Best Foods), 1 tbsp.	2.4
Sandwich Spread (Hellmann's), 1 tbsp.	2.4

HORS D'OEUVRE, Frozen
1 piece

	Carbohydrate Grams
Bean and Bacon Burrito Rolls (Patio)	4.4
Beef Burrito Rolls (Patio)	3.98
Beef Puffs (Durkee)	3.10

	Carbohydrate Grams
Cheese Puffs (Durkee)	2.89
Cheese Straws (Durkee)	1.20
Chicken Burrito Rolls (Patio)	4.5
Chicken Puffs (Durkee)	3.05
Chicken Liver Puffs (Durkee)	3.10
Cocktail Tacos (Patio)	4.85
Frank-N-Blankets (Durkee)	1.01
Shrimp Puffs (Durkee)	3.

SOUPS AND CHOWDERS
Canned

	Carbohydrate Grams
Alphabet Vegetable (Lipton), 1 envelope	36.6
Asparagus, Cream of (Campbell's), 3½ oz.	9.4
Bean with Bacon (Campbell's), 3½ oz.	17.1
Bean, Hot Dog (Campbell's), 3½ oz.	18
Bean with Smoked Pork (Heinz), 1 cup	19.1
Beef (Campbell's), 3½ oz.	9.2
Beef Bouillon, Cubes (Knorr-Swiss), 8 oz.	0
Beef Bouillon, Cubes (Maggi), 1 cube	0.5
Beef Bouillon, Instant (Maggi), 1 tsp.	0.5
Beef Broth (Campbell's), 3½ oz.	2.1
Beef Broth (College Inn), 1 cup	7.4
Beef Noodle (Campbell's), 3½ oz.	7.2
Beef Noodle (Heinz), 1 cup	6.7
Beef Noodle (Lipton), 1 envelope	32.6
Black Bean (Campbell's), 3½ oz.	12.2
Black Bean (Crosse & Blackwell), 6½ oz., ½ can	15.5
Celery, Cream of (Campbell's), 3½ oz.	6.4
Celery, Cream of (Heinz), 1 cup	9.0
Cheddar Cheese (Campbell's), 3½ oz.	8.5
Chicken Bouillon, Cubes (Knorr-Swiss), 8 oz.	0

Carbohydrate
Grams

Chicken Bouillon, Cubes (Maggi), 1 cube	1.1
Chicken Bouillon, Instant (Maggi), 1 tsp.	1.1
Chicken Broth (Campbell's), 3½ oz.	1.2
Chicken, Cream of (Campbell's), 3½ oz.	6.3
Chicken, Cream of (Heinz), 1 cup	8.3
Chicken Gumbo (Campbell's), 3½ oz.	7.5
Chicken 'n Dumplings (Campbell's), 3½ oz.	4.2
Chicken Noodle (Campbell's), 3½ oz.	7.2
Chicken Noodle (Heinz), 1 cup	9.5
Chicken Noodle (Lipton), 1 envelope	26.8
Chicken Noodle-O's (Campbell's), 3½ oz.	7.9
Chicken Noodle with Diced Chicken Meat (Lipton), 1 envelope	29.2
Chicken Rice (Lipton), 1 envelope	23.8
Chicken with Rice (Campbell's), 3½ oz.	4.9
Chicken with Rice (Heinz), 1 cup	6.7
Chicken with Rice (Richardson & Robbins), 1 cup	1.37
Chicken and Stars (Campbell's), 3½ oz.	6.1
Chicken and Stars Noodle (Heinz), 1 cup	7.9
Chicken Vegetable (Campbell's), 3½ oz.	7.6
Chicken Vegetable (Heinz), 1 cup	9.3
Chicken Vegetable (Lipton), 1 envelope	29.8
Chili Beef (Campbell's), 3½ oz.	18.3
Chili with Beef (Heinz), 1 cup	21.2
Clam Chowder, Manhattan Style (Campbell's), 3½ oz.	9.2
Clam Chowder, Manhattan Style (Crosse & Blackwell), 6½ oz., ½ can	12.9
Clam Chowder, New England Style (Crosse & Blackwell), 6½ oz., 1 can	10.3
Consomme (Campbell's), 3½ oz.	2.5
Consomme Madrilene, Clear (Crosse & Blackwell), 6½ oz., ½ can	2.4

Carbohydrate
Grams

Consomme Madrilene, Red (Crosse & Blackwell), 6½ oz., ½ can	2.4
Consomme Beef Flavor, Instant Soupmix (Knorr-Swiss), 6 oz.	0.3
Consomme Celestine, Instant Soupmix (Knorr-Swiss), 6 oz.	5.4
Consomme, Chicken Flavor, Instant Soupmix (Knorr-Swiss), 6 oz.	0.2
Consomme, Oxtail Flavor, Instant Soupmix (Knorr-Swiss), 6 oz.	0.5
Crab (Crosse & Blackwell), 6½ oz., ½ can	8.3
Gazpacho (Crosse & Blackwell), 6½ oz., ½ can	6.8
Green Pea (Campbell's), 3½ oz.	18.5
Green Pea Soupmix (Knorr-Swiss), 6 oz.	6.3
Green Pea (Lipton), 1 envelope	67.4
Leek Soupmix (Knorr-Swiss), 6 oz.	7.7
Lobster, Cream of (Crosse & Blackwell), 6½ oz., ½ can	6.5
Minestrone (Campbell's), 3½ oz.	9.2
Mushroom (Campbell's), 3½ oz.	6.8
Mushroom (Lipton), 1 envelope	24.1
Mushroom, Cream of (Campbell's), 3½ oz.	7.5
Mushroom, Cream of (Heinz), 1 cup	10.4
Mushroom Bisque (Crosse & Blackwell), 6½ oz., ½ can	8.3
Noodle Soupmix (Knorr-Swiss), 6 oz.	7.6
Noodles & Ground Beef (Campbell's), 3½ oz.	8.1
Onion (Campbell's), 3½ oz.	2.7
Onion, French (Crosse & Blackwell), 6½ oz., ½ can	4.8
Onion Soupmix and Dip Mix (Knorr-Swiss), 6 oz.	5.7
Onion (Lipton), 1 envelope	22.1

**Carbohydrate
Grams**

Oxtail Soupmix (Knorr-Swiss), 6 oz.	6.2
Oyster Stew (Campbell's), 3½ oz.	5.3
Pepper Pot (Campbell's), 3½ oz.	7.6
Petite Marmite (Crosse & Blackwell), 6½ oz., ½ can	3.7
Potato (Lipton), 1 envelope	57.4
Potato, Cream of (Campbell's), 3½ oz.	9.1
Scotch Broth (Campbell's), 3½ oz.	8.6
Senegalese (Crosse & Blackwell), 6½ oz., ½ can	6.8
Shrimp, Cream of (Crosse & Blackwell), 6½ oz., ½ can	6.5
Split Pea with Ham (Campbell's), 3½ oz.	19.1
Split Pea with Ham (Heinz), 1 cup	23.0
Tomato (Campbell's), 3½ oz.	12.3
Tomato (Heinz), 1 cup	18.3
Tomato Beef Noodle-O's (Campbell's), 3½ oz.	13.6
Tomato, Bisque (Campbell's), 3½ oz.	18.4
Tomato Rice, Old Fashioned (Campbell's), 3½ oz.	14.7
Tomato Vegetable (Lipton), 1 envelope	48.2
Tuna Creole (Crosse & Blackwell), 6½ oz., ½ can	6.6
Turkey Noodle (Campbell's), 3½ oz.	6.6
Turkey Noodle (Heinz), 1 cup	10.0
Turkey Vegetable (Campbell's), 3½ oz.	7.0
Vegetable (Campbell's), 3½ oz.	11.1
Vegetable Soupmix (Knorr-Swiss), 6 oz.	4.1
Vegetable, Old Fashioned (Campbell's), 3½ oz.	7.2
Vegetable Beef (Campbell's), 3½ oz.	6.4
Vegetable Beef (Heinz), 1 cup	9.6
Vegetable Beef (Lipton), 1 envelope	22.0

	Carbohydrate Grams
Vegetable and Beef Stockpot (Campbell's), 3½ oz.	7.5
Vegetable with Beef Stock (Heinz), 1 cup	13.4
Vegetable, Golden Noodle-O's (Campbell's), 3½ oz.	8.5
Vegetarian Vegetable (Campbell's), 3½ oz.	10.4
Vegetable Vegetarian (Heinz), 1 cup	14.2
Vermicelli Soupmix with Meatballs (Knorr-Swiss), 6 oz.	7.8

Low Sodium Soups, (Campbell's) ready to serve, 8 oz.

Green Pea	24.1
Mushroom, Cream of	8.9
Tomato	17.6
Turkey Noodle	5.4
Vegetable	12.9
Vegetable Beef	7.7

SOUPS AND CHOWDERS, Frozen (Campbell's), 1/3 can, 1 serving

	Carbohydrate Grams
Clam Chowder, New England Style	8.9
Green Pea with Ham	14.5
Oyster Stew	6.9
Potato, Cream of	10.1
Shrimp, Cream of	6.9
Vegetable with Beef, Old Fashioned	6.6

MEATS, Packaged and Fresh, per slice, except as noted

	Carbohydrate Grams
Bacon (Oscar Mayer)	0
Canadian Bacon (Oscar Mayer), 6 oz.	0

Carbohydrate
Grams

Bar-B-Q Loaf (Oscar Mayer)	2.7
Beef Jerky (Slim Jim), 1 piece	.7
Beef Loaf, Jellied (Oscar Mayer)	0.4
Beef, Thin-Sliced (Oscar Mayer), 1 oz.	0.7
Bologna, All Meat (Armour), 100 grams	0
Bologna, Bar-S (Cudahy)	trace
Bologna, All Meat (Oscar Mayer)	0.7
Bologna, Pure Beef (Oscar Mayer)	0.6
Bologna, Pure Beef Lebanon (Oscar Mayer)	0.4
Cheese Smokes (Oscar Mayer), 1 link	1.3
Cocktail Loaf (Oscar Mayer)	3.9
Corned Beef, Jellied Loaf (Oscar Mayer)	0.4
Franks, All Meat (Armour Star), 100 grams	0
Franks, Pure Beef (Oscar Mayer), 1 link	1.5
Franks, Machiaeh Brand, Pure Beef (Oscar Mayer), 1 link	2.6
Ham, Boneless, Jubilee (Oscar Mayer), whole, per oz.	0
Ham and Cheese Loaf (Oscar Mayer)	0.4
Ham, Chopped (Oscar Mayer)	1.0
Ham, Minced (Oscar Mayer)	2.0
Ham, Smoked Cooked (Oscar Mayer), 6 oz.	0
Ham, Thin-Sliced (Oscar Mayer)	0
Ham and Cheese Roll (Oscar Mayer), meat spread, 1 oz.	.9
Head Cheese (Oscar Mayer)	1.3
Honey Loaf (Oscar Mayer)	0.9
Liver Cheese (Oscar Mayer)	0.6
Liver Loaf, Bar-S (Cudahy)	trace
Luncheon Meat, All Meat (Oscar Mayer)	1.3
Luncheon Meat, Pure Beef (Oscar Mayer)	1.3
Luxury Loaf (Oscar Mayer)	1.6
Old Fashioned Loaf (Oscar Mayer)	3.8

**Carbohydrate
Grams**

Olive Loaf (Oscar Mayer)	4.7
Peppered Loaf (Oscar Mayer)	1.9
Pickle and Pimento Loaf (Oscar Mayer)	3.9
Picnic Loaf (Oscar Mayer)	2.2
Salami, for Beer (Oscar Mayer)	0.3
Salami, Cotto, Pure Beef (Oscar Mayer)	0.6
Salami, Cotto, Bar-S (Cudahy)	trace
Salami, Cotto, All Meat (Oscar Mayer)	0.6
Salami, Hard, All Meat (Oscar Mayer)	0.2
Salami, Machiaeh Brand, Pure Beef (Oscar Mayer)	0.8
Sausage, Smoke Breakfast, All Meat (Oscar Mayer), 1 link	2.2
Sausage, Braunschweiger Liver (Oscar Mayer), 1 oz.	0.4
Sausage, Chubbie, All Meat (Oscar Mayer), 1 link	2.4
Sausage, Luncheon Roll (Oscar Mayer)	1.5
Sausage, Minced Roll, All Meat (Oscar Mayer)	0.8
Sausage, New England Brand, All Meat (Oscar Mayer)	0.8
Sausage, Polish, All Meat (Oscar Mayer), ¾ lb. ring	0
Sausage, All Beef, Polish (Slim Jim), 1 piece	.4
Sausage, Pork (Armour Star), 100 grams	0
Sausage, Pork, Pure (Oscar Mayer), 1 link cooked	0
Sausage, Smokie Links, All Meat (Oscar Mayer), 1 link	1.3
Sausage, Little Smokies, All Meat (Oscar Mayer), 1 link	0.2
Sausage, Thuringer Cervelat, All Meat (Oscar Mayer)	0.4

	Carbohydrate Grams
Sausage, Thuringer Cervelat, Pure Beef Summer (Oscar Mayer)	0.6
Slim Jims (Slim Jim), 1 piece	.4
Turkey Breast Meat, cured-pressed-smoked-cooked (Oscar Mayer)	0
Wieners, All Meat (Oscar Mayer), 1 link	1.5
Wieners, Bar-S (Cudahy), 1 link	trace
Little Wieners, All Meat (Oscar Mayer), 1 link	0.3

MEATS AND POULTRY
Canned

	Carbohydrate Grams
Barbecue Manwich (Hunt's), 15 oz.	69.1
Beef, Chopped (Armour), 12 oz.	43.2
Beef Stew (Armour Star), 24 oz.	61.5
Beef Stew (B & M), 1 cup	14.7
Beef Stew (Bounty), ⅓-½ cup	7.2
Beef Stroganoff (Lipton), 1 package	97.1
Chicken a la King (College Inn), 1 cup	8.9
Chicken a la King (Richardson & Robbins), 1 cup	5.9
Chicken Baronet (Lipton), 1 package	90.6
Chicken, Boned (Richardson & Robbins), 3 oz.	0.7
Chicken, Boned (College Inn), 1 oz.	0
Chicken Fricassee (Richardson & Robbins), 1 cup	5.2
Chicken Fricassee (College Inn), 1 cup	14.8
Chicken & Egg Noodles (College Inn), 1 cup	52.9
Chicken Noodle Dinner (Heinz), 1 can	18.9
Chicken Stew (B&M), 1 cup	14.2
Chicken Stew (Bounty), ⅓-½ cup	6.8
Chicken Stew with Dumplings (Heinz), 1 can	22.1
Chicken Stroganoff (Lipton), 1 package	90.3

	Carbohydrate Grams
Chicken Supreme (Lipton), 1 package	94.3
Corned Beef Hash (Armour), 15½ oz.	35.4
Corned Beef Hash (Bounty), ⅓-½ can	8.2
Ham Chedderton (Lipton), 1 package	91.5
Ham, Chopped (Armour), 12 oz.	45
Ham, Parti-Style (Armour), 100 grams	0.1
Lamb Stew (B & M), 1 cup	13.2
Manwich, (Hunt's), 15 oz.	57.9
Potted Meat (Armour), 3¼ oz.	10.7
Treet (Armour), 12 oz.	41.5
Turkey Primavera (Lipton), 1 package	86.5

MEATS AND POULTRY
Frozen

	Carbohydrate Grams
Beans with Franks Dinner (Morton), 11 oz.	57.6
Beans and Franks, TV Brand (Swanson), 1 complete dinner	70.1
Beans and Franks (Banquet), 10.75 oz.	20.26
Beef in Red Wine Sauce (Seabrook Farms), ½ cup	1.5
Beef Dinner, TV Brand (Swanson), 1 complete dinner	32.5
Beef Dinner (Banquet), 11 oz.	6.49
Beef Dinner (Swanson), 3 course dinner	65.4
Beef, sliced, gravy (Banquet), 5 oz.	3
Beef, sliced, gravy (Banquet Buffet Supper), 32 oz.	2.34
Beef, sliced, BBQ Sauce (Banquet), 5 oz.	9
Beef, macaroni, TV Brand (Swanson), 1 complete dinner	35
Beef, macaroni (Banquet Buffet Supper), 32 oz.	10.65
Beef, macaroni in Tomato Sauce, EfficienC (Swanson), 1 entree	26.7

Carbohydrate
Grams

Beef, braised short ribs, EfficienC (Swanson),
   1 entree   2.9

Beef, chopped (Banquet), 9 oz.   10.55

Beef, corned beef hash, TV Brand (Swanson),
   1 complete dinner   55.0

Beef, creamed chipped (Banquet), 5 oz.   8.30

Beef, Enchilada Dinner (Patio), 12 oz.   87.5

Beef Goulash (Seabrook Farms), ½ cup   7.5

Beef Pie (Stouffer's), 10 oz.   42.9

Beef Pot Pie (Morton), 8¼ oz.   37.6

Beef, deep dish meat pie (Swanson), 1 lb.   51.3

Beef, Meat Pie (Swanson), 8 oz.   37.0

Beef Pot Pie (Banquet), 36 oz.   12.62

Beef Pot Pie (Banquet), 8 oz.   17.86

Beef Ragout Specialty (Swanson),
   1 complete dinner   13.7

Beef Stew (Seabrook Farms), ½ cup   7.5

Beef Stew (Banquet Buffet Supper), 32 oz.   9.07

Beef Stew, EfficienC (Swanson), 1 entree   15.8

Beef Stroganoff Specialty (Swanson),
   1 complete dinner   5.8

Chicken a la King, EfficienC (Swanson),
   1 entree   5.2

Chicken a la King (Banquet), cook in bag,
   5 oz.   6.35

Chicken, White Wine Cream Sauce Specialty
   (Swanson), 1 complete dinner   3.7

Chicken, Dumplings (Banquet Buffet
   Dinner), 32 oz.   12.21

Chicken, Noodles (Banquet Buffet Supper),
   32 oz.   7.04

Chicken, Noodles, TV Brand (Swanson),
   1 complete dinner   46.0

Carbohydrate
Grams

Chicken, Noodles Specialty (Swanson), 1 complete dinner	17.3
Chicken, Noodles, EfficienC (Swanson), 1 entree	16.6
Chicken, Creamed (Stouffer's), 11½ oz.	16.2
Chicken Dinner (Banquet), 11 oz.	15.47
Chicken, Escalloped, Noodles (Stouffer's), 11½ oz.	35.9
Chicken, Fried, Dinner (Morton), 11 oz.	22
Chicken, Fried (Banquet), 10 pieces, 32 oz.	12.46
Chicken, Fried (Banquet), 5 pieces, 14 oz.	7
Chicken, Fried, TV Brand (Swanson), 1 complete dinner	46.6
Chicken, Fried, (Swanson), 3-course dinner	90.8
Chicken, Fried, TV Brand (Swanson), 1 entree	37.8
Chicken Pot Pie (Banquet), 8 oz.	16.64
Chicken Pie (Stouffer's), 10 oz.	44.2
Chicken Pot Pie (Morton), 8¼ oz.	37.2
Chicken, Meat Pie (Swanson), 8 oz.	52.9
Chicken, Deep Dish Meat Pie (Swanson), 1 lb.	57.7
Ham Dinner (Morton), 10 oz.	54.4
Ham Dinner (Banquet), 10 oz.	18.78
Ham Dinner, TV Brand (Swanson), 1 complete dinner	42.1
Macaroni and Beef Dinner (Morton), 11 oz.	58.3
Macaroni and Beef with Tomatoes (Stouffer's), 11½ oz.	39
Meatballs and Brown Gravy, EfficienC, (Swanson), 1 entree	4.9
Meat Loaf Dinner (Swanson), 3-course dinner	51.1

Carbohydrate
Grams

Meat Loaf Dinner (Banquet), cook-in bag, 5 oz.	7.29
Meat Loaf Dinner, TV Brand (Swanson), 1 complete dinner	42.2
Meat Loaf Dinner (Banquet), 11 oz.	9.22
Meat Loaf Dinner (Morton), 11 oz.	23.6
Meat Loaf Dinner with Tomato Sauce, EfficienC (Swanson), 1 entree	13.9
Pork, Loin, TV Brand (Swanson), 1 complete dinner	40.5
Pork, Loin with Gravy and Dressing, EfficienC (Swanson), 1 entree	16.4
Salisbury Steak Dinner (Morton), 11 oz.	16.4
Salisbury Steak, TV Brand (Swanson), 1 entree	35.4
Salisbury Steak Dinner (Swanson), 3-course dinner	50.2
Salisbury Steak (Banquet Buffet Supper), 32 oz.	5.13
Salisbury Steak (Banquet), 11 oz.	6.74
Salisbury Steak with gravy (Banquet), 5 oz.	5.11
Salisbury Steak with Mushroom Gravy, EfficienC (Swanson), 1 entree	8.3
Sirloin, Chopped, TV Brand (Swanson), 1 complete dinner	40.0
Swiss Steak (Stouffer's), 1 complete dinner	14
Swiss Steak with Gravy EfficienC (Swanson), 1 entree	5.1
Swiss Steak, TV Brand (Swanson), 1 complete dinner	35
Turkey Dinner (Morton), 11 oz.	25.7
Turkey Dinner (Banquet), 11.50 oz.	8.66

Carbohydrate
Grams

Turkey Dinner, TV Brand (Swanson), 1 entree	33.7
Turkey Dinner (Swanson), 3-course dinner	67.6
Turkey Dinner, TV Brand (Swanson), 1 complete dinner	43.7
Turkey Pot Pie (Morton), 8¼ oz.	39.5
Turkey Pot Pie (Banquet), 8 oz.	16.75
Turkey Meat Pie (Banquet), 36 oz.	11.87
Turkey Meat Pie (Swanson), 8 oz.	40.1
Turkey, Deep Dish Pie (Swanson), 1 lb.	53.1
Turkey, Sliced and Giblet Gravy (Banquet Buffet Supper), 32 oz.	2.43
Turkey, Sliced and Giblet Gravy (Banquet), 5 oz.	4.06
Turkey, Sliced with Dressing and Gravy, EfficienC (Swanson), 1 entree	15.5
Veal Parmigiana, Breaded, EfficienC (Swanson), 1 entree	13.9
Veal Parmigiana, TV Brand (Swanson), 1 complete dinner	47.7
German Style International Dinner (Swanson), 1 complete dinner	42.2
Stuffed Green Pepper with Tomato Sauce, EfficienC (Swanson), 1 entree	21.3
Sloppy Joe (Banquet), 5 oz.	7.76

FISH AND SEAFOOD
Canned

Carbohydrate
Grams

Anchovy Paste (Crosse & Blackwell), 1 tbsp.	1.0
Brislings, Norwegian (Reese), 3¾ oz.	0.6
Clams, Steamed, New England Style (Lord Mott's), 6 clams	1.1
Crab, Alaska King (Del Monte), ½ cup flakes	0.9

	Carbohydrate Grams
Oysters, Smoked (Reese), 3¾ oz.	12.8
Salmon, Red Sockeye (Del Monte), ⅖ cup	0
Salmon, Pink (Del Monte), ⅖ cup	0
Salmon, (S & W Blue Label), ¼ can	2.6
Sardines, Norwegian, in oil (Underwood), 3 oz. drained	0.66
Sardines, Norwegian, in mustard sauce (Underwood), 3 oz. plus 1 oz. sauce	1.55
Sardines, in mustard sauce (Del Monte), 1½ large	1.7
Sardines, in tomato sauce (Del Monte), 1½ large	1.7
Sardines, Portuguese (Reese), 3¾ oz.	0.6
Tuna Fish, White, in oil (Del Monte), ¾ cup	0

FISH AND SEAFOOD
Frozen

	Carbohydrate Grams
Cod Filets, uncooked (Gorton's), approx. 5-oz. serving	0
Crab, Alaska King Newberg (Stouffer's), 12 oz.	13.6
Fish and Chips (Gorton's) 16 oz. package, 8-oz. serving	39
Fish 'n' French Fries, TV Brand (Swanson), 1 complete dinner	41.4
Fish Dinner (Morton's), 8¾ oz.	28.2
Fish Filet Crisps (Gorton's), 8 oz. package, 4-oz. serving	10
Fish Puffs, (Gorton's), 8 oz. package, 4-oz. serving	9
Fish Sticks, (Gorton's), 8 oz. package, 4-oz. serving	8
Flounder, Filets, uncooked (Gorton's), approx. 5-oz. serving	0

	Carbohydrate Grams
Haddock (Banquet), 8.8 oz.	17.89
Haddock, Filets, uncooked (Gorton's), 16 oz. package, approx. 5-oz. serving	0
Haddock, Filet, TV Brand (Swanson), 1 complete dinner	36.5
Lobster Newburg (Stouffer's), 11½ oz.	16
Perch, Ocean (Banquet), 8.8 oz.	19.69
Perch, Ocean Filets (Gorton's), 16 oz. package, approx. 5-oz. serving	0
Perch, Ocean, Breaded (Gorton's), 11 oz. package, approx. 4-oz. serving	9
Scallop Crisps (Gorton's), 7 oz. package, approx. 3½-oz. serving	8
Shrimp, breaded (Gorton's), 4-oz. serving	23
Shrimp Dinner (Morton), 7¾ oz.	33.3
Shrimp Scampi (Gorton's), approx. 4-oz. serving	7
Shrimp, Fried, TV Brand (Swanson), 1 complete dinner	41.5
Sole, Filets (Gorton's), 16 oz. package, approx. 5-oz. serving	0
Sole, in Lemon Butter (Gorton's), 3-oz. serving	2
Sole, Filet, Bonne Femme, EfficienC (Swanson), 1 entree	16.4
Tuna, Noodle Casserole (Stouffer's), 11½ oz.	36.7
Tuna, Pot Pie (Banquet), 8 oz.	17.75
Tuna, Meat Pie (Swanson), 8 oz.	38.1
Tuna and Noodles, EfficienC (Swanson), 1 entree	16.4

DAIRY PRODUCTS
CHEESE, 1 oz.,
except as noted

Carbohydrate
Grams

American:

American Dairy Association	1
Borden's	1
Kraft	1
Kraft Old English	1
"Vera-Sharp"	1
American Pasteurized, Process (Sealtest)	.5
American Process Cheese Food (American Dairy Association) , 1 slice	1
Blue, Blue Moon (Foremost)	0.6
Blue, domestic (American Dairy Association)	1
Blue, Danish (Borden's)	1
Blue (Gerber) , 1 tbsp.	1.6
Blue (Kraft)	1
Brie	1
Camembert (Borden's)	1
Camembert (Kraft)	1
Cheddar (American Dairy Association)	1
Cheddar (Borden's)	1
Cheddar, Sharp (Gerber) , 1 tbsp.	50
Cheddar (Kraft)	1
Edam (Kraft)	1
Farmer, Midget (Breakstone), 4 oz.	3.18
Feta	1
Gorgonzola (Kraft)	1
Gruyere (Borden's)	1
Gruyere (Gerber) , 1 tbsp.	.5
Gruyere (Kraft)	1
Gruyere (Swiss Knight)	1
Liederkranz Brand	0
Limburger (American Dairy Association)	1
Limburger (Kraft)	1

	Carbohydrate Grams
Muenster, Processed (Kraft)	1
Mysost	15
Parmesan (Kraft)	2
Pabst-ett	2
Pimento (Borden's)	2
Pimento-American (Kraft)	2
Provolone (Borden's)	1
Provolone (Kraft)	1
Ricotta (Breakstone), 4 oz.	1.13
Roquefort (Kraft)	1
Swiss:	
Domestic (American Dairy Association)	.5
Natural (Borden's)	.5
Domestic (Sealtest)	.5
Natural (Borden's)	1
Natural (Dorman's Endeco)	1
Natural (Kraft)	1
Processed (Borden's)	1
Velveeta	3

GRATED CHEESE

American (Borden's), 1 tbsp.	0
Cheddar, 1 cup	2
Parmesan (Buitoni, Kraft, La Rosa, Borden's), 1 tbsp.	0

CREAM CHEESE, foil wrapped and/or in jars, 1 oz.

American Dairy Association	0
Plain (Borden's)	0
Plain (Breakstone)	.57
Plain (Kraft)	.6
Plain (Sealtest)	.6
Whipped, Temp-Tee (Breakstone)	.57
Neufchatel (Kraft)	2

CHEESE SPREAD	Carbohydrate Grams
Snack Mate Pasteurized Process, American, 100 grams	7.5
Snack Mate Pasteurized Process, Cheddar, 100 grams	7.5
Snack Mate Pasteurized Process, Pimiento, 100 grams	1.7
Pimiento (Sealtest), 1 oz.	1.7

COTTAGE CHEESE, 1/2 cup, except where noted

California Style (Breakstone)	2.95
Chive (Breakstone)	2.95
Creamed, Chive (Sealtest)	2.4
Creamed, Chive-Pepper (Sealtest)	2.7
Creamed, Peach-Pineapple (Sealtest)	9.0
Creamed, Pineapple (Sealtest)	8.0
Creamed, Spring Garden	3.4
Creamed (Sealtest)	2.4
Creamed (American Dairy Association), 1 oz.	1
Creamed (Foremost)	2.7
Creamed (Deans), 100 grams	2.4
Diet (Pet)	3.2
Dry, Uncreamed (Sealtest)	0.8
Light n' Lively (Sealtest)	2.8
Low Fat (So-Lo)	3.2
Low Fat, 2% Fat (Sealtest)	3.6
Low Fat (Breakstone)	2.95
Pineapple (Breakstone)	2.83
Pot Style, (Breakstone)	1.93
Regular, 4% Fat (Pet)	3.5
Regular (Breakstone)	2.83
Skim Milk (Breakstone)	1.93
Tiny Soft Curd (Breakstone)	2.83
Uncreamed (Kraft)	3

	Carbohydrate Grams
Uncreamed (Sealtest)	3
Uncreamed (American Dairy Association), 1 oz.	1

YOGURT, 8 oz. container, except when noted

Bokoo (Dannon), 4-oz. cuplet	31.92
Apple, Spiced (Sealtest)	47.2
Apricot (Dannon)	41.9
Apricot (Breakstone Regular)	53.21
Banana (Dannon)	41.9
Black Cherry (Breakstone Swiss Parfait), 5 oz.	34.60
Blueberry (Breakstone Regular)	53.21
Blueberry (Dannon)	41.9
Blueberry (Sealtest)	50.6
Blueberry (Breakstone Swiss Parfait)	56.80
Boysenberry (Dannon)	41.9
Cinnamon Apple (Breakstone Regular)	53.21
Lemon (Sealtest)	43.4
Mandarin Orange (Breakstone Swiss Parfait), 8 oz.	57.40
Mandarin Orange (Breakstone Swiss Parfait), 5 oz.	35.80
Natural, Low Fat (Yami)	12.8
Peach (Breakstone Swiss Parfait)	53.70
Peach (Sealtest)	49.3
Peach Melba (Breakstone Swiss Parfait), 5 oz.	37.70
Pineapple-Orange (Dannon)	41.9
Pineapple (Breakstone Regular)	53.99
Plain (Pet)	12.2
Plain (Dannon)	12.4
Plain (Sealtest)	16.8
Plain (Breakstone Regular)	13.40

	Carbohydrate Grams
Prune (Sealtest)	50.8
Prune Whip (Dannon)	41.9
Prune Whip (Breakstone Regular)	53.21
Raspberry (Breakstone Regular)	53.21
Red Raspberry (Breakstone Swiss Parfait)	54.40
Red Raspberry (Dannon)	41.9
Red Raspberry (Sealtest)	41.8
Royale, Low Fat (Yami)	38.8
Strawberry (Dannon)	41.9
Strawberry (Sealtest)	44.3
Strawberry (Breakstone Regular)	53.73
Strawberry (Breakstone Swiss Parfait), 5 oz.	33.60
Strawberry (Breakstone Swiss Parfait), 8 oz.	54.10
Vanilla (Breakstone Regular)	30.62
Vanilla (Sealtest)	32.7
Vanilla (Dannon)	26.7
Vanilla, Low Fat (Yami)	22.6

MILK, CREAM, and CREAM SUBSTITUTES
8 oz., except as noted

Buttermilk, 0.1% fat (Pet)	11.7
Buttermilk (Dean), 100 grams	4.7
Buttermilk (Golden Nugget)	10
Buttermilk (Light n' Lively)	10.5
Buttermilk, Bulgarian (Sealtest)	11
Buttermilk, Cultured, 1.5% fat (Foremost)	11.2
Buttermilk, Lowfat (Sealtest)	9.3
Buttermilk, Skimmilk (Sealtest)	9.3
Egg Nog, Dairy Packed, 6% fat (Foremost)	53.8
Egg Nog, (Sealtest), ½ cup	18
Evaporated Milk (Sealtest), 4 oz.	12

	Carbohydrate **Grams**
Evaporated Milk (Sego)	24
Evaporated Milk (Golden Key)	24
Evaporated Milk (Pet)	24
Evaporated Milk (Carnation)	24.4
Evaporated Skim Milk (Pet 99)	26
Whole Milk, 3.25% fat (Sealtest)	10.8
Whole Milk, 3.3% fat (Foremost)	11.1
Whole Milk, 3.5% (Sealtest)	11
Whole Milk, 3.7% fat (Sealtest)	11.1
Whole Milk, 3.7% fat (Pet)	11.3
Whole Milk, (Dean), 100 grams	4.5
Chocolate Milk, 3.3% fat (Foremost)	17.9
Chocolate Milk (Dean), 100 grams	10.2
Chocolate Milk, 0.5% fat (Sealtest)	26.2
Chocolate Milk, 1.0% fat (Sealtest)	26.2
Chocolate Milk, 2.0% fat (Sealtest)	26.1
Chocolate Milk, 3.4% fat (Sealtest)	25.9
Lowfat Milk (Light n' Lively)	13.6
So-Lo Fortified Low Fat Milk, 2% fat (Foremost)	13.0
Multivitamin (Sealtest)	11.0
Profile Nonfat, 0.1% fat (Foremost)	13.0
Sweetened Condensed (Sealtest)	10.9
Skim Milk, 0.1% fat (Pet), 1 cup	11.7
Skim Milk (Sealtest), 1 cup	11.3
Skim Milk, Chocolate (Dean), 100 grams	10.5
Skim Milk, Diet (Sealtest)	13.8
Skim Milk, Profile, 0.5% fat (Foremost)	13
Value 3 (Sealtest)	11.0
Vita-Lure, 2% fat (Sealtest)	13.6

INSTANT DAIRY PRODUCTS
8 oz., except as noted

Milk (Carnation), 1 cup reconstituted	11.6
Milk, Dry (Milkman), 1 quart reconstituted	48.8

	Carbohydrate Grams
Milk, Dry Nonfat (Pet), reconstituted	12.0
Milk, Dry Nonfat (Sealtest), ¼ cup	14.5
Milk, Dry Whole (Sealtest), ¼ cup	10.7
Great Shakes Mix, all flavors (Birds Eye), whole milk, 1 cup	37
Great Shakes Mix, all flavors (Birds Eye), nonfat, 1 cup	38
Chocolate Drink (Ghiradelli), 1 tsp.	10.8

Instant Breakfast, prepared with 8 oz. whole milk:

Chocolate (Carnation)	34.00
Strawberry (Carnation)	35.53
Vanilla (Carnation)	35.37
Milk Chocolate, Dutch Chocolate, Chocolate Fudge, Coffee, Cherry Vanilla, Vanilla, Strawberry (Foremost)	34.2
Breakfast Plus, Chocolate, Chocolate Fudge (Pet)	34.1
Breakfast Plus, Chocolate Malt (Pet)	34.7
Breakfast Plus, Strawberry, Vanilla (Pet)	35.2
Chocolate (Pillsbury), 1 oz.	19
Chocolate Malt (Pillsbury), 1 oz.	18.8
Strawberry (Pillsbury), 1 oz.	19.2
Vanilla (Pillsbury), 1 oz.	17.9
Malted Milk Powder, Plain, (Sealtest) 3 tbsp.	20.8
Malted Milk Powder, Chocolate, (Sealtest) 3 tbsp.	22.8

CREAM:

Half and Half, 10.5% fat (Foremost), 1 tbsp.	0.6
Half and Half, 10.5% fat (Sealtest), 1 cup	5.1

**Carbohydrate
Grams**

Half and Half, 12.0% fat (Foremost), 1 tbsp.	0.6
Half and Half, 12.0% fat (Sealtest), ½ cup	5.0
Half and Half, 12.0% fat (Pet), 1 tbsp.	0.7
Half and Half, 12.0% fat (Dean), 100 grams	4.7
Heavy or Whipping Cream:	
(Dean), 100 grams	3.1
30% fat (Sealtest), 1 tbsp.	0.5
36% fat (Sealtest), 1 tbsp.	0.5
Light Cream:	
(Foremost), 1 tbsp.	0.6
(Sealtest), 1 tbsp.	0.6
16% fat (Sealtest), 1 tbsp.	0.6
25% fat (Sealtest), 1 tbsp.	0.5
Sour Cream:	
(Pet), 1 tbsp.	0.6
18% fat (Foremost), 1 tbsp.	0.6
20% fat (Foremost), 1 tbsp.	0.6
(Dean), 2 tbsp.	1.0
(Sealtest), 2 tbsp.	1.0
Sour Cream-Imitation-Canned:	
(Pet), 1 tbsp.	0.7
Non-dairy (Sealtest), 2 tbsp.	2.2
Sour Half and Half, 10.5% fat (Foremost), 1 tbsp.	0.6
Sour Half and Half, 12.0% fat (Foremost), 1 tbsp.	0.6
Sour Half and Half, 12.0% fat (Sealtest), 2 tbsp.	1.0
Coffee Twin, frozen (Sealtest), ½ oz.	1.9
Coffee Creamer, Non-Dairy (Pet), 1 tbsp.	3.0
Coffee Creamer, Non-Dairy, Frozen (Pet), 100 grams	52

ICE CREAM, ICE MILK, SHERBET and RELATED PRODUCTS

ICE CREAM

Vanilla, 10.2% fat (Sealtest), ¼ pint	15.8
Vanilla, 12.1% fat (Sealtest), ¼ pint	16.1
Vanilla, Party Slice (Sealtest), ¼ pint	15.8
Vanilla, French, Prestige (Sealtest), ¼ pint	15.8
Vanilla, Fudge Royal (Sealtest), ¼ pint	18.2
Vanilla, Dutch Pride, Imitation, 10.65% fat (Foremost), ½ pint	31
Vanilla, 10.35% fat (Foremost), ½ pint	31
Vanilla (Carnation), ⅓ pint	18.7
Vanillla, 4.20% fat, Big Dip (Seatest), ½ pint	34
Chocolate (Carnation), ⅓ pint	18.7
Chocolate Chip (Carnation), ⅓ pint	18.7
Chocolate, Prestige (Sealtest), ¼ pint	18.0
Chocolate (Sealtest), ¼ pint	17.3
Chocolate, 9.15% fat (Foremost), ½ pint	34
Chocolate, Dutch Pride, Imitation, 10.71% fat (Foremost), ½ pint	31
Strawberry (Carnation), ⅓ pint	19.5
Strawberry (Sealtest), ¼ pint	19.5
Strawberry, 8.65% fat (Foremost), ½ pint	31
Strawberry, Dutch Pride, Imitation, 10.11% fat (Foremost)	31

ICE MILK

Ice Milk, 3% (Pet), ½ pint	28.9
Ice Milk, 4% fat (Pet), ½ pint	33.5
Vanilla (Light n' Lively), ¼ pint	16.7
Vanilla, Dutch Pride, Imitation, 7% fat (Foremost), ½ pint	28
Vanilla-Chocolate-Strawberry (Light n' Lively), ¼ pint	17.1

**Carbohydrate
Grams**

Vanilla Fudge (Light n' Lively) , ¼ pint	18.5
Almond, Buttered (Light n' Lively) , ¼ pint	16.4
Chocolate, Big Dip, 4.40% fat (Foremost) , ½ pint	34
Chocolate (Light n' Lively) , ¼ pint	17.6
Chocolate, Dutch Pride, Imitation, 7% fat (Foremost), ½ pint	27
Orange Pineapple (Light n' Lively) , ¼ pint	16.7
Peach (Light n' Lively) , ¼ pint	17.6
Strawberry (Light n' Lively) , ¼ pint	17.1
Strawberry, Dutch Pride, Imitation, 6.65% fat (Foremost) , ½ pint	28
Strawberry, Big Dip, 3.75% fat (Foremost) , ½ pint	34

SHERBET

Lemon, 1.20% fat (Foremost) , ½ pint	52
Lime, 1.20% fat (Foremost), ½ pint	52
Orange, 1.20% fat (Foremost) , ½ pint	52
Orange (Sealtest) , ¼ pint	26.5
Pineapple, 1.02% fat (Foremost) , ½ pint	50
Raspberry, 1.05% fat (Foremost) , ½ pint	50
Orange Ice (Sealtest) , ¼ pint	32.6

Popsicle Industries Products:

Creamsicle, 3 fl. oz.	15.6
Fudgsicle, 2½ fl. oz.	23.4
Popsicle, 3 fl. oz.	16.4

Sealtest Ice Cream Novelties, 2½ fl. oz., except as noted:

Chocolate Coated Ice Cream Bar	12.1
Chocolate Coated Ice Milk Bar	13.6
Choco-Nut Sundae Cone	21.5
Fudge Bar	18.6

	Carbohydrate Grams
Ice Cream Sandwich, 3 fl. oz.	26.1
Orange Creame Bar	17.6
Toffee Krunch Bar, 3 fl. oz.	11.9

MARGARINE, 1 pat, 1 tbsp., except as noted

	Carbohydrate Grams
Blue Bonnet	0.3
Blue Bonnet Soft	0.3
Blue Bonnet, Whipped	0.3
Fleischmann's, Salted	0.3
Fleischmann's, Unsalted	0.3
Fleischmann's Soft	0.3
Fleischmann's, Diet	0.3
Good Luck, 100 grams	0.82
Golden Glow, 100 grams	0.88
Imperial, 100 grams	0.84
Imperial Sof-Spread	0.88
Mazola	0.1
Mazola, Unsalted	0
Nucoa	0.1
Parkay	0
Pet	0.1

VEGETABLES
Canned and Jarred

	Carbohydrate Grams
Asparagus (Diet Delight), ½ cup	2.1
Asparagus (Musselman), ½ cup	2.8
Asparagus, Green (Del Monte), 6 spears	3.9
Asparagus, Whole Spears (Green Giant), ½ cup	1.8
Asparagus, White (Del Monte), 6 spears	7.7
Asparagus, All Green (S & W Blue Label), 5 whole	1.96

Carbohydrate Grams

Beans, baked, New England Style Sauce (B & M) , 1 cup	60.4
Beans, baked, with Pork in Molasses Sauce (Green Giant) , ½ cup	26.2
Beans, Barbecue (Campbell's) , ⅓-½ cup	22.5
Beans, Campside (Heinz) , 1 cup	51.1
Beans 'n' Beef in Tomato Sauce (Campbell's) , ⅓-½ cup	15.3
Beans and Franks in Tomato Sauce (Campbell's) , ⅓-½ cup	15.7
Beans in Molasses Sauce (Heinz) , 1 cup	52.8
Beans in Tomato Sauce, Vegetarian (Heinz) , 1 cup	48.9
Beans, Kidney (Hunt Wesson) , ½ cup	22.2
Pork 'n'Beans with Tomato Sauce (Campbell's), ⅓-½ cup	18.8
Pork and Beans and Tomato Sauce (Heinz) , 1 cup	48.5
Pork and Beans (Hunt Wesson) , ½ cup	27.6
Pork and Beans and Molasses Sauce, Boston Style (Heinz) , 1 cup	50.8
Red Beans (Hunt Wesson) , ½ cup	20.4
Beans, Chili (Hunt Wesson) , ½ cup	20.8
Beans, Green (Lord Mott's) , ½ cup	3.25
Beans, Green (Diet Delight) , ½ cup	2.7
Beans, Green, Diagonal Cut (Green Giant) , ½ cup	3.3
Beans, Cut Green (S & W Blue Label) , ½ cup	2.81
Beans, Green in Brine (Del Monte) , 1 cup, cut, without liquid	7.3
Beans, Lima (Del Monte) , 1 cup, without liquid	31.8
Beans, Wax (Del Monte) , 1 cup, cut,	

Carbohydrate
Grams

without liquid	7.03
Beans, Wax Whole (Green Giant), ½ cup	2.2
Beets (Lord Mott's), ½ cup	6.2
Beets (Del Monte), diced, 1 cup	14.3
Beets (Del Monte), sliced, 1 cup	15.5
Beets (Del Monte), whole, 1 cup	14.0
Beets, sliced (S & W Blue Label), ½ cup	5.93
Beets, Harvard (Lord Mott's), ½ cup	10.
Cabbage, Sweet n' Sour Red (Lord Mott's), ½ cup	15
Carrots (Del Monte), 1 cup, without liquid	10.7
Carrots (Lord Mott's), ½ cup	5.0
Carrots, Sliced (S & W Blue Label), ½ cup	4.64
Corn, Cream Style (S & W Blue Label), ½ cup	17.33
Corn, Cream Style (Del Monte), 1 cup, solid and liquid	50
Corn, Family Style (Del Monte), 1 cup without liquid	34.4
Corn, Cream Style (Green Giant), ½ cup	21.4
Corn, Whole Kernel (S & W Blue Label), ½ cup	10.47
Corn, Whole Kernel (Diet Delight), ½ cup	13.2
Corn, Whole Kernel, Brine Pack (Green Giant), ½ cup	14.3
Corn, Whole Kernel, Vacuum Packed (Green Giant), ½ cup	21.4
Corn, Vacuum Packed (Del Monte), 1 cup	43.4
Mixed Vegetables (Del Monte), 1 cup without liquid	17.7
Mushroom Buttons (Reese), 4 oz., drained	3.7
Mushrooms, Broiled-in-Butter (Grocery Store Products), 1 can, including broth	4.1
Onion Rings (Old London), 1 piece	0.4

Carbohydrate
Grams

Onions, in Cream Style Sauce (Lord Motts),
  ½ cup   13

Onions, Whole Broiled (Lord Mott's), ½ cup   5.0

Peas (Del Monte), 1 cup   25.8

Peas (Lord Mott's), ½ cup   20.7

Peas (Diet Delight), ½ cup   6.1

Peas, Early June (Le Sueur), ½ cup   8.8

Peas, Sweet (S & W Blue Label), ½ cup   5.96

Peas, Sweets (Green Giant), ½ cup   7.3

Peas, Blackeyed (Lord Mott's), ½ cup   21.7

Peas & Carrots (Diet Delight), ½ cup   5.7

Peas and Carrots (Lord Mott's), ½ cup   13.5

Peas and Carrots (S & W Blue Label), ½ cup   5.74

Peas and Carrots (Del Monte), 1 cup,
  without liquid   19.5

Potatoes, Whole (Hunt Wesson), ½ cup   4.10

Potatoes (Del Monte), ⅔ cup   9.8

Potatoes, Whole White (Lord Mott's), ½ cup 11.14

Pumpkin (Del Monte), 1 cup   19.2

Sauerkraut, Chopped or Shredded
  (Del Monte), ⅔ cup   4.0

Spinach (Del Monte), 1 cup, without liquid   8.0

Spinach, Chopped (Lord Mott's), ½ cup   3.2

Spinach in Cream-Style Sauce (Lord Mott's),
  ½ cup   9.7

Spinach, Leaf (Lord Mott's), ½ cup   3.2

Sweet Potatoes (Del Monte), 1 cup,
  with liquid   67.3

Sweet Potatoes (Lord Mott's), ½ cup   27.5

Tomatoes (Del Monte) 1 cup,
  solids and liquid   10.2

Tomatoes, Pureed (Lord Mott's), ½ cup   10.1

Tomatoes, Stewed (Del Monte), 1 cup   15.5

Zucchini (Del Monte), 1 cup   9.0

POTATO MIXES

	Carbohydrate Grams
Au Gratin (French's), 5½ oz.	95
Mashed, Country Style (French's), 1⅓ cup	60
Mashed, Instant (French's), 3¼ oz.	73
Pancakes (French's), 3 oz.	62
Scalloped (French's), 5⅝ oz.	117
Scalloped (Pillsbury), 1 oz.	20.2

VEGETABLES, Frozen
1/2 cup, except as noted

	Carbohydrate Grams
Artichoke Hearts (Birds Eye Deluxe), 5 or 6 hearts	4
Asparagus Cuts (Birds Eye)	3.3
Asparagus, Cuts and Tips (Seabrook Farms)	2.5
Asparagus, Cuts and Tips in Hollandaise Sauce (Seabrook Farms)	5
Asparagus Spears (Birds Eye), ⅓ package	3.6
Asparagus Spears (Seabrook Farms), 5 spears	1.5
Asparagus, Whole Cuts, in Butter Sauce (Green Giant)	5.4
Beans, Baby Butter (Birds Eye), 1 package	57.9
Beans, Green, Cut (Birds Eye)	5.1
Beans, Whole Green (Birds Eye Deluxe)	5.2
Beans, Green, Cut (Seabrook Farms)	4
Beans, Green, Diagonal Cut in Butter Sauce (Green Giant)	8.5
Beans, Green, Diagonal Cut, in Mushroom Sauce (Green Giant)	1.9
Beans, Green, French-Style (Birds Eye)	5.2
Beans, Green, Italian (Birds Eye)	5.2
Beans, Green, French-Style (Seabrook Farms)	4.5
Beans, Green, French-Style, with Toasted Almonds (Birds Eye)	5.9

	Carbohydrate Grams
Beans, Green, French-Style, with Sauteed Mushrooms (Birds Eye)	5.7
Beans, Green, French-Style in Deluxe Sauce (Birds Eye)	4.5
Beans, Green, French-Style, in Mushroom Sauce (Seabrook Farms)	6.5
Beans, Lima, Baby (Birds Eye)	21.1
Beans, Lima, Baby (Seabrook Farms)	18
Beans, Lima, Fordhook (Birds Eye)	17.9
Beans, Lima, Fordhook (Seabrook Farms)	16
Beans, Lima, Fordhook, in Butter Sauce (Birds Eye)	21.2
Beans, Lima, Baby in Butter Sauce (Green Giant)	21.3
Beans, Lima, in Cheese Sauce (Seabrook Farms)	23.5
Beans, Wax, Cut (Seabrook Farms)	4
Beans Wax (Birds Eye)	5.3
Beets, Sliced in Orange Flavor Glaze (Birds Eye)	12.9
Broccoli, Chopped (Seabrook Farms)	4
Broccoli, Spears, in Butter Sauce (Green Giant)	5.4
Broccoli, Cuts, in Cheese Sauce (Green Giant)	6.3
Broccoli, Spears (Birds Eye)	3.7
Broccoli, Spears, Baby (Birds Eye Deluxe)	3.7
Broccoli, Spears, in Deluxe Butter Sauce (Birds Eye)	4
Broccoli, Spears with Hollandaise Sauce (Birds Eye)	3.2
Brussels Sprouts (Seabrook Farms)	6
Brussels Sprouts (Birds Eye)	5.7
Brussels Sprouts, Baby (Birds Eye Deluxe)	5.7

Carbohydrate
Grams

Brussels Sprouts, in Butter Sauce (Green Giant)	5.0
Butterbeans (Seabrook Farms)	19.5
Carrots, in Butter Sauce (Green Giant)	6.7
Carrots, Sliced, in Deluxe Butter Sauce (Birds Eye)	7.7
Carrots, with Brown Sugar Glaze (Birds Eye)	15.5
Cauliflower (Seabrook Farms)	3.5
Cauliflower (Birds Eye)	3.3
Cauliflower, Cut, Young, in Butter Sauce (Green Giant)	2.7
Cauliflower, Cut, Young, in Cheese Sauce (Green Giant)	9.1
Cauliflower Au Gratin (Stouffer's), 10 oz.	17.9
Collard Greens (Seabrook Farms)	4
Collard Greens, Chopped (Birds Eye)	4.5
Corn on the Cob (Birds Eye), 1 ear	21.9
Corn, Whole Kernel, in Butter Sauce (Green Giant)	14.8
Corn, Whole Kernel, with Peppers and Butter Sauce (Green Giant)	17.6
Corn, Whole Kernel, White, in Butter Sauce (Green Giant)	19.3
Corn, Sweet, White (Birds Eye Deluxe)	18
Corn, Cut (Seabrook Farms)	16.5
Corn, in Deluxe Butter Sauce (Birds Eye)	15.6
Corn, Cream Style (Birds Eye)	19.2
Corn and Peas, with Tomatoes (Birds Eye)	14.8
Corn Souffle (Stouffer's), 12 oz.	57
Kale, Chopped Leaf (Seabrook Farms)	5
Kale, Chopped (Birds Eye)	4.3
Mushrooms, Whole in Butter Sauce (Green Giant)	2.3
Mustard Greens, Chopped (Birds Eye)	2.2
Mustard Greens, Chopped, Leaf (Seabrook Farms)	3.5

Carbohydrate
Grams

Okra, Cut (Birds Eye)	7.6
Okra, Cut and Whole (Seabrook Farms)	6
Okra, Whole (Birds Eye)	7.6
Onions, Chopped (Birds Eye) , ¼ cup	3.2
Onions with Cream Sauce (Birds Eye)	12.2
Onions in Cream Sauce (Seabrook Farms)	5.5
Onions, Small, in Cream Sauce (Green Giant)	7.2
Onion Rings, French Fried (Birds Eye)	17.2
Onions, Small Whole (Birds Eye) , ⅙ package	10.8
Peas, Green Sweet (Seabrook Farms)	9
Peas, Green (Birds Eye)	12.2
Peas, Tender, Tiny (Birds Eye Deluxe)	12.2
Peas, Green in Deluxe Butter Sauce (Birds Eye)	10.6
Peas, Green, Early June, in Butter Sauce (Le Sueur)	11.1
Peas, Green, with Sauteed Mushrooms (Birds Eye)	11.8
Peas, Green, in Onion Sauce (Seabrook Farms)	10
Peas, Sweets, in Butter Sauce (Green Giant)	10.5
Peas and Carrots (Seabrook Farms)	7.5
Peas, Green and Carrots (Birds Eye)	10.7
Peas, Green and Celery (Birds Eye)	10.2
Peas, Green and Pearl Onions (Birds Eye)	12.4
Peas, Sweets, with Onion in Butter Sauce (Green Giant)	10.6
Peas, Green and Potatoes with Cream Sauce (Birds Eye)	14.3
Potatoes, Buttered Parsley (Seabrook Farms)	14.5
Potatoes, Whole Boiled (Seabrook Farms)	16.5
Potatoes Au Gratin (Stouffer's) , 11½ oz.	35.6
Potatoes Au Gratin Specialty (Swanson)	16.8
Potatoes Au Gratin (General Mills)	20.8
Potato Buds (General Mills)	17.1

Carbohydrate Grams

Potatoes, Creamed with Peas (Stouffer's), 10 oz.	35.2
Potatoes, French Fried (Seabrook Farms), 17 pieces	19
Potatoes, Scalloped (Stouffer's), 12 oz.	48.4
Potatoes, Scalloped (General Mills)	22.2
Potatoes, Sweet, Candied (Birds Eye)	53.1
Potatoes, Sweet, with Brown Sugar Pineapple Glaze (Birds Eye)	31.1
Rice and Peas with Mushrooms (Birds Eye)	7.4
Spinach, Leaf (Birds Eye), ½ package	3.2
Spinach, Leaf in Butter Sauce (Green Giant)	11.
Spinach, Leaf (Seabrook Farms)	4
Spinach, Leaf, in Butter Sauce (Green Giant)	11
Spinach, Chopped (Seabrook Farms)	4
Spinach, Chopped (Birds Eye)	2.8
Spinach, Chopped, in Deluxe Butter Sauce (Birds Eye)	3
Spinach, Chopped, Creamed (Seabrook Farms)	6.5
Spinach, Creamed (Birds Eye)	5
Spinach, Creamed (Green Giant)	9.4
Spinach Souffle (Stouffer's), 12 oz.	29
Spinach Souffle (Swanson)	15.9
Squash, Cooked (Birds Eye)	9
Squash, Cooked, Sliced Summer (Birds Eye)	3.8
Squash, Cooked (Seabrook Farms)	11
Succotash (Seabrook Farms)	19.5
Succotash (Birds Eye)	18.9
Turnip Greens, Leaf and Chopped	3.5
Turnip Greens (Birds Eye)	2.7
Vegetable Jubilee (Birds Eye)	18.7
Vegetables, Mixed (Birds Eye)	12.5
Vegetables, Mixed (Seabrook Farms)	10.5
Vegetables, Mixed, in Butter Sauce (Green Giant)	9.8

	Carbohydrate Grams
Vegetables, Mixed, in Onion Sauce (Birds Eye)	11
Vegetables, Mixed in Deluxe Butter Sauce (Birds Eye)	11.3

FRUITS, Canned and Dried
1/2 cup, except as noted

	Carbohydrate Grams
Apples, dried, uncooked (Del Monte), 1 cup	61.7
Apple, sliced (Musselman)	26.9
Apples and Apricots, mixed, in jars (Mott's Fruit Treats)	25.83
Apples and Cherries, mixed, in jars (Mott's Fruit Treats)	26.85
Apples and Pineapples, mixed, in jars (Mott's Fruit Treats)	31.16
Apples and Raspberries, mixed, in jars (Mott's Fruit Treats)	27.27
Apples and Strawberries, mixed, in jars (Mott's Fruit Treats)	25.83
Apple Rings, spiced (Musselman)	5.2
Apple Sauce (Musselman)	26.9
Apple Sauce, Dietetic (Musselman)	12.3
Apple Sauce (Diet Delight)	10.7
Apple Sauce with Cinnamon, Country Style (Mott's)	26.18
Apple Sauce, Golden Delicious (Mott's)	26.18
Apple Sauce, McIntosh (Mott's)	26.18
Applesauce (S & W Blue Label)	11.46
Applesauce (S & W Red Label)	11.45
Applesauce (S. P.)	67
Applesauce (Del Monte), 1 cup	62.4
Applesauce, in jars (Mott's)	26.68
Apricots (Del Monte), Juice Pack, 1 cup with liquid	32.6
Apricots (Del Monte), Heavy Syrup, 1 cup with liquid	55.4

**Carbohydrate
Grams**

Apricots (Del Monte), Light Syrup, 1 cup with liquid	41.5
Apricots (Hunt Wesson)	26.4
Apricots, halves (S & W Blue Label), 4 halves	8.69
Apricots, halves (Diet Delight)	8.0
Apricots, halves (S & W Red Label), 4 halves	9.14
Apricots, dried, uncooked (Del Monte)	84.4
Apricots, Whole, Peeled (Diet Delight)	7.1
Blackberries (Musselman)	23.6
Blackberries (S & W Red Label)	7.88
Blueberries (Musselman)	25.6
Cranberry Sauce, jellied, canned (Ocean Spray), 100 grams	37.4
Cranberry Sauce, Whole, canned (Ocean Spray), 100 grams	38.6
Cherries, Sweet (Musselman)	20.5
Cherries, Water pack (Musselman)	14.0
Cherries (Del Monte), 1 cup, with light syrup	41.3
Cherries, Royal Anne (S & W Blue Label), 14 whole cherries	10.65
Cherries, Royal Anne (Diet Delight)	11.3
Cherries, Royal Anne (S & W Red Label), 14 whole cherries	11.29
Cherries, Dark Sweet (S & W Red Label)	12.49
Citrus Salad (Del Monte), 1 cup, with liquid	46.1
Crabapples (Musselman), 1 crabapple	8.7
Dates, chopped (Dromedary), 100 grams	81.1
Figs (Del Monte), Light Syrup, 1 cup	40.8
Figs (Del Monte), Heavy Syrup, 1 cup	54.1
Figs (Del Monte), Extra Heavy Syrup, 1 cup	67.6
Figs, Whole (S & W Blue Label), 6 whole figs	12.24
Figs, Whole, Kadota (Diet Delight)	11.1
Figs, Whole (S & W Red Label)	11.51

Carbohydrate Grams

Fruit Cocktail (Del Monte), Light Syrup, 1 cup	37.9
Fruit Cocktail (Del Monte), Heavy Syrup, 1 cup	48.4
Fruit Cocktail (S & W Blue Label)	10.65
Fruit Cocktail (Diet Delight)	8.1
Fruit Cocktail (S & W Red Label)	8.18
Fruit Cocktail (Hunt Wesson)	29.8
Fruit for Salad (Diet Delight)	6.9
Fruit for Salad (Del Monte), Light Syrup, 1 cup	37.5
Fruit for Salad (Del Monte), Heavy Syrup, 1 cup	47.7
Grapefruit Sections (S & W Red Label)	7.87
Grapefruit Sections (Diet Delight)	7.3
Oranges, Mandarin (Del Monte), 1 cup with light syrup	4.71
Oranges, Mandarin, Segments (Diet Delight)	6.1
Peaches (Del Monte), Juice Pack, 1 cup	29.1
Peaches (Del Monte), Light Syrup, 1 cup	38.5
Peaches (Del Monte), Heavy Syrup, 1 cup	52.3
Peaches, Cling Slices (S & W Blue Label)	5.11
Peaches, Cling Slices (Diet Delight)	6.4
Peaches, Cling Slices (S & W Red Label)	5.60
Peaches, Cling Halves (Diet Delight)	5.9
Peaches, Freestone Halves (S & W Red Label)	5.92
Peaches, Freestone, Halves (Diet Delight)	5.8
Peaches, Freestone, Slices (S & W Red Label)	5.49
Peaches, Freestone, Slices (Diet Delight)	5.5
Peaches (Hunt Wesson)	25.2
Peaches, dried, uncooked (Del Monte), 1 cup	120.2
Pears, Halves (S & W Blue Label), 2 halves	7.15
Pears, Halves & Quarters (Diet Delight)	7.6
Pears, Halves (S & W Red Label)	6.53
Pears, quartered (S & W Red Label)	6.15

Carbohydrate
Grams

Pears (Hunt Wesson)	23.2
Pears (Del Monte), Juice Pack, 1 cup	26.6
Pears (Del Monte), Light Syrup, 1 cup	35.7
Pears (Del Monte), Heavy Syrup, 1 cup	45.6
Pears, quartered (S & W Blue Label)	6.46
Pineapple, Chunks (Diet Delight)	11.4
Pineapple, Crushed (Diet Delight)	13.1
Pineapple, sliced (S & W Blue Label), 2½ slices	16.67
Pineapple, sliced (Diet Delight)	8.6
Pineapple, sliced (S & W Red Label)	13.05
Pineapple (Del Monte), Juice Pack, 1 cup	42.0
Pineapple (Del Monte), Light Syrup, 1 cup	43.0
Pineapple (Del Monte), Heavy Syrup, 1 cup	54.9
Pineapple, Tidbits (S & W Blue Label)	16.55
Pineapple, Tidbits (Diet Delight)	10.8
Pineapple, Tidbits (S & W Red Label)	11.07
Plums, Purple (S & W Red Label)	11.88
Plums, Purple (Diet Delight)	12.6
Plums, Purple (Del Monte), 1 cup, Heavy Syrup	50.5
Plums (Musselman)	25.5
Prunes, cooked (Del Monte), 1 cup	83.5
Prunes (Del Monte), ready to eat, 1 cup	126.0
Raspberries, Black (Musselman)	24.1
Raisins (Del Monte), 1 cup	110.7
Salad Fruits (S & W Blue Label)	8.67
Salad Fruits (S & W Red Label)	7.94
Snack Pack Fruit (Hunt Wesson), 5½ oz.	30.3
Snack Pack Peaches (Hunt Wesson), 5 oz.	27.7
Snack Pack Applesauce (Hunt Wesson), 5 oz.	24.4
Strawberries (S & W Red Label)	4.33

FRUITS, Frozen
1/2 cup, except as noted

Carbohydrate
Grams

Apples, Escalloped (Stouffer's), 12 oz.	93.3
Blueberries (Birds Eye)	30.2

	Carbohydrate Grams
Blueberries, Unsweetened (Seabrook Farms)	11
Cherries, Bing (Birds Eye)	30.8
Mixed Fruit (Birds Eye)	28.2
Peaches (Birds Eye)	23.3
Peaches, Sliced, Sweetened (Seabrook Farms)	28
Peaches and Strawberries (Birds Eye)	20.4
Raspberries (Birds Eye)	32.2
Raspberries, Sweetened (Seabrook Farms)	31
Rhubarb (Birds Eye), ¼ package	34.9
Strawberries, Whole, Unsweetened (Seabrook Farms)	10
Strawberries, Halves (Birds Eye)	39.2
Strawberries, Sliced (Seabrook Farms)	36
Strawberries, Whole (Birds Eye)	30.7

FRUIT JUICES
Canned or Bottled

	Carbohydrate Grams
Apple (Musselman), 6 oz.	19.5
Apple (Mott's), 6 oz.	21.9
Apple (Sealtest), 4 oz.	15.1
Apple-Apricot-Prune (Sunsweet), 6 oz.	24
AM-PM (Mott's), 6 oz.	22.8
Apricot Nectar (Diet Delight), ½ cup	5.4
Apricot Nectar (S & W Red Label), ½ cup	7
Apricot Nectar (Heinz), 5½ oz.	19.3
Apricot Nectar (Del Monte), 1 cup	35.9
Apricot Nectar (Mott's), 6 oz.	27
Apricot and Pineapple Nectar (S & W Blue Label), ½ cup	7.3
Cider, Sweet (Mott's), 6 oz.	21.9
Cranberry Cocktail, Low Calorie, (Ocean Spray), 100 grams	4.9
Cranberry Cocktail (Ocean Spray), 100 grams	15.2
Cranberry-Apple, Low Calorie (Cranapple), 100 grams	3.8
Cranberry-Apple (Cranapple), 100 grams	18.1

**Carbohydrate
Grams**

Cranberry-Grape (Grapeberry), 100 grams	15.4
Cranberry-Prune (Cranprune), 100 grams	15.9
Apple Cranberry (Mott's), 6 oz.	21.9
Cranberry Flavored (Mott's), 6 oz.	21.9
Grape (S & W Blue Label), ½ cup	15.4
Grape (Heinz), 5½ oz.	27
Grapefruit, Unsweetened (Diet Delight), ½ cup	9.7
Grapefruit (Del Monte), Sweetened, 1 cup	31.4
Grapefruit (Del Monte), Unsweetened, 1 cup	24
Grapefruit (Sealtest), ½ cup	12
Grapefruit and Orange (Del Monte), 1 cup	29.8
Orange, Fresh (Pet), 6 oz.	17.8
Orange (Heinz), 5½ oz.	15.1
Orange (Del Monte), Sweetened, 1 cup	29.8
Orange (Del Monte), Unsweetened, 1 cup	27.4
Orange (Sealtest), ½ cup	13.3
Orange (Sealtest), 6 oz.	21.7
Peach Nectar (Del Monte), 1 cup	30.5
Pear Nectar (S & W Red Label), ½ cup	6.8
Pear Nectar (Del Monte), 1 cup	32.4
Pineapple (S & W Blue Label), ½ cup	14.2
Pineapple (Heinz), 5½ oz.	19.8
Pineapple, Unsweetened (Del Monte), 1 cup	33.1
Prune (Del Monte), 1 cup	46.5
Prune (Sunsweet), 6 oz.	28.4
Prune (Sealtest), 4 oz.	23
Prune with Lemon (Sunsweet), 6 oz.	28.4
Juices with Tomato:	
Beef-a-mato (Mott's), 6 oz.	13.7
Clamato (Mott's), 6 oz.	16
Tomato (S & W Blue Label), ½ cup	4.2
Tomato (Campbell's), ⅓-½ cup	4
Tomato (Diet Delight), ½ cup	4
Tomato (Heinz), 5½ oz.	7.8

	Carbohydrate Grams
Tomato (Musselman), 6 oz.	7.7
Tomato (Del Monte), 1 cup	10.5
Tomato (Sealtest), ½ cup	4.5
Vegetable (V-8), ⅓-½ cup	3.6
Vegetable Juice Cocktail (S & W Blue Label), ½ cup	4.2

PASTA, Canned and Mixes

	Carbohydrate Grams
Macaroni 'n Beef in Tomato Sauce (Franco-American), ⅓-½ cup	11
Mac-A-Roni and Cheddar (Golden Grain), ¾ cup	27.7
Macaroni and Cheddar (General Mills), ¾ cup	36.7
Macaroni and Cheese (Franco-American), ⅓-½ cup	11
Macaroni and Cheese, Stir 'n Serve (Golden Grain), ½ cup	22.4
Macaroni with Cheese Sauce (Heinz), 8 oz.	27
Macaroni Creole (Heinz), 1 can	28.4
Macaroni O's with Cheese Sauce (Franco-American), ⅓-½ cup	9.8
Macaroni Monte Bello (General Mills), 1 cup	38.9
Noodles, Almondine (General Mills), ½ cup	26.2
Noolles, Italiano (General Mills), ½ cup	27.6
Noodles, Romanoff (General Mills), ½ cup	26.4
Noodles, Canton Dinner (General Mills), 1 cup	33.1
Noodles Stroganoff (General Mills), 1 cup	41.6
Noodles with Beef (Heinz), 1 can	18.1
Noodle Roni Almondine (Golden Grain), ½ cup	19.1
Noodle Roni Au Gratin (Golden Grain), ⅔ cup	19.6
Noodle Roni Parmesano (Golden Grain), ¾ cup	22.5

**Carbohydrate
Grams**

Noodle Roni Romanoff (Golden Grain), ½ cup	19.8
Noodle Roni Stroganoff (Golden Grain), ½ cup	16.4
Beef Rice-A-Roni (Golden Grain), ½ cup	26.7
Cheese Rice-A-Roni (Golden Grain), ½ cup	20.5
Chicken Rice-A-Roni (Golden Grain), ½ cup	25.7
Drumstick (Minute), ½ cup	24.1
Fried Rice-A-Roni (Golden Grain), ½ cup	24.5
Ham Rice-A-Roni (Golden Grain), ½ cup	14
Rice Teriyaki (General Mills), 1 cup	39
Rib Roast (Minute), ½ cup	24.2
Spanish Rice (Heinz), 1 can	20
Spanish Rice (Minute), ½ cup	25.3
Spanish Rice (El Paso), ½ cup	21.8
Spanish Rice-A-Roni (Golden Grain), ½ cup	18.1
Turkey Rice-A-Roni (Golden Grain), ½ cup	26
Wild Rice-A-Roni (Golden Grain), ½ cup	21.2
Spaghetti 'n Beef in Tomato Sauce (Franco-American), ⅓-½ cup	15.6
Spaghetti and Franks in Tomato Sauce (Heinz), 1 can	28.2
Spaghetti, Italian Style (Franco-American), ⅓-½ cup	13.6
Spaghetti, Italiano (Golden Grain), ½ cup	25.7
Spaghetti with Meatballs (Franco-American), ⅓-½ cup	10.7
Spaghetti with Meat Sauce (Heinz), 1 can	20.6
Spaghetti in Tomato Sauce with Cheese (Franco-American), ⅓-½ cup	15.6
Spaghetti in Tomato Sauce with Cheese (Heinz), 8 oz.	31.1
Spaghetti O's with Sliced Franks (Franco-American), ⅓-½ cup	11.3
Spaghetti O's in Tomato and Cheese Sauce (Franco-American), ⅓-½ cup	15.2

PASTA, Frozen

Macaroni and Beef Dinner (Morton), 11 oz.	58.3
Macaroni and Beef with Tomatoes (Stouffer's), 11½ oz.	39
Macaroni and Cheese, TV Brand (Swanson), 1 complete dinner	48.4
Macaroni and Cheese, EfficienC (Swanson), 1 entree	18.6
Macaroni and Cheese (Stouffer's), 12 oz.	52.1
Macaroni and Cheese (Banquet), 8 oz.	15.76
Macaroni and Cheese (Banquet), 12 oz.	13.82
Macaroni and Cheese (Banquet), 20 oz.	14.46
Macaroni and Cheese (Banquet), cook-in bag, 8 oz.	15.87
Macaroni and Cheese Dinner (Morton), 12¾ oz.	66.6
Macaroni and Cheese Specialty (Swanson), 1 complete dinner	29.2
Macaroni and Cheese Casserole (Morton), 8 oz.	28.8
Spaghetti with Meat Sauce (Banquet), 8 oz.	13.27

PASTA, Packaged Dinners (Kraft), 1/2 cup, prepared according to package directions

Italian Macaroni Style	23
Macaroni and Cheese	22.5
Macaroni and Cheese Deluxe	22.4
Mexican Macaroni Style	27.1
Noodles and Cheese	24.6
Noodles with Chicken	23.1
Noodles Romanoff	22.2
Spaghetti, Mild American Style	26.7
Spaghetti with Meat Sauce, Deluxe	27.5
Spaghetti, Tangy Italian Style	23.2

RICE, Frozen, 1/2 cup

Medley, with Peas and Mushrooms (Green Giant)	20.1
Pilaf, with Mushroom and Onions (Green Giant)	26.1
Spanish (Green Giant)	17.2
Verdi, with Bell Peppers and Parsley (Green Giant)	22.6
White and Wild (Green Giant)	24.5

ITALIAN FOODS, Frozen

Carbohydrate Grams

Chicken Cacciatore (Seabrook Farms), ½ cup	8
Lasagna with Meat Sauce, EfficienC (Swanson), 1 entree	30.5
Italian Style (Banquet), 11 oz.	14.10
Italian Style International Dinner (Swanson), 1 complete dinner	54.1
Spaghetti & Meatballs (Banquet), 11.5 oz.	17.56
Spaghetti & Meatballs (Banquet Buffet Supper), 32 oz.	11.46
Spaghetti and Meatballs, EfficienC (Swanson), 1 entree	26.6
Spaghetti and Meatballs, TV Brand (Swanson), 1 complete dinner	44.4
Spaghetti with Meat Balls Dinner (Morton), 11 oz.	85.8
Spaghetti with Meat Sauce (Banquet), cook in bag, 8 oz.	14.88
Spaghetti with Meat Sauce Specialty (Swanson), 1 entree	28.5
Spaghetti and Meat Sauce, EfficienC (Swanson), 1 complete dinner	25.7
Turkey Tetrazzini (Stouffer's), 12 oz.	68.7

LATIN AMERICAN FOODS

Carbohydrate Grams

Chili Con Carne (El Paso), 8 oz.	16.4
Chili without Beans (Armour), 15½ oz.	20.6
Chili with Beans (Armour), 15½ oz.	41.7
Chili with Beans (El Paso), 8 oz.	32.3
Chili Con Carne with Beans (Bounty), ⅓-½ cup	9.6
Chili Con Carne with Beans (Heinz), 1 can	28.2
Chili, Green, with Meat and Beans (El Paso), 8 oz.	16.9
Chili Con Carne with Beans (Banquet), 8 oz.	9.48
Chili Con Carne with Beans, TV Brand (Swanson), 1 complete dinner	58.6
Enchilada in Chili Gravy (Patio), 1 piece	5.5
Enchilada, Beef, (Banquet), 12.5 oz.	17.23
Enchilada, Beef, with Sauce (Banquet), cook in bag, 8 oz.	17.05
Enchilada Dinner, Beef (Patio), 12 oz.	87.5
Enchilada Dinner, Cheese (Patio), 12 oz.	88.13
Enchilada, Cheese (Banquet), 12.5 oz.	16.45
Mexican Style Dinner (Banquet), 16.25 oz.	16.05
Mexican Style Dinner (Patio), 15 oz.	83.3
Mexican Style Combination Dinner (Patio), 12 oz.	63.8
Mexican Style International Dinner (Swanson), 1 complete dinner	67.3
Tacos (Patio), 1 piece	15.1
Tamales (El Paso), 1 piece	7.5
Tamales and Beef Chili Gravy (Patio), 1 piece	6.3
Tamales with Sauce, (Banquet), Cook-in Bag, 6 oz.	10.29
Tortillas (Patio), 1 piece	6.9
Tortillas (El Paso), 1 piece	13.7

ORIENTAL FOOD, Canned
1 cup, except as noted

Carbohydrate Grams

Bamboo Shoots, sliced (La Choy), ½ cup	1
Bamboo Shoots (Chun King)	2.4
Bamboo Sprouts (La Choy)	1.9
Bean Sprouts (Chun King)	2.5
Beef Chow Mein (Chun King)	10.97
Beef Chow Mein (La Choy)	4.4
Beef Chow Mein, Bi-Pack (La Choy)	7.4
Beef Chow Mein, Divider-Pak (Chun King)	9.15
Chicken Chow Mein-303 (La Choy)	8.4
Chicken Chow Mein (Chun King)	11.19
Chicken Chow Mein, 2 can package (La Choy)	5.0
Chicken Chow Mein Divider-Pak (Chun King)	12.37
Mixed Chinese Vegetables (La Choy)	3.9
Chinese Vegetables (Chun King)	3.1
Mushroom Chow Mein, Bi-Pack (La Choy)	7.7
Mushroom Chow Mein, Divider-Pak (Chun King)	8.48
Chop Suey Vegetable (La Choy)	5.3
Chow Mein Noodles (Chun King)	23.2
Chow Mein Noodles (La Choy), ½ cup	14.4
Chow Mein Vegetables (Chun King)	3.5
Meatless Chow Mein-303 (La Choy)	5.4
Meatless Chow Mein (Chun King)	9.37
Pork Chow Mein, Divider-Pak (Chun King)	7.2
Fried Rice (La Choy), ½ cup	27.7
Meatless Fried Rice (Chun King)	46.6
Fried Rice with Chicken (La Choy), ½ cup	25.4
Chicken Fried Rice (Chun King)	55.96
Pork Fried Rice (Chun King)	52.9
Shrimp Fried Rice (Chun King)	50.72
Shrimp Chow Mein-303 (La Choy)	4.7
Shrimp Chow Mein, Bi-Pack (La Choy)	8.2

	Carbohydrate Grams
Shrimp Chow Mein, Divider-Pak (Chun King)	9.12
Water Chestnuts (La Choy), ½ cup	4.6
Water Chestnuts (Chun King)	15

ORIENTAL FOOD, Frozen

	Carbohydrate Grams
Egg Rolls, Meat and Shrimp (Chun King), 1 roll	3.7
Egg Rolls, Shrimp (Chun King), 1 roll	3.7
Egg Rolls, Chicken (Chun King), 1 roll	3.17
Egg Rolls, Lobster and Meat (Chun King), 1 roll	3.7
Egg Foo Young (Chun King), 6 oz.	10.9
Egg Foo Young, Premium Dinner (Chun King), 11 oz.	45.25
Chow Mein, Beef Premium Dinner (Chun King), 11 oz.	47.87
Chow Mein, Beef (Chun King), 1 cup	10.5
Chow Mein, Chicken (Chun King), 1 cup	11
Chow Mein, Chicken (Stouffer's), 11½ oz.	39.4
Chow Mein, Chicken Premium Dinner (Chun King), 11 oz.	39.89
Chow Mein, Chicken, EfficienC (Swanson), 1 entree	8
Chow Mein, Chicken (Banquet), 7 oz., per 100 grams	4.83
Chow Mein, Chicken (Banquet), 11 oz., per 100 grams	10.26
Chow Mein, Chicken (Banquet), 32 oz., per 100 grams	4.83
Chow Mein, Shrimp (Chun King), 1 cup	13.5
Chow Mein, Shrimp Premium Dinner (Chun King), 11 oz.	44.9
Chow Mein, Vegetable, EfficienC (Swanson), 1 entree	12.1

	Carbohydrate Grams
Chop Suey, Beef (Banquet), 7 oz., per 100 grams	4.42
Chop Suey, Beef (Banquet), 11 oz., per 100 grams	11.21
Chop Suey, Beef (Banquet), 32 oz., per 100 grams	4.42
Rice, Fried with Chicken (Chun King), 1 cup	35.4
Rice, Fried with Meat (Chun King), 1 cup	31.9
Pork, Sweet and Sour (Chun King), 1 cup	27.5
Chinese Style International Dinner (Swanson), 1 complete dinner	40.9

TOMATO PRODUCTS

	Carbohydrate Grams

TOMATO PASTE AND PUREE:

Paste, canned (Contadina), 6 oz.	35.4
Paste, canned (Del Monte), 1 cup	48
Paste, canned (Hunt's), ½ cup	24.5
Puree, canned (Contadina), ½ cup	9.1
Puree, canned (Hunt's), ½ cup	10.5

TOMATO SAUCE, 1 cup, exectp at noted:

Tomato Sauce (Contadina)	10.1
Tomato Sauce (Hunt's)	17.9
Tomato Sauce with Cheese (Hunt's)	18.1
Tomato Sauce with Mushrooms (Hunt's)	17.2
Tomato Sauce with Onions (Hunt's)	21.3
Tomato Sauce with Tomato Bits (Hunt's)	17.0

TOMATOES:

Tomatoes, Sliced Baby (Contadina), ½ cup	5.3
Tomatoes, Round, Peeled (Contadina), ½ cup	3.5
Tomatoes, Whole, Peeled (Diet Delight), ½ cup	4.2

SAUCES, GRAVIES, CONDIMENTS, AND SEASONINGS

A La King Sauce without Chicken (Durkee), 1⅛ cups, prepared	17.5
All Purpose Soy Sauce (Chun King), 1 tbsp.	.34
Au Jus Gravy (McCormick), 1 oz.	10
Au Jus Gravy Mix (French's), ¼ cup	1.1
Barbecue Sauce-Open Pit (Good Seasons), 1½ tbsp.	9.3
Barbecue Sauce Mix (Kraft), ½ cup	36.4
Beef Gravy (Franco-American), ⅓-½ cups	6.3
Beef Stew Seasoning Mix (McCormick), 1½ oz.	19
Beef Stew Seasoning (French's), 1.78 oz.	25.9
Beef Stroganoff Sauce (French's), 1⅓ cup	37.0
Bordelaise Sauce (General Mills), ¼ cup	5.2
Brown Gravy Mix (Kraft), ½ cup	6.0
Brown Gravy (McCormick), ⅞ oz.	13.0
Brown Gravy (Lawry's), ½ cup, prepared	120.2
Brown Gravy Mix (Durkee), 1 cup, prepared	11.2
Brown Gravy Mix (French's), ¼ cup	2.6
Butter Flavored Salt, Imitation (Durkee), 1 tsp.	12.1
Cheddar Cheese Sauce Mix (Kraft), ½ cup	7.8
Cheese Sauce (General Mills), ¼ cup	1.1
Cheese Omelet Seasoning Mix (McCormick), 1¼ oz.	12
Cheese Sauce Mix (McCormick), 1 package	4.75
Cheese Sauce Mix (French's), 1 cup	18.7
Cheese Sauce Mix (Durkee), 1 cup prepared	14.4
Chicken Barbecue Sauce (Compliment), ½ cup	27.4
Chicken Gravy (Franco-American), ⅓-½ cup	5.5
Chicken Gravy (McCormick), ⅞ oz.	14

Carbohydrate
Grams

Chicken Gravy Mix (Kraft), ½ cup	9.1
Chicken Gravy Mix (French's), ¼ cup	3.9
Chicken Gravy Mix (Durkee), 1 cup prepared	14.4
Chicken Supreme Sauce (Compliment), ½ cup	8.7
Chili Seasoning Mix (McCormick), 1¼ oz., including tomato sauce	13
Chili Con Carne Mix, without Meat and Beans (Durkee), 1¼ cups, prepared	44.66
Chili Con Carne Mix, with Meat and Beans (Durkee), 2½ cups, prepared	94.0
Chili Dog Sauce Mix (McCormick), 25 grams per serving	.2
Chili-O (French's), 1.75 oz.	23.8
Chop Suey Sauce Mix (Durkee), 1¼ cups, prepared	18.57
Enchilada Seasoning Mix (McCormick), 1½ oz.	24
Enchilada Sauce, Hot (El Paso), 1 oz.	2.2
Enchilada Sauce, Mild (El Paso), 1 oz.	2.2
Famous Sauce (Durkee), 6½ oz. or 13 tbsp.	22.1
Famous Sauce (Durkee), 10 oz. or 20 tbsp.	34.0
Garlic Spread (Lawry's), 1 tbsp.	13
Giblet Gravy (Franco-American), ⅓-½ cup	4.9
Gravy for Pork (French's), ¼ cup	2.3
Gravy for Turkey (French's), ¼ cup	2.5
Ground Beef Seasoning with Onions (French's), 1⅛ oz.	16.6
Ground Beef Seasoning with Garlic (French's), 1 oz.	14.8
Hawaiian Barbecue Sauce (Chun King), 1 tbsp.	3.5
Herb Gravy (McCormick), ¼ cup	10
Hollandaise Sauce (McCormick), 2 oz.	4.0

Carbohydrate Grams

Hollandaise Sauce Mix (Durkee), ⅔ cup, prepared	11.7
Hollandaise Sauce Mix (French's), ¾ cup	6.8
Hollandaise Sauce (Lord Mott's), ½ cup	7.2
Hollandaise Sauce (General Mills), ¼ cup	4.0
Horseradish Dressing (Reese), 1 tbsp.	2.2
Italian Sauce (Cookbook), ½ cup	11.6
Hamburger & Meat Loaf (McCormick), 1½ oz.	29
Meat Loaf Sauce (Compliment), ½ cup	15.5
Meat Loaf Sauce (Cookbook), ½ cup	13.6
Meat Marinade Seasoning Mix, Instant (McCormick), 1⅛ oz.	17
Meat Marinade, 15 Minute (Adolph's), 0.8 oz.	26
Meat Tenderizer, Seasoned, Instant (Adolph's), 1 tsp.	trace
Mushroom Gravy (McCormick), ¾ oz.	13
Mushroom Gravy (Franco-American), ⅓-½ cup	5.0
Mushroom Gravy Mix (Durkee), 1 cup, prepared	13.6
Mushroom Gravy Mix (French's), ¼ cup	1.5
Mushroom Sauce (Cookbook), ½ cup	9.6
Mushroom Sauce (General Mills), ¼ cup	5.0
Mushroom Omelet Seasoning Mix (McCormick), 1¼ oz.	17
Newburg (General Mills), ¼ cup	5.9
Onion Burger Seasoning Mix (McCormick), 1 oz.	16
Onion Gravy (McCormick), ⅞ oz.	14
Onion Gravy Mix (Kraft), ½ cup	7.8
Onion Gravy Mix (French's), ¼ cup	3.1
Onion Gravy Mix (Durkee), 1 cup, prepared	16.8
Oven Barbecue Sauce (Cookbook), ½ cup	28.0
Pepper, Lemon (Durkee), 1 tsp.	0.7
Pizza Sauce (French's), 12 servings	48.8

**Carbohydrate
Grams**

Pizza Sauce (Contadina), ½ cup	11.3
Pork Barbecue (Compliment) ½ cup	23.5
Sauces for Cooking (Compliment), ½ cup	5.7
Savory Pork Chop Sauce (Compliment), ½ cup	9.7
Seafood Cocktail Sauce (Reese), 1 tbsp.	3.8
Sloppy Joes Seasoning Mix (McCormick), 1 ⁵⁄₁₆ oz.	25
Sloppy Joe with Meat and Tomato Paste (Durkee), 3 cups, prepared	100.37
Sloppy Joe Sauce Mix with Meat and Tomato Sauce (McCormick), 3 oz. per serving	4.5
Sloppy Joe Seasoning (French), 1.5 oz.	2.6
Sour Cream Sauce (French's), ⅔ cup	18.0
Sour Cream Sauce (McCormick), 2 oz.	2.5
Sour Cream Sauce Mix (Durkee) prepared with whole milk, ⅔ cup	11.4
Sour Cream Sauce Mix (Durkee), prepared with skim milk, ⅔ cup	12.0
Sour Cream Sauce Mix (Kraft), ½ cup	16.3
Spaghetti Sauce Mix (Kraft), ½ cup	9.8
Spaghetti Sauce Mix, without Meat (Durkee), 1½ cups	31.08
Spaghetti Sauce without Meat (McCormick), 1½ oz.	13.0
Spaghetti Sauce, Italian (French's), 2½ cups	53.7
Spaghetti Sauce with Meat (Franco- American), ⅓-½ cup	7.9
Spaghetti Sauce with Meat (Heinz), 8 oz.	30.8
Spaghetti Sauce without Meat (Heinz), 8 oz.	30.7
Spaghetti Sauce Mix with Mushrooms (Lawry's), 2 cups, prepared	47
Spaghetti Sauce with Mushrooms (Heinz), 8 oz.	27.5
Spaghetti Sauce with Mushrooms (Franco- American), ⅓-½ cup	10.9

	Carbohydrate Grams
Spaghetti Sauce with Mushrooms (French's), 2½ cups	49.2
Spaghetti Sauce Mix with Mushrooms and Tomato Paste (Durkee), 3 cups	84.03
Spaghetti Sauce with Mushrooms and Meat (Heinz), 8 oz.	27.9
Stroganoff Sauce (Cookbook), ½ cup	9.2
Sweet-Sour Sauce (Durkee), 1½ cups	44.59
Sweet-Sour Sauce (Chun King), 1 tbsp.	12.6
Swiss Steak Seasoning Mix (McCormick), 1 oz.	10
Swiss Steak Sauce (Cookbook), ½ cup	9.2
Tomato Swiss Steak (Compliment), ½ cup	6.7
Taco Seasoning (French's), 1.75 oz.	23.8
Taco Sauce (El Paso), 1 oz.	1.9
Taco Seasoning Mix (McCormick), 1¼ oz.	15
Taco Seasoning Mix (Lawry's), 2 cups prepared	21.9
Tartar Sauce (Reese), 1 tbsp.	1.9
Teriyaki Sauce (Chun King), 1 tbsp.	1.4
Turkey Gravy (McCormick), ⅞ oz.	15
Western Style Omelet Seasoning Mix (McCormick), 1¼ oz.	15
White Roquefort Dressing Sauce (Reese), 1 tbsp.	1.2
White Sauce Mix (Kraft), ½ cup	11.3
White Sauce Supreme (McCormick), 2 oz.	4.0

SALAD DRESSINGS

	Carbohydrate Grams
Bacon Dressing Mix (Lawry's), 1 tbsp., prepared	12.1
Blue Cheese (Diet Delight), ½ cup	1.9
Blue Cheese, French Style (Wish-Bone), 1 tsp.	.49
Blue Cheese (Lawry's), 8 oz.	7.5

Blue Cheese Dressing Mix (Lawry's), 1 tbsp. prepared	12.9
Caesar Garlic Cheese Mix (Lawry's), 1 tbsp. prepared	13.5
Cheddar-Blue Cheese (Hellmann's/Best Foods), 1 tbsp.	2
French (Lawry's), 1 tbsp., prepared	16.4
French (Heinz), 1 tbsp.	2
French, Old Fashioned (Lawry's), 8 oz.	17.2
French (Hellmann's/Best Foods Family), 1 tbsp.	3
French, Classic (Wish-Bone), 1 tsp.	.88
French, Deluxe (Wish-Bone), 1 tsp.	.75
French, Low Cal (Wish-Bone), 1 tsp.	1.10
Garlic (Good Seasons), 1 tbsp.	.7
Garlic French (Wish-Bone), 1 tsp.	1.20
Garlic French, Low Cal (Wish-Bone), 1 tsp.	.92
French, San Francisco Mix (Lawry's), 1 tbsp., prepared	13.3
Green Goodess Mix (Lawry's), 9 oz.	13.5
Green Goddess Mix (Lawry's), 1 tbsp. prepared	13
Green Goddess (Wish-Bone), 1 tsp.	.41
Hickory Bits (Wish-Bone), 1 tsp.	.24
Italian (Good Seasons), 1 tbsp.	.7
Italian, True (Hellmann's/Best Foods), 1 tbsp.	1
Italian (Lawry's), 1 tbsp. bottled	13.9
Italian, Mix (Lawry's), 1 tbsp. prepared	11.8
Italian, Golden (Wish-Bone), 1 tsp.	.34
Italian, Swiss (Hellmann's/Best Foods), 1 tbsp.	2
Italian, Low Cal (Wish-Bone), 1 tsp.	.37
Italian Rosé (Wish-Bone), 1 tsp.	.23
Italian with Cheese Dressing Mix (Lawry's), 8 oz.	12.6

	Carbohydrate Grams
Italian with Cheese Dressing Mix (Lawry's), 1 tbsp., prepared	13.9
Mayonnaise (Best Foods), 1 tbsp.	0.2
Mayonnaise (Hellmann's), 1 tbsp.	0.2
Onion, Creamy (Wish-Bone), 1 tsp.	.33
Russian (Wish-Bone), 1 tsp.	2.40
Russian, Low Cal (Wish-Bone), 1 tsp.	1.76
Salad Dressing (Heinz), 1 tbsp.	2
Salad Supreme (McCormick), 1 oz.	2
Thousand Island (Good Seasons), 1 tbsp.	.6
Thousand Island (Kraft), ½ oz.	40.1
Thousand Island (Lawry's), 1 tbsp.	13.2
Thousand Island (Wish-Bone), 1 tsp.	.90
Whipped Dressing (Diet Delight), ½ cup	3.6

CEREALS, Ready to Cook

	Carbohydrate Grams
Barley, Pearled (Quaker Scotch Brand), ¼ cup, uncooked	37
Barley, Quick Pearled (Quaker Scotch Brand), ¼ cup, uncooked	37
Corn Meal (Quaker or Aunt Jemima), ⅙ cup, uncooked	19
Cream of Wheat, Instant, 100 grams	74.4
Cream of Wheat, Quick, 100 grams	74.4
Cream of Wheat, Regular, 100 grams	77
Cream of Wheat, Mix 'n Eat, 100 grams	73
Hominy Grits (Quaker or Aunt Jemima), ⅙ cup, uncooked	23
Farina, Enriched (Quaker), ⅙ cup, uncooked	22
Farina, Creamed (H-O), 1 cup	135
Masa Farina (Quaker), 2-6 tortillas	26
Oatmeal, Instant (H-O), ½ cup, uncooked	21.2
Oatmeal, Instant (Quaker), 1-oz. packet	19
Oatmeal, Instant, with Apples and Cinnamon (Quaker), 1⅛-oz. packet	24

*Carbohydrate
Grams*

Oatmeal, Instant, with Raisins and Spice (Quaker), 1½-oz. packet	32
Oats (H-O Quick), ½ cup, uncooked	21.2
Oats, Old Fashioned (H-O), ½ cup, uncooked	21.2
Oats, Quick or Old Fashioned (Quaker Oats), ⅓ cup, uncooked	19
Oats (Ralston), 5 tbsp., uncooked	18.29
Ralston, Hot Instant (Ralston Purina), 4 tbsp., uncooked	20.27
Ralston, Hot Regular (Ralston Purina), 3⅓ tbsp., uncooked	20.27
Rice, Cream of (Grocery Store Products), ½ cup	15.8
Wheat Oata (Ralston-Purina), ¼ cup, uncooked	19.56
Whole Wheat, Rolled (Quaker Pettijohns), ⅓ cup, uncooked	21

CEREALS, Ready to Eat

*Carbohydrate
Grams*

General Mills:

Cheerios, 1¼ cups	20.2
Clackers, 1 cup	22.1
Cocoa Puffs, 1 cup	25.0
Corn Bursts, 1 cup	25.6
Corn Flakes, 1⅓ cups	24.4
Frost O's, ¾ cup	23.9
Kix, 1⅓ cups	23.0
Luckey Charms, 1¼ cups	23.0
Stax, 1 cup	21.9
Sugar Jets, ⅞ cup	23.7
Total, 1 cup	23.1
Trix, 1 cup	25.0
Twinkles, ⅞ cup	24.2
Wheaties, 1 cup	23.1

	Carbohydrate Grams
Kellogg's:	
Apple Jacks, 1 cup	25.5
All-Bran, ½ cup	21.4
Bran Buds, ½ cup	22.5
40% Bran Flakes, ¾ cup	22.6
Bran, Raisin, ⅔ cup	22.4
Cocoa Krispies, 1 cup	23.8
Concentrate, ⅓ cup	15.3
Corn Flakes, 1⅓ cups	24.4
Froot Loops, 1 cup	24.1
Frosted Flakes, Sugar, ¾ cup	25.4
Krumbles, ¾ cup	23.8
Pep Wheat Flakes, 1 cup	23.0
Product 19, 1 cup	23.0
Puffa Puffa Rice, 1 cup	23.9
Rice Krispies, 1 cup	24.6
Shredded Wheat, 2 biscuits	30.4
Special K, 1½ cups	20.8
Stars, 1 cup	25.0
Sugar Smacks, 1 cup	25.0
Sugar Pops, 1 cup	25.4
Nabisco, 100 grams:	
100% Bran	68.5
Rice Honeys	87.2
Shredded Wheat Biscuit	76.5
Team Flakes	85.6
Wheat Honeys	83.7
Quaker Oats:	
Cap'n Crunch, ¾ cup	23
Life, ⅔ cup	20
Puffed Rice, 1¼ cups	13
Puffed Wheat, 1⅓ cups	11
Quake, 1 cup	23
Quisp, 1 1/16 cups	23
Rice Puffs, Diet Frosted, 1 cup	13
Shredded Wheat, 2 biscuits	30

Carbohydrate Grams

Posts:

Alpha Bits Sugar Frosted Oat, 1 cup	23.7
Bran and Prime Flakes, ¾ cup	23.2
40% Bran Flakes, ⅔ cup	22.7
Crispy Critters Oat, 1 cup	23.2
Grape Nuts Brand, ¼ cup	23.7
Grape Nuts Flakes, ⅔ cup	23.5
Honecomb Sweet Crisp Corn, 1⅓ cups	25.5
Fortified Oat, ⅔ cup	24.4
Post Toasties Corn Flakes, 1 cup	21.7
Raisin Bran ½ cup	25.7
Super Sugar Crisp Puffed Wheat, ¾ cup	25.7
Sugar Rice Krinkles, ⅔ cup	25.9

Ralston Purina:

Corn Chex, 1¼ cups	24.69
Corn Flakes, 1 cup	24.44
Rice Chex, 1⅛ cups	24.86
Wheat Chex, ⅔ cup	23.33

Sunshine:

Shredded Wheat, 1 biscuit	22.3

BREAKFAST TARTS

Animal, all flavors (Toast 'Em), 1 tart	33.5
Brown Sugar-Cinnamon, Plain or Frosted (Kellogg's Pop Tarts), 1.8 oz.	34.6
Danka Toaster Danish (Toast 'Em), 1 tart	24.5
Frosted Pop Ups all flavors (Toast 'Em), 1 tart	37.4
Fruit Filled (Kellogg's Pop Tarts), 1.8 oz.	36.9
Fruit Filled, Frosted (Kellogg's Pop Tarts), 1.8 oz.	36.6
Pop-Ups, fruit flavors (Toast 'Em), 1 tart	32.5
Toastettes, Apple, 100 grams	68.2

BREADS, Refrigerated

Biscuits, 1 oz.

Baking Powder (Tenderflake)	11.1
Butter Tastin' (Hungry Jack)	10.4
Buttermilk (Pillsbury)	12.8
Buttermilk, Flaky (Hungry Jack)	10.9
Buttermilk (Hungry Jack)	12.2
Buttermilk, Baking Powder (Tenderflake)	11.1
Buttermilk (Tenderflake)	11.1
Buttermilk, Extra Light (Pilllsbury)	12.0
Country Style (Pillsbury)	12.8
Flaky (Hungry Jack)	10.6
Ovenready (Ballard)	12.8
Tenderburst (Pillsbury)	11.0

Rolls, 1 oz.

Butterflake Dinner (Pillsbury)	11.9
Cinnamon with Icing (Pillsbury)	14.0
Crescent Dinner (Pillsbury)	10.8
Parkerhouse Dinner (Pillsbury)	12.6
Snowflake Dinner (Pillsbury)	11.9

PANCAKES, WAFFLES
Mixes

Carbohydrate Grams

Pancake, prepared (Aunt Jemima), 3/4" pancakes	24
Pancake, prepared (Hungry Jack), 1 oz.	19.9
Pancake Mix, prepared, Deluxe Easy Pour (Aunt Jemima), 3/4" pancakes	33
Pancake, Blueberry, Extra Light (Hungry Jack), 1 oz.	20.6
Pancake, Extra Light (Hungry Jack), 1 oz.	20.2
Pancake, Buckwheat, prepared (Aunt Jemima), 3/4" pancakes	25
Pancake, Buckwheat, prepared (Hungry Jack), 1 oz.	20.2
Pancake, Buttermilk, prepared (Aunt Jemima), 3/4" pancakes	28

**Carbohydrate
Grams**

Pancake, Buttermilk, prepared (Hungry Jack), 1 oz.	20.5
Pancake, Sweet Cream (Hungry Jack), 1 oz.	20.2
Waffle, prepared (Aunt Jemima), 3/4" waffles	24

CRACKERS, 1 piece
as packaged, except as noted

**Carbohydrate
Grams**

Bacon flavored Thins (Nabisco), 100 grams	59.1
Barbecue Snack Wafers (Sunshine)	2
Cheese Snack (Sunshine)	2.2
Cheese Tid-Bits, 100 grams	57.3
Cheeze-it (Sunshine)	6
Chicken in a Biskit (Nabisco), 100 grams	60.9
Chipsters, Potato Snacks, 100 grams	67.2
French Onion (Nabisco), 100 grams	67.3
Hi-Ho (Sunshine)	2
Krispy Saltines (Sunshine)	2.1
Meal Mates Sesame Bread Wafers (Nabisco), 100 grams	61.1
Oyster (Sunshine)	.7
Premium Saltines, 100 grams	71.9
Ritz (Nabisco), 100 grams	65.8
Ry-Krisp, Seasoned (Ralston Purina)	4.52
Ry-Krisp, Traditional (Ralston Purina)	4.84
Shapies, Cheese Flavored Dip Delights (Nabisco), 100 grams	47.5
Sip 'N Chips Snacks (Nabisco), 100 grams	60.2
Sociables (Nabisco), 100 grams	62.9
Smack Wafers (Sunshine)	1.2
Tomato Onion (Sunshine)	2.5
Waverly Wafers (Nabisco), 100 grams	68.6
Wheat, Shredded (Triscuit Wafers), 100 grams	67.4

COOKIES, Packaged
 1 cookie, as packaged,
 except as noted

Carbohydrate
Grams

Burry Vending Products, 6 cookies:

Chocolate-Vanilla Creme, 1⅝ oz.	31.4
Chocolate-Vanilla Creme, 2⅜ oz.	45.9
Lemon Sandwich Creme, 1⅝ oz.	30
Lemon Sandwich Creme, 2⅜ oz.	43
Mr. Chips, Chocolate, 1¼ oz.	23.3
Peanut Butter & Cheese, 1½ oz.	32.6
Peanut Butter & Jelly (Imitation) 1⅝ oz.	28.9

Nabisco, 100 grams:

Brown Edge	71
Chocolate Cakes, Pinwheels	69.1
Chocolate Chip	71
Chocolate Wafers	75.3
Creme Sandwich, Chocolate, Oreo	70.8
Creme Sandwich, Social Tea	70.1
Fancy Crests	72.9
Fig Newton Cakes	71.1
Ginger Snaps, Old Fashioned	76.8
Graham Crackers	76.8
Grahams Crackers, Honeymaid	80.7
Marshmallow, Sandwich	73.4
Social Tea Biscuits	76.2
Sugar Rings	72.5
Vanilla Wafers	70.4

Sunshine:

Animal Crackers	1.8
Applesauce	4.4
Applesauce, Iced	14.1
Arrowroot	2.9
Butter Flavored	3.5
Chocolate Wafers	2.6
Chocolate Ice Box Wafers	4.8
Chocolate Chip	4.8
Chocolate Chip Nuggets	3.3
Chocolate Chip, Coconut	9.9

**Carbohydrate
Grams**

Cinnamon Wafers	3.2
Clover Leaves	3.7
Coconut Bars	7.6
Chocolate Fudge Sandwich	9.3
Creme Sandwich, Coconut, Orbit	7.4
Creme Sandwich, Vanilla, Cup Custard	10.3
Date and Nut	14.7
Delito Grahams	5.5
Devil's Cake	10.9
Dutch Rusk	10.5
Fig Bars	8.8
Frosted Cakes	14.8
Ginger Snaps, large	5.7
Ginger Snaps, small	2.5
Golden Fruit	16.2
Graham Crackers	3.0
Graham Crackers, Sugar Honey	5.2
Hydrox	6.7
Kreenalined Wafers	6.2
Macaroons	12.1
Macaroons, Butter-Flavored	4.9
Macaroons, Coconut	12.8
Marshmallow, Chocolate Covered, Chocolate Puffs	10.6
Marshmallow, Chocolate Covered Kings	19.6
Marshmallow, Nut Sundae	12.0
Mallo Puffs, with Coconut	13.1
Milco Dandees	12.3
Milco Sugar Wafers	10.1
Oatmeal	8.9
Peanut	3.8
Peanut Butter	8.1
Peanut Butter	4.2
Pecan Krunch	8.4
Shortbread, Scottie	4.9
Sugar Wafers	6.8

	Carbohydrate Grams
Sugar Wafers, Regent	3.4
Sugar Wafers, Chocolate Covered, Ice Box	4.8
Toy Cookies	2.1
Vanilla Wafers	2.1
Vienna Finger Sandwich	11.1
Yum,Yum	10.4
Zweiback	5.3
Fortune Cookies (Chun King)	4.6

COOKIES
Refrigerated, 1 oz.

	Carbohydrate Grams
Butterscotch Nut (Pillsbury)	15.2
Chocolate Chip (Pillsbury)	17.0
Fudge Nut (Pillsbury)	15.9
Oatmeal Raisin (Pillsbury)	16.8
Peanut Butter (Pillsbury)	16.0
Sugar (Pillsbury)	16.1

CAKES, COOKIES, BREADS, Mixes

	Carbohydrate Grams

CAKES

	Carbohydrate Grams
Angel Food, Traditional (General Mills), 1/16	22.8
Angel Food (General Mills), 1/16	26.2
Angel Food, Confetti (General Mills), 1/16	26.8
Angel Food, Lemon Custard (General Mills), 1/16	26.0
Angel Food, Raspberry Swirl (Pillsbury), 1 oz.	23.6
Angel Food, Strawberry (General Mills), 1/16	27.1
Angel Food, White (Pillsbury), 1 oz.	23.3
Applesauce Spice (Pillsbury), 1 oz.	22.7
Banana, Chiquita (General Mills), 1/12	36.6
Banana Flavor (Pillsbury), 1 oz.	22.7
Banana Flavor, Loaf (Pillsbury), 1 oz.	22.6
Black Walnut (General Mills), 1/12	36.3

	Carbohydrate Grams
Butter Flavor (Pillsbury), 1 oz.	21.9
Butter Brickle (General Mills), 1/12	35.9
Caramel Apple (General Mills), 1/12	35.1
Cherry Chip (General Mills), 1/12	37.6
Cherry Fudge (General Mills), 1/12	35.8
Chocolate, German (General Mills), 1/12	35.9
Chocolate, German (Pillsbury), 1 oz.	22.0
Chocolate Fudge (Pillsbury), 1 oz.	22.1
Chocolate, Loaf (Pillsbury), 1 oz.	21.8
Chocolate Malt (General Mills), 1/12	35.8
Chocolate, Milk (General Mills), 1/12	35.0
Chocolate, Sour Cream, Fudge (General Mills), 1/12	35.4
Coffee Cake (Aunt Jemima Easy Mix), 1 piece	30
Dark Chocolate Fudge (General Mills), 1/12	35.2
Devil's Food (General Mills), 1/12	35.8
Devil's Food, Butter Recipe (General Mills), 1/12	37.0
Dessert, Boston Cream Pie (General Mills) 1/8	47.9
Double Dutch (Pillsbury), 1 oz.	21.5
Fudge Macaroon (Pillsbury), 1 oz.	21.2
Fudge, Sour Cream Flavored (Pillsbury), 1 oz.	21.2
Fudge, Toffee (Pillsbury), 1 oz.	21.7
Gingerbread (General Mills), 1/9	36.1
Gingerbread (Pillsbury), 1 oz.	22.1
Honey Spice (General Mills), 1/12	36.1
Lemon Chiffon, Sunkist (General Mills), 1/12	26.8
Lemon, Sunkist (General Mills), 1/12	36.1
Lemon Cream, Moist (Pillsbury), 1 oz.	21.8
Marble (General Mills), 1/12	37.2
Orange (Pillsbury), 1 oz.	21.9
Orange, Sunkist (General Mills), 1/12	36.8
Orange Chiffon, Sunkist (General Mills), 1/12	27.1

	Carbohydrate Grams
Pineapple (Pillsbury), 1 oz.	21.8
Pineapple Chiffon, Dole (General Mills), 1/12	26.8
Pineapple, Dole (General Mills), 1/12	36.1
Pound Cake (Dromedary), 100 grams	50.1
Pound, Golden (General Mills), 1/12	28.0
Pudding Cake, Apple Cinnamon (General Mills), 1/6	44.5
Pudding Cake, Caramel (General Mills), 1/6	44.4
Pudding, Chocolate (General Mills), 1/6	44.0
Pudding, Sunkist Lemon (General Mills), 1/6	45.4
Red Devil's Food (Pillsbury), 1 oz.	21.5
Spice 'N Apple with Raisins (General Mills), 1/12	37.7
Upside Down, Apple Cinnamon (General Mills), 1/9	44.2
Upside Down, Cherry (General Mills), 1/9	43.4
Upside Down, Pineapple (General Mills), 1/9	42.3
White Cake (General Mills), 1/12	35.5
White (Pillsbury), 1 oz.	21.4
White, Loaf (Pillsbury), 1 oz.	21.8
White, Sour Cream (General Mills), 1/12	34.1
White, Whiping Cream (Pillsbury), 1 oz.	20.8
Yellow (Pillsbury), 1 oz.	21.9
Yellow (General Mills), 1/12	35.5
Yellow, Butter Recipe (General Mills), 1/12	37.0
Yellow, Loaf (Pillsbury), 1 oz.	21.6

COOKIES

Coconut Macaroon (General Mills), 1	10.2
Cookie Mix with Morsels (Nestle's), 1 cookie with egg	7.2
Cookie Mix without Morsels (Nestle's), 1 cookie with egg	5.7
Date Bar (General Mills), 1	8.8
Vienna Dream Bar (General Mills), 1	10.3

BREADS	*Carbohydrate Grams*
Corn (Aunt Jemima Easy Mix), 1 piece	35
Corn (Ballard), 1 oz.	19.2
Rolls (Pillsbury), 1 oz.	19.2
Muffins:	
Apple Cinnamon (General Mills), 1	26.4
Chiquita Banana Nut (General Mills), 1	24.6
Blueberry (General Mills), 1	19.3
Butter Pecan (General Mills), 1	21.3
Corn (General Mills), 1	24.8
Corn (Flako), 1	21
Date Nut (General Mills), 1	21.8
Golden Corn (Pillsbury), 1 oz.	18.8
Honey Bran (General Mills), 1	26.2
Oatmeal (General Mills), 1	23.8
Spice (General Mills), 1	23.4
Sunkist Lemon (General Mills), 1	23.5
Sunkist Orange (General Mills), 1	26.6

BROWNIES

Butterscotch (General Mills), 1½″ square	9.6
Fudge (General Mills), 1½″ square	9.6
Fudge (Pillsbury), 1 oz.	21.7
Fudge Supreme (General Mills), 1½″ square	9.9
German Chocolate (General Mills), 1½″ square	12.0
Walnut (General Mills), 1½″ square	9.5
Walnut (Pillsbury), 1 oz.	20.5

FROSTINGS (General Mills), 1/2 portion, except as noted	*Carbohydrate Grams*
Butter Brickle	29.7
Caramel Apple	29.5
Cherry Fluff	16.6
Cherry Fudge	28.5

	Carbohydrate Grams
Chiquita Banana	29.5
Chocolate Flavor Walnut	26.6
Chocolate Fudge	28.6
Chocolate Malt	28.7
Coconut Pecan	29.3
Creamy Cherry	28.4
Creamy Spice	29.2
Creamy White	29.8
Dark Chocolate Fudge	27.4
Dole Pineapple	28.4
Fluffy Chocolate	12.8
Fluffy White	14.9
Fudge Nugget	28.6
Golden Caramel	29.6
Milk Chocolate	28.9
Sour Cream Chocolate Flavor Fudge	27.5
Sour Cream White	29
Sunkist Lemon	28.5
Sunkist Lemon Fluff	14.9
Sunkist Orange	28.3
Toasted Coconut	28.7
Ready-to-Spread, 1/12 portion:	
Butterscotch	27.8
Cherry	28.0
Chocolate	25.0
Dark Dutch Fudge	24.7
Sunkist Lemon	28.0
Milk Chocolate	27.2
Vanilla	28.0
Canned, (Pillsbury), 1 oz. Pink, Red, Yellow, Green	21.0

TOPPINGS, SYRUPS, and RELATED PRODUCTS

	Carbohydrate Grams
Baking Chocolate (Hershey), 1 oz.	6.6
Bosco Milk Amplifier, 1 tbs.	10.4

**Carbohydrate
Grams**

Coco-Bake, Pre-melted Chocolate (Nestle's), 1 oz.	10.2
Chocolate Chips, Semi-Sweet (Baker's), 1/6 cup	19.1
Chocolate Flavored Syrup (Hershey), 1 oz.	16.5
Chocolate Topping (Diet Delight), 1/2 cup	7.3
Cocoa (Hershey), 1 oz.	11.8
Cocoa Mix, Instant (Hershey), 1 oz.	25.0
Coconut, Angel Flake (Baker's), 1/4 cup	11.7
Coconut Crunchies (Baker's), 1/4 cup	10.8
Coconut, Premium Shred & Cookie (Baker's), 1/4 cup	12.1
Cool n' Creamy (Birds Eye), 1/2 cup	28.2
Milk Chocolate Fudge Topping (Hershey), 1 oz.	15.7
Syrup (Mrs. Butterworth's), 1 tablespoon	67 per 100 grams
Syrup (Brer Rabbit), Light Gold Label, 1 tbsp.	14.6
Syrup (Brer Rabbit), Dark Green Label, 1 tbsp.	13.3
Syrup (Aunt Jemima), 1/4 cup	52
Syrup (Log Cabin), 1 tbsp.	13.2
Syrup (Old Manse), 1 tbsp.	13
Syrup, Buttered (Log Cabin), 1 tbsp.	13
Syrup, Corn, Dark (Karo), 1 tbsp.	14.6
Syrup, Corn, Light (Karo), 1 tbsp.	14.6
Syrup, Maple Imitation (Karo), 1 tbsp.	14.6
Syrup, Pancake and Waffle (Log Cabin), 1 tbsp.	13.2
Syrup, Pancake and Waffle (Karo), 1 tbsp.	14.6
Syrup (Vermont Maid), 1 tbsp.	13.4
Hard Sauce (Crosse & Blackwell), 1 tbsp.	8.3
Whipped Topping (D-Zerta), 1 tbsp.	0.3
Whipped Topping (Dream Whip), 1 tbsp.	1.2

	Carbohydrate Grams
Lucky Whip Dessert Topping (Imperial Lever), 1 tbsp.	11 per 100 grams
Lucky Whip Dessert Topping Mix (Imperial Lever), 1 tbsp.	50 per 100 grams
Frozen Non-dairy Whipped Topping (Pet)	92.4 per 100 grams
Zip Whipt Aerosol, Real Cream Topping, 1.5 oz.	17

PIES, CAKES, PASTRIES, and RELATED PRODUCTS Frozen

	Carbohydrate Grams
Apple Danish (Sara Lee), 1 oz.	11
Apple Nut Kuchen (Durkee), 1 piece	5.5
Apple Pie (Banquet), 20 oz.	34.9
Apple Pie (Morton), 1 whole pie	217.2
Banana Pie (Banquet), 14 oz.	35.26
Blackberry Pie (Banquet), 20 oz.	39.15
Blueberry Pie (Banquet), 20 oz.	39.33
Blueberry Rings (Sara Lee), 1 oz.	15
Boysenberry Pie (Banquet), 20 oz.	38.27
Butterscotch Pie (Banquet), 14 oz.	38.08
Caramel Nut Roll (Durkee), 1 piece	9.54
Cherry Danish (Sara Lee), 1 oz.	11
Cherry Pie (Morton), 1 whole pie	221
Cherry Pie (Banquet), 20 oz.	35.45
Chocolate Cake (Sara Lee), 1 oz.	16
Chocolate Cream Pie (Morton), 1 whole pie	162.5
Chocolate Pie (Banquet), 14 oz.	40.2
Cinnamon Whirl (Durkee), 1 piece	5.53
Cinnamon Sticks (Aunt Jemima), 3 sticks	22
Coconut Pie (Banquet), 14 oz.	34.2
Custard Pie (Banquet), 20 oz.	29.10
Custard, Coconut Pie (Banquet), 20 oz.	28.04

	Carbohydrate Grams
Doughnuts, Sugar and Spice (Morton), 1 doughnut	6.9
German Chocolate Cake (Sara Lee), 1 oz.	12
Key Lime Pie (Banquet), 14 oz.	38.78
Lemon Pie (Banquet), 14 oz.	35.97
Lemon Puffs, Sweet (Durkee), 1 piece	12.83
Mincemeat Pie (Banquet), 20 oz.	44.27
Neapolitan Pie (Banquet), 14 oz.	38.43
Orange Cake (Sara Lee), 1 oz.	15
Peach Pie (Banquet), 20 oz.	32.10
Pound Cake (Sara Lee), 1 oz.	13
Pumpkin Pie (Banquet), 20 oz.	32.8
Raspberry Rings (Sara Lee), 1 oz.	15
Strawberry Pie (Banquet), 14 oz.	38.79
Strawberry Cream Pie (Morton), 1 whole pie	123.7

GELATIN, PIE FILLINGS, PUDDINGS, and CUSTARDS

Carbohydrate Grams

GELATIN, 1/2 cup

All Flavors (Jell-O)	18.2
All Flavors (Jells Best)	18.7
All Flavors (Royal)	11.5
All Flavors (D-Zerta)	0

PIE FILLING

Apple (Musselman), 4 oz.	28.1
Apple (Mott's), 25 oz.	213
Apple, French (Comstock), 21 oz.	163.8
Apple (Comstock), 21 oz.	178.5
Apricot (Comstock), 21 oz.	153.72
Blackberry (Comstock), 21 oz.	212.31
Blueberry (Comstock), 21 oz.	162.33
Blueberry (Musselman), 4 oz.	28.1
Blueberry (Mott's), 25 oz.	200
Boysenberry (Comstock), 21 oz.	160.65

	Carbohydrate Grams
Cherry (Comstock), 21 oz.	165.69
Cherry (Musselman), 4 oz.	28.1
Cherry (Mott's), 25 oz.	241
Lemon (Comstock), 22 oz.	180.18
Mincemeat (Comstock), 22 oz.	196.24
Mincemeat (None Such Rum & Brandy), 18 oz.	223.02
Mincemeat (Non Such), 28 oz.	364.28
Peach (Comstock), 22 oz.	183.96
Peach (Musselman), 4 oz.	28.1
Pineapple (Comstock), 21 oz.	139.44
Pumpkin (Comstock), 29.4 oz.	165.52
Pumpkin (Del Monte), 1 cup	56.8
Raisin (Comstock), 22 oz.	192.28
Red Raspberry (Comstock), 21 oz.	203.07
Strawberry (Comstock), 21 oz.	155.19

PUDDINGS AND CUSTARDS
1/2 cup, except where noted

Banana, Regular (Royal)	28
Banana Cream (Jell-O)	30.5
Banana Cream (My-T-Fine)	32.6
Banana Cream, Instant (Jell-O)	30.5
Banana Cream, Instant (Royal)	30
Bavarian Cream (My-T-Fine)	32.5
Bavarian Custard Rice-A-Roni (Golden Grain)	43.4
Butterscotch (Hunt Wesson), Snack Pack, 5 oz.	30.3
Butterscotch (Jell-O), whole milk	29.4
Butterscotch (Jell-O), nonfat milk	29.9
Butterscotch (My-T-Fine)	32.5
Butterscotch (D-Zerta), whole milk	12.2
Butterscotch (D-Zerta), nonfat milk	12.7
Butterscotch (Sealtest)	20.6
Butterscotch (Royal)	34

	Carbohydrate Grams
Butterscotch (Del Monte), 5 oz.	32.7
Butterscotch, Instant (Jell-O)	30.5
Butterscotch (Mott's), Snack Pack, 4¾ oz.	26.62
Butterscotch, Instant (Royal)	30
Butter Pecan (My-T-Fine)	32.5
Caramel Nut, Instant (Royal)	32
Caramel Rich 'N Ready (My-T-Fine)	35.1
Cherry Vanilla (Mott's), Snack Pack, 4¾ oz.	26.62
Chocolate, Dutch (Bounty)	28.0
Chocolate (Hunt Wesson), Snack Pack, 5 oz.	30.3
Chocolate (Jell-O), whole milk	27.1
Chocolate (Jell-O), nonfat milk	27.6
Chocolate (My-T-Fine)	31.3
Chocolate (Sealtest)	22.8
Chocolate (Royal)	32
Chocolate (Mott's), Snack Pack, 4¾ oz.	26.62
Chocolate, Instant (Jell-O)	33.8
Chocolate, Rich 'N Ready (My-T-Fine)	32.9
Chocolate, Instant (Royal)	34
Chocolate (Royal Shake-a-Pudd'n)	41
Chocolate Malt (Royal Shake-a-Pudd'n)	48
Chocolate with Nuts (My-T-Fine)	31.2
Chocolate Fudge, Rich 'N Ready (My-T-Fine)	34.3
Chocolate Fudge (My-T-Fine)	31.2
Chocolate Fudge (Del Monte), 5 oz.	32.2
Chocolate Fudge (Mott's), Snack Pack, 4¾ oz.	26.62
Coconut, Toasted, Instant (Royal)	30
Coconut Cream (Jell-O), whole milk	27.1
Coconut Cream (Jell-O), nonfat milk	27.6
Coconut Cream, Instant (Jell-O)	27.9
Custard (Royal)	30
Custard, Egg (Jell-O)	23
Custard, Egg (Sealtest), ½ cup	24.3
Dark 'N' Sweet (Royal)	32
Dark 'N' Sweet, Instant (Royal)	34

	Carbohydrate Grams
Lemon (Hunt Wesson), Snack Pack, 5 oz.	35.3
Lemon (Jell-O)	38.8
Lemon (My-T-Fine)	31.7
Lemon, Instant (Jell-O)	30.5
Mince Meat (Crosse & Blackwell), 1 tbsp.	14.3
Mocha Nut, Instant (Royal)	33
Pistachio Nut, Instant (Royal)	32
Plum Pudding (Crosse & Blackwell), 4 oz.	62.4
Rice Pudding (Dean)	22.7
Rice Pudding (Bounty), 1/3-1/2 cup	22.6
Strawberry (Royal Shake-a-Pudd'n)	38
Tapioca (Dean)	23.4
Tapioca, Chocolate (Jell-O)	27.7
Tapioca, Chocolate (Royal)	30
Tapioca, Lemon (Jell-O)	27.7
Tapioca (Minute)	23.1
Tapioca, Orange (Jell-O)	27.7
Tapioca, Vanilla (Sealtest)	21.7
Tapioca, Vanilla (Jell-O)	27.7
Tapioca, Vanilla (Royal)	30
Tapioca, Vanilla (My-T-Fine)	25.2
Vanilla, French (Bounty)	18.8
Vanilla (Hunt Wesson), Snack Pack, 5 oz.	30.2
Vanilla (Del Monte), 5 oz.	32.4
Vanilla (My-T-Fine)	32.7
Vanilla, Rich 'N Ready (My-T-Fine)	34.4
Vanilla (Sealtest)	20.9
Vanilla (Royal Shake-a-Pudd'n)	34
Vanilla (Mott's), Snack Pack, 4¾ oz.	26.62
Vanilla, Instant (Royal)	32
Whip and Chill, ½ cup, made with whole milk:	
Chocolate	18.6
Lemon	18.6
Strawberry	17.3
Vanilla	18.6
1-2-3-Dessert, All Flavors, ⅔ cup average	24.8

	Carbohydrate Grams
Ready-To-Serve (General Mills), ½ cup:	
Butterscotch	29.2
Chocolate	29.8
Chocolate Fudge	30.0
Lemon	40.1
Rice	29.5
Vanilla	28.0

JAMS, JELLIES, PRESERVES, HONEY SPREADS, 1 tbsp., except as noted

	Carbohydrate Grams
Apple Butter (Musselman)	8.4
Jelly, all flavors (Crosse & Blackwell)	12.8
Jam, Strawberry (Musselman)	14.1
Jelly, Mint with leaves (Reese)	14.5
Jelly, all flavors (Musselman)	13.5
Marmalade (Crosse & Blackwell)	14.9
Marmalade, Orange (Musselman)	13
Peanut Butter (Planter's), 1 jar	2.3
Peanut Butter, Chunk Style (Skippy)	2.3
Peanut Butter, Creamy Style (Skippy)	2.3
Preserves, all flavors (Crosse & Blackwell)	14.8
Preserves (Reese), Wild Strawberry	14.2
Preserves (Reese), Wild Blueberry	14.1
Preserves (Reese), Quince	14.5
Nutradiet (S & W Red Label), Low Calorie Artificially Sweetened, 1 tsp.:	
Apple Jelly	4.5
Apricot, Pineapple Preserves	3.4
Blackberry Jam	3.5
Boysenberry Preserves	3.6
Red Tart Cherry Preserves	3.7
Concord Grape Jelly	3.4
Orange Marmalade	3.6
Raspberry Jam	3.4
Strawberry Jam	4.1

RELISHES, GARNISHES, COCKTAIL ACCOMPANIMENTS, and RELATED PRODUCTS

Carbohydrate Grams

Barbecue Sauce with Bits of Onion (Heinz), Regular, 1 tbsp.	4.2
Barbecue Sauce with Bits of Onion (Heinz), Hickory Smoked, 1 tbsp.	2.8
Brown Sauce (La Choy), ¼ cup	78.5
Capers (Crosse & Blackwell), 1 tbsp.	1
Chili Sauce (Hunt's), ½ cup	35.5
Chili Sauce (Del Monte), 1 cup	61.3
Chow Chow (Crosse & Blackwell), 1 tbsp.	1
57 Sauce (Heinz), 1 tbsp.	2.6
Mint Sauce (Crosse & Blackwell), 1 tbsp.	4
Mustard, Brown (Heinz), 1 tsp.	0.5
Mustard, Cream Style (French's), 1 tbsp.	0.94
Mustard with Horseradish (Best Foods), 1 tbsp.	1.2
Mustard, Yellow (Heinz), 1 tsp.	0.5
Onions, Cocktail (Crosse & Blackwell), 1 tbsp.	0.3
Pickles, Bread & Butter (Fannings), 3 slices	3.6
Pickles, Dill (Del Monte), 1 large	2.2
Pickles, Dill (Heinz), 1, 4" long	1.1
Pickles, Dill, Processed (Heinz), 1, 3" long	0.1
Pickles, Dill Hamburger Slices (Crosse & Blackwell), 1 tbsp.	0.5
Pickles, Dill Hamburger Slices (Heinz), 3 slices	0.1
Pickles, Fresh Cucumber (Del Monte), 12 slices	17.9
Pickles, Kosher Dill Slices (Cross & Blackwell), 1 tbsp.	0.5
Pickles, Sour (Del Monte), 1 large	2.0
Pickles, Sour (Heinz), 1, 2" long	1.6
Pickles, Sweet Chips (Crosse & Blackwell), 1 tbsp.	4.2
Pickles, Sweet Cucumber Slices (Crosse & Blackwell), 1 tbsp.	3.7

**Carbohydrate
Grams**

Pickles, Sweet (Del Monte), 1 large	36.5
Pickles, Sweet Cucumber Slices (Heinz), 3 slices	4.7
Pickles, Sweet Gherkins (Heinz), 1, 2" long	3.9
Pickles, Kosher Dill Gherkins (Crosse & Blackwell), 1 tbsp.	0.5
Pickles, Sweet Mixed (Heinz), 3 slices	5.6
Pickles, Sweet Mustard (Heinz), 1 tbsp.	6.8
Relish, Barbecue (Heinz), 1 tbsp.	8.5
Relish, Corn (Crosse & Blackwell), 1 tbsp.	3.6
Relish, Hamburger (Crosse & Blackwell), 1 tbsp.	4.7
Relish, Hamburger (Heinz), 1 tbsp.	3.6
Relish, Hot Dog (Heinz), 1 tbsp.	3.9
Relish, Hot Dog, Barbecue (Crosse & Blackwell), 1 tbsp.	5.4
Relish, India (Heinz), 1 tbsp.	3.9
Relish, Piccalilli (Heinz), 1 tbsp.	5.3
Relish, Piccalilli, India (Crosse & Blackwell), 1 tbsp.	6.3
Relish, Sweet (Heinz), 1 tbsp.	6.6
Relish, Sweet (Del Monte), 2 tbsp.	17
Relish, Sour (Del Monte), 2 tbsp.	1.0
Savory Sauce (Heinz), 1 tbsp.	1.5
Seafood Cocktail Sauce (Crosse & Blackwell), 1 tbsp.	4.9
Soy Sauce (La Choy), ½ cup	8.3
Steak Sauce (Crosse & Blackwell), 1 tbsp.	4.8
Sweet & Sour Sauce (Contadina), ½ cup	30.8
Sweet & Sour Sauce (La Choy), ½ cup	54.7
Tartar Sauce (Best Foods), 1 tbsp.	0.3
Tartar Sauce (Hellmann's), 1 tbsp.	0.3
Tomato Catsup (Del Monte), 1 cup	71.6
Tomato Catsup (Hunt's), ½ cup	40.9
Tomato Ketchup (Heinz), 1 tbsp.	3.8
Worcestershire Sauce (Crosse & Blackwell), 1 tbsp.	3.6

	Carbohydrate Grams
Worcestershire Sauce (Heinz), 1 tbsp.	2.5
Worcestershire Sauce (French), 5 oz.	13.89
Watermelon Rind (Crosse & Blackwell), 1 tbsp.	9.3

SNACKS

	Carbohydrate Grams
Bacon Bits, Imitation (Durkee), 1 tsp.	1.92
Bacon Bits, Imitation (McCormick), 1 tbsp.	5
Bacon Rinds (Wonder), 0.9 oz.	.75
Bows (General Mills), 152 pieces	52.5
Bows (General Mills), 22 pieces	7.5
Bugles (General Mills), 104 pieces	52.5
Bugles (General Mills), 15 pieces	7.5
Buttons (General Mills), 339 pieces	54.7
Buttons (General Mills), 48 pieces	7.8
Caramel Popcorn (Old London), 1 piece	0.8
Cheese Twists (Wonder), 1¾ oz.	22.5
Chee Tos (Frito-Lay), 100 grams	53.0
Cheez-Doodles (Old London), 1 piece	.3
Corn Cheese (Tom Huston), 10 pieces	1.9
Corn Chips, Regular and King Size (Fritos), 100 grams	53.2
Corn Chips (Wonder), 1¾ oz.	25.5
Corn Chips, Popped, Intermission (Frito-Lay), 100 grams	56.2
Corn Snacks, Fandangos (Frito-Lay), 100 grams	53.2
Corn Sticks (Wonder), 1¾ oz.	27.5
Daisy's (General Mills), 198 pieces	61.8
Daisy's (General Mills), 28 pieces	8.8
Danish Salama Sticks (Reese), 1 oz.	.03
Dipsy Doodles (Old London), 1 piece	.9
Nutty Doodles (Old London), 1 piece	.8
Onion Flavored, Funyuns (Frito-Lay), 100 grams	62.7
Pop Corn (Wonder), 1¾ oz.	29.5
Pop Corn (Old London), 1 piece	.15

	Carbohydrate Grams
Popcorn (Tom Huston), 1 cup	8.9
Potato Chips (Tom Huston), 1 cup	10.
Potato Chips, Lay's (Frito-Lay), 100 grams	48.6
Potato Chips, Ruffles (Frito-Lay), 100 grams	48.6
Potato Crisps, Munchos (Frito-Lay), 100 grams	55
Pretzels, Nuggets (Old London), 1 piece	0.7
Pretzels, Rold Gold (Frito-Lay), 100 grams	75.3
Pretzels, Mister Salty (Nabisco), 100 grams	75.7
Rounds (Old London), 1 piece	1.5
Taco (Old London), 1 piece	.2
Toast (Old London), 1 piece	3
Tortilla Chips, Doritos (Frito-Lay), 100 grams	64
Tortilla (Old London), 1 piece	.2
Space Food Sticks, Peanut Butter Flavor (Pillsbury), 1 oz.	19.8
Space Food Sticks, Chocolate Flavor (Pillsbury), 1 oz.	19.8
Space Food Sticks, Caramel Flavor (Pillsbury), 1 oz.	19.8
Space Food Sticks, Chocolate Malt Flavor (Pillsbury), 1 oz.	19.8
Whistles (General Mills), 20 pieces	56.1
Whistles (General Mills), 17 pieces	8
Waffies (Old London), 1 piece	1.9

NUTS

	Carbohydrate Grams
Almonds, Roasted (Funsten), 1 oz.	4.8
Almonds, Dry Roasted (Planter's), 1 jar	5
Cashews (Tom Huston), 15 nuts	8.8
Cashews, Dry Roasted (Planter's), 1 jar	8
Cashews, Dry Roasted (Skippy), 1 oz.	8.4
Cashews, Oil Roasted (Planter's), 1 can	8
Cashews, Salted (Skippy), 1 oz.	8
English Walnuts (Funsten), 1 oz.	3.9
Mixed Salted Nuts (Skippy), 1 oz.	5.9

	Carbohydrate Grams
Mixed, Dry Roasted (Planter's), 1 jar	6
Mixed, Dry Roasted (Skippy), 1 oz.	6.3
Mixed, Oil Roasted, without Peanuts (Planter's), 1 can	6
Mixed, Oil Roasted with Peanuts (Planter's), 1 can	6
Peanuts, Dry Roasted, Lay's (Frito-Lay), 100 grams	52
Peanuts, Dry Roasted (Planter's), 1 jar	5.5
Peanuts, Dry Roasted (Skippy), 1 oz.	5.4
Peanuts, Oil Roasted, Cocktail (Planter's), 1 bag	4
Peanuts, Oil Roasted, Cocktail (Planter's), 1 can	5
Peanuts, Salted (Skippy), 1 oz.	5.2
Peanuts, Toasted (Tom Huston), 2 tbsp.	5.6
Pecans, Dry Roasted (Planter's), 1 jar	3.5
Pecans (Funsten), 1 oz.	3.5
Spanish, Dry Roasted (Planter's), 1 jar	3.5
Spanish Peanuts, Oil Roasted (Planter's), 1 can	3.5
Walnuts (Diamond), ½ cup	15.6
Walnuts, Black (Funsten), 1 oz.	3.7

CANDY AND OTHER CONFECTIONS

	Carbohydrate Grams
Almond Chocolate Bar (Nestle's), 1 oz.	15.3
Almond Candy Bar (Ghiradelli), 10¢ size	17.6
Bonanza Chocolate Bar (Nestle's), 1 oz.	13.6
Butter Chip Bar (Hershey), 1 oz.	18.7
Butterscotch Morsels (Nestle's), 6 oz.	102.1
Caramel Cream Chocolate Bar (Nestle's), 1 oz.	18.3
Caramels (Whirligigs), 100 grams	82
Caramel Pop (Sugar Daddy), 100 grams	87.7
Cashew Crunch (Planter's), 1 can	14

	Carbohydrate Grams
Chocolate Chips (Ghiradelli), ⅓ cup	35.6
Crisp and Milk Chocolate Candy Bar (Ghiradelli), 10¢ size	17.6
Divinity (Stuckey's), 1 piece	22.9
Eagle Bar (Ghiradelli), 1 square	16.7
Full Dinner (Tom Huston), 1 bar	29.7
Fudge (Stuckey's), 1 oz.	20.8
Fudge Chocolate (Tom Huston), 1 bar	29.0
Fudge with Black Walnuts (Stuckey's), 1 oz.	19.0
Milk Chocolate Bar (Nestle's), 1 oz.	13.1
Milk Chocolate Bar, Plain (Hershey), 1 oz.	15.9
Block Milk Chocolate (Hershey), 1 oz.	17.8
Block Milk Chocolate (Ghiradelli), 10¢ size	19.7
Milk Chocolate Bar with Almonds (Hershey), 1 oz.	13.8
Milk Chocolate Covered Candy Coated Almonds (Hershey), 1 oz.	16.9
Milk Chocolate Chips (Hershey), 1 oz.	15.9
Milk Chocolate Kisses (Hershey), 1 oz.	15.9
Milk Chocolate Covered Coated Peanuts (Hershey), 1 oz.	17.9
Mint Chocolate (Ghiradelli), 10¢ size	18.7
Pecan Log Roll (Stuckey's), 1 oz.	17.4
Peppermint Cream Chocolate Bar (Nestle's), 1 oz.	20.5
Praline, Coconut (Stuckey's), 1 praline	21.1
Praline, Maple (Stuckey's), 1 praline	21.1
Raisin Bar (Ghiradelli), 1 bar, 10¢ size	52.8
Semi-Sweet Chocolate Bar (Hershey), 1 oz.	17.0
Semi-Sweet Chocolate Bar (Nestle's), 1 oz.	17.3
Semi-Sweet Chocolate Chips (Hershey), 1 oz.	17.2
Semi-Sweet Chocolate Morsels (Nestle's), 6 oz.	108.4
Sweet Chocolate Sprigs (Hershey), 1 oz.	18.3
Coconut Cream Egg (Hershey), 1 oz.	20.4
Crunch Chocolate Bar (Nestle's), 1 oz.	17.8
Fruit 'n Nut Chocolate Bar (Nestle's), 1 oz.	16.5

	Carbohydrate Grams
Triple Decker Chocolate Bar (Nestle's), 1 oz.	16.8
Cracker Jack, Regular, 1⅜ oz.	37.6
Cracker Jack Pass-Around Pack, 6 oz.	146
Cracker Jack, Park Pack, 3 oz.	73
Candy Coated Hershey-Ets (Hershey), 1 oz.	21.0
Krackel Bar (Hershey), 1 oz.	15.0
Marshmallows, Old Fashioned (Campfire), 1 marshmallow	4.75
Marshmallows, Super Soft (Campfire), 1 marshmallow	4.75
Marshmallows, Miniature (Campfire), 1 marshmallow	.47
Mr. Goodbar (Hershey), 1 oz.	12.5
$100,000 Chocolate Bar (Nestle's), 1 oz.	18.9
Jumbo Peanut Block (Planters), 1 bar	14
Peanuts, double coated (Tom Huston), 1 oz.	10.9
Peanut Brittle (Stuckey's), 1 oz.	20.9
Peanut Plank (Tom Huston), 1 bar	19.8
Reese's Peanut Butter Cup (Hershey), 1 oz.	15.4
Reese's Peanut Butter Egg (Hershey), 1 oz.	12.4
Doublemint Gum (Wrigley), 1 stick	2.3
Juicy Fruit Gum (Wrigley), 1 stick	2.4
Spearmint Gum Wrigley), 1 stick	2.2
Thin Mints (Nabisco), 100 grams	80.5
Tootsie Rolls Midgies and 1¢ piece, per piece	4.96
Tootsie Roll, 2¢ per piece	8.08
Tootsie Roll, 5¢ per piece	21.5
Tootsie Roll, 10¢ per piece	37.7
Tootsie Roll Pop Sucker	13.21
Tootsie Roll Pop Drop, per piece	4.4

BEVERAGES
Canned and Bottled, 1 cup, except as noted

	Carbohydrate Grams
Apple Drink (Del Monte)	26.7
Apricot Apple (Betty Crocker)	32.6
Cherry Apple (Betty Crocker)	35.0

	Carbohydrate Grams
Cider (Mott's), 6 oz.	21.9
Cider, Cherry Flavored (Mott's), 6 oz.	21.9
Coffee, Ground (Yuban, Maxwell House, Sanka)	.4
Fruit Punch (Del Monte)	34.3
Grape Ade (Sealtest)	32.4
Grape Apple (Betty Crocker)	36.9
Grape Drink (Del Monte)	33.1
Hawaiian Punch, all flavors	28.35
Hawaiian Punch Sunshine Orange (exception)	28.75
Lemon Drink (Sealtest)	30.1
Lemonade (Sealtest	26.7
Orange Ade (Sealtest)	31.3
Orange Drink (Del Monte)	29.9
Orange Drink (Sealtest)	28.4
Orange Drink Deluxe (Sealtest), 50% orange juice	26.9
Orange Apricot (Betty Crocker)	31.1
Orange Apricot Juice Drink (Del Monte)	26.0
Orange Banana (Betty Crocker)	31.1
Orange Grapefruit (Betty Crocker)	31.1
Orange Pineapple (Betty Crocker)	32.7
Pineapple-Apricot Juice (Del Monte)	22.8
Merry Pineapple Cherry (Del Monte)	29.9
Pineapple Grapefruit Juice Drink (Del Monte)	31.1
Pineapple Orange Juice Drink (Del Monte)	30.1
Pineapple-Pear Juice Drink (Del Monte)	31.4
Pink Pineapple-Grapefruit (Del Monte)	29.2
Tropical Fruit (Mott's), 6 oz.	22.5

BEVERAGES, Instant

	Carbohydrate Grams
Coffee (Maxwell House, Yuban, Sanka), 1 cup	.7
Coffee, Freeze Dried (Maxim), 1 cup	.7
Coffee, Freeze Dried (Sanka), 1 cup	.8

	Carbohydrate Grams
Nescafé (Nestles), 1 slightly rounded tsp.	.7
Decaf (Nestles), 1 tsp.	.6
Kool-Aid Soft Drink Mix, average all flavors, 1 cup	25.4
Nestea (Nestles), 1 level tsp.	.09
Nestea, Iced (Nestles), all flavors, sweetened with sugar, 3 tsp.	15.1
Nestea, Iced (Nestles), all flavors, sweetened without sugar, 2 tsp.	3.4
Postum, 1 cup	2.9
Replay, Orange, 1 cup	21.7
Replay, Citrus, 1 cup	22.1
Start, ½ cup	15
Tang, ½ cup	14.9
Twist, Sugar Sweetened Imitation Lemonade Mix, 1 cup	19.6

BEVERAGES, Frozen

	Carbohydrate Grams
Awake, for Imitation Orange Juice (Birds Eye), ½ cup	12.6
Fruit Juicy Red, prepared as directed (Hawaiian Punch), 1 cup	28.35
Great Grape, prepared as directed (Hawaiian Punch), 1 cup	28.35
Orange Plus, Imitation Orange Juice (Birds Eye), ½ cup	16.6

SODA

	Carbohydrate Grams
Bitter Lemon (Schweppes), 1 oz.	3.74
Black Cherry (Shasta), sugar sweetened, 8 oz.	32.54
Black Cherry (Shasta), diet, 8 oz.	0.16
Citrus (Gatorade), 1 oz.	1.3
Cherry Cola (Shasta), sugar sweetened, 8 oz.	27.35
Cherry Crush (Crush International), 1 oz.	4.07
Cherry Crush (Crush International), 10 oz.	40.7
Cherry Cola (Shasta), diet, 8 oz.	0.11
Cola (Gatorade), 1 oz.	1.2

Carbohydrate
Grams

Cola (Royal Crown), 1 oz.	3.42
Cola (Shasta), sugar sweetened, 8 oz.	26
Cola, New Cyclamate Free Diet-Rite (Royal Crown), 1 oz.	1.5
Cola (Shasta), diet, 8 oz.	.12
Collins (Shasta), 8 oz.	22.25
Cream Soda (Shasta), sugar sweetened, 8 oz.	29.76
Cream Soda (Shasta), diet, 8 oz.	.05
Dr. Pepper, regular, 1 oz.	2.9
Dr. Pepper, New Diet, 1 oz.	.06
Ginger Ale (Shasta), sugar sweetened, 8 oz.	24.69
Ginger Ale (Shasta), diet, 8 oz.	0.10
Ginger Ale (Schweppes), 1 oz.	2.71
Ginger Beer (Schweppes), 1 oz.	2.94
Grape Soda (Shasta), sugar sweetened, 8 oz.	29.76
Grape (Nehi), 1 oz.	3.87
Grape Soda (Shasta), diet, 8 oz.	0.10
Grape Crush (Crush International), 1 oz.	4.26
Grape Crush (Crush International), 10 oz.	42.6
Grapefruit Crush (Crush International), 1 oz.	3.2
Grapefruit Crush (Crush International), 10 oz.	32.
Lemon Juice (Rose's), 1 oz.	2.6
Lemon-Lime (Shasta), sugar sweetened, 8 oz.	24.69
Lemon-Lime (Shasta), diet, 8 oz.	0.17
Lime Juice (Rose's), 1 oz.	12.0
Orange (Shasta), sugar sweetened, 8 oz.	32.54
Orange (Nehi), 1 oz.	4.14
Orange (Shasta), diet, 8 oz.	0.11
Orange Crush (Crush International), 1 oz.	3.95
Orange Crush (Crush International), 10 oz.	39.5
Quinine (Shasta), sugar sweetened, 8 oz.	19.22
Raspberry (Shasta), diet, 8 oz.	.17
Root Beer (Hires), 1 oz.	3.1
Root Beer (Hires), 10 oz.	31

	Carbohydrate Grams
Root Beer (Nehi), 1 oz.	3.87
Root Beer (Shasta), sugar sweetened, 8 oz.	28.63
Root Beer (Shasta), diet, 8 oz.	0.11
Sun-drop (Crush International), 1 oz.	3.7
Sun-drop (Crush International), 10 oz.	37
Strawberry (Shasta), sugar sweetened, 8 oz.	27.35
Strawberry (Shasta), diet, 9 oz.	0.16
Strawberry Crush (Crush International), 1 oz.	4.07
Strawberry Crush (Crush International), 10 oz.	40.7
Swing (Shasta), sugar sweetened, 8 oz.	28.63
Swing (Shasta), diet, 8 oz.	0.14
Tiki (Shasta), sugar sweetened, 8 oz.	28.63
Tiki (Shasta), diet, 8 oz.	0.05
Tonic Water (Schweppes), 1 oz.	2.75
Whiskey Sour (Shasta), 8 oz.	22.25
No-Cal:	
Coffee	0.051
Cola	0.006
Cream	0.002
Ginger	0.001
Root Beer	0.005
Pink Grapefruit	0.008
Black Raspberry	0.048
Black Cherry	none
Citrus	none
Grape	none
Lemon	none
Quinine Water	none
Orange	none

COCKTAILS, LIQUEURS, LIQUORS, WINES

Carbohydrate Grams

COCKTAILS

	Carbohydrate Grams
Daiquiri (Calvert), 3 oz.	9.5
Gin Sour (Calvert), 3 oz.	10.4

	Carbohydrate Grams
Manhattan (Calvert), 3 oz.	2.0
Margarita (Calvert), 3 oz.	9.5
Martini (Calvert), 3 oz.	0
Tequila Sour (Calvert), 3 oz.	11.4
Vodka Martini (Calvert), 3 oz.	0
Whiskey Sour (Calvert), 3 oz.	9.5

LIQUEURS

Absinthe (Leroux Liqueurs-American), 3 oz.	2.9
Anesone (Leroux Liqueurs-American), 3 oz.	8.5
Anisette (Bois), 50 proof, 1 oz.	13.9
Anisette, White or Red (Leroux Liqueurs-American), 3 oz.	29.7
Apricot, (Leroux Liqueurs-American), 3 oz.	26.6
Apricot (Leroux Flavored Brandy), 3 oz.	25.7
Aquavit (Leroux Liqueurs-American), 3 oz.	0
Banana (Leroux Liqueurs-American), 3 oz.	34.2
Blackberry Brandy and All Flavored Brandies (Bois), 70 proof, 1 oz.	7.4
Blackberry Liqueur and all Fruit Liqueurs (Bois), 60 proof, 1 oz.	8.9
Blackberry (Leroux Liqueurs-American), 3 oz.	21.4
Blackberry (Leroux Flavored Brandy), 3 oz.	24.8
Brandy and Coffee (Leroux Flavored), 3 oz.	24.8
Casanove, Italy (Leroux Liqueurs-American), 3 oz.	28.6
Cheri Suisse (Leroux Liqueurs-Imported), 3 oz.	30.6
Cherry (Leroux Liqueurs-American), 3 oz.	22.8
Cherry (Leroux Flavored Brandy), 3 oz.	24.8
Cherry Karise (Leroux Liqueurs-American), 3 oz.	22.8
Cherry Kijafa (Seagram), 3 oz.	15.3
Claristan (Leroux Liqueurs-American), 3 oz.	32.3

	Carbohydrate Grams
Creme de Cocoa (Bois), 54 proof, 1 oz.	11.8
Creme de Cacao, Brown (Leroux Liqueurs-American), 3 oz.	42.8
Creme de Cacao, White (Leroux Liqueurs-American), 3 oz.	39.9
Creme de Cafe (Leroux Liqueurs-American), 3 oz.	40.9
Creme de Cassis (Leroux Liqueurs-American), 3 oz.	44.7
Creme de Menthe (Bois), 60 proof, 1 oz.	13.0
Creme de Menthe, Green (Leroux Liqueurs-American), 3 oz.	45.6
Creme de Menthe, White (Leroux Liqueurs-American), 3 oz.	38.5
Creme de Noyaux (Bois), 60 proof, 1 oz.	13.7
Creme de Noyaux (Leroux Liqueurs-American), 3 oz.	43.7
Curacao, Blue (Bois), 64 proof, 1 oz.	10.3
Curacao, Orange (Bois), 64 proof, 1 oz.	8.8
Curacao (Leroux Liqueurs-American), 3 oz.	28.5
Deluxe Brandy (Leroux), 3 oz.	0.4
Five Star Brandy (Leroux), 3 oz.	0.4
Ginger (Leroux Flavored Brandy), 3 oz.	13.3
Ginger, Sharp (Leroux Flavored Brandy), 3 oz.	14.2
Gold-O-Mint (Leroux Liqueurs-American), 3 oz.	45.6
Grenadine (Leroux Liqueurs-American), 3 oz.	45.6
Kirschwasser (Leroux Brandy), 3 oz.	0
Kummel (Liqueurs-American), 3 oz.	12.4
Lechan Ora (Leroux Liqueurs-Imported), 3 oz.	23.3
Maraschino (Leroux Liqueurs-American), 3 oz.	29.1
Pasha Turkish Coffee (Leroux Liquers-Imported), 3 oz.	39.8

Carbohydrate
Grams

Peach (Leroux Liqueurs-American) , 3 oz.	26.6
Peach (Leroux Flavored Brandy) , 3 oz.	26.6
Peppermint Schnapps (Leroux Liqueurs-American) , 3 oz.	27.7
Polish Blackberry (Leroux Flavored Brandy) , 3 oz.	25.7
Raspberry (Leroux Liqueurs-American) , 3 oz.	24.8
Rock & Rye (Leroux Liqueurs-American) , 3 oz.	31.4
Rock & Rye, Irish Moss (Leroux Liqueurs-American) , 3 oz.	39.0
Sabra (Leroux Liqueurs-Imported) , 3 oz.	31.2
Strawberry (Leroux Liqueurs-American) , 3 oz.	24.8
Triple Sec (Bois) , 78 proof, 1 oz.	8.8
Triple Sec (Leroux Liqueurs-American) , 3 oz.	26.6
Vandermint (Leroux Liqueurs-Imported) , 3 oz.	30.5

LIQUORS

Canadian-Gold Pennant (Brown-Forman) 86.18 proof, 1 oz.	0.4
King Blend (Brown-Forman) , 86 proof, 1 oz.	0.1
Mint Gin (Leroux Flavored) , 3 oz.	8.5
Orange Gin (Leroux Flavored) , 3 oz.	8.5
Sloe Gin (Bois) , 66 proof, 1 oz.	4.7
Sloe Gin (Leroux Flavored) , 3 oz.	18.0

WINES

Beaujolais St. Louis, Burgundy Red French (Barton & Guestier) , 3 oz.	0.1
Bolla; Cello; Frescobaldi; Vaselli; Asti (Brown-Forman) , 1 oz.	6.0
Chablis (Barton & Geustier) , 3 oz.	0.1
Champagnes, Veuve Clicquot (Brown-Forman) , 1 oz.	0.2

**Carbohydrate
Grams**

Chateauneuf du Pape (Barton & Guestier), 3 oz.	0.5
Chiante Classico (Brolio), 3 oz.	0.3
Cordon Rouge Brut (Mumm's), 3 oz.	1.4
Extra Dry Champagne (Mumm's), 3 oz.	5.6
Graacher Himmelreich, German Moselle (Seagram), 3 oz.	2.5
Graves (Barton & Guestier), 3 oz.	0.6
Liebfraumilch, Anheuser (Brown-Forman), 1 oz.	0.3
Liebfraumilch Glockenspiel (Julius Kayser), 3 oz.	1.8
Margaux (Barton & Guestier), 3 oz.	0.4
Nectarose Vin Rose (Seagram), 3 oz.	2.6
Niersteiner (Julius Kayser), 3 oz.	0.9
Nuits St. George (Barton & Guestier), 3 oz.	0.5
Piesporter Riesling, German Moselle (Seagram), 3 oz.	1.7
Pommard (Barton & Guestier), 3 oz.	0.4
Pouilly Fuisse (Barton & Guestier), 3 oz.	0.3
Pouilly Fume (Barton & Guestier), 3 oz.	0.1
Prince Blanc (Barton & Guestier), 3 oz.	0.6
Prince Noir (Barton & Guestier), 3 oz.	0.35
Puligny Montrachet (Barton & Guestier), 3 oz.	0.3
St. Emilion (Barton & Guestier), 3 oz.	0.7
Sancerre (Barton & Guestier), 3 oz.	0.3
Sauternes, Bordeuax White French (Barton & Guestier), 3 oz.	7.6
Sauternes, Haut, Bordeaux White French (Barton & Guestier), 3 oz.	8.7
Sparkling Burgundy, Red French (Barton & Guestier), 3 oz.	2.2
Vermouth (Brown-Forman), Rosso, 1 oz.	2.3
Vermouth (Brown-Forman), Bianco, 1 oz.	2.6
Vermouth, Dry (Noilly Prat), 3 oz.	1.6
Vermouth, Sweet (Noilly Prat), 3 oz.	12.1